THE LATER JACOBEAN AND CAROLINE DRAMATISTS

Advisory Editor: Alfred Harbage

The Later Jacobean
and Caroline Dramatists

A Survey and Bibliography of Recent Studies in English
Renaissance Drama

Edited by
Terence P. Logan and Denzell S. Smith

UNIVERSITY OF NEBRASKA PRESS
LINCOLN AND LONDON

Publishers on the Plains

UNP

Most recent printing shown by first digit below:
1   2   3   4   5   6   7   8   9   10

Library of Congress Cataloging in Publication Data

Logan, Terence P.
  The later Jacobean and Caroline dramatists.

  (Their A survey and bibliography of recent studies
in English Renaissance drama)
  Includes index.
  1. English drama—17th century—History and
criticism—Bibliography. I. Smith, Denzell S.,
joint author. II. Title. III. Series.
Z2014.D7L816   016.822'3'09   77-25265
ISBN 0-8032-2850-3

MANUFACTURED IN THE UNITED STATES OF AMERICA

For
Alfred Harbage
This volume and the series

CONTENTS

PREFACE

The Later Jacobean and Caroline Dramatists is the fourth and last volume of Recent Studies in English Renaissance Drama, a series which gives a comprehensive account of recent scholarship on English plays and playwrights, exclusive of Shakespeare, from 1580 to 1642. The first volume, *The Predecessors of Shakespeare* (1973), deals with anonymous plays first performed between 1580 and 1593 and playwrights who wrote most of their plays in those years; the next two volumes, *The Popular School* (1975) and *The New Intellectuals* (1977), jointly cover the period from 1593 to 1616. *The Popular School* includes dramatists primarily associated with the public open-air theaters, and anonymous plays first performed in them; *The New Intellectuals* treats dramatists who either wrote principally for the private theaters or were significantly influenced by them, and the anonymous plays first performed in them. *The Later Jacobean and Caroline Dramatists* includes plays and playwrights of both popular and private theaters for the period from 1616 to 1642. The determinations of theater types and first performance dates were made principally by reference to Alfred Harbage, *Annals of English Drama*, revised by Samuel Schoenbaum (1964), to the *Supplements to the Revised Edition* by Schoenbaum (1966, 1970), and by consultation with Professor Harbage.

The publication date of the initial volumes of G. E. Bentley's *The Jacobean and Caroline Stage*, 7 vols. (1941–68), provided the anterior limits for the survey of scholarship and criticism in this volume. An anterior limit of 1923, the publication date of E. K. Chambers's *The Elizabethan Stage*, 4 vols. (1923), was selectively used for those authors whose pre-1616 plays receive extended discussion in Chambers. Contributors to *The Later Jacobean and Caroline Dramatists* used annual bibliographies published from 1923 or 1941 through 1976 and were encouraged to include especially important material published both before and after those limits. The chief sources for the items included in this volume were the author and title entries in twelve bibliographies and lists: *Essay and General Literature Index, International Index* (since 1965, *Social Sciences and Humanities Index*), *MLA International Bibliography, Modern Humanities Research Association Annual Bibliography of English Language and Literature, Readers' Guide to Periodical Literature, Research Opportunities in Renaissance Drama, Shakespeare Quarterly, Shakespeare Survey, Studies in Bibliography, Studies in Philology, Yearbook of Comparative and General Literature,* and *The Year's Work in English Studies.* Those entries were supplemented by selected general studies of Elizabethan, Jacobean, and Caroline drama surveyed for discussions of individual playwrights, and by the additional research of individual contributors. Entries were restricted to published material except in the treatment of anonymous plays, where edition theses were included.

Each essay begins with a general section, including, when available, biographical material, general studies of the plays, and studies of the works at large. (It is assumed that later sections, particularly those dealing with individual plays, will be used in conjunction with this general section.) The next section discusses criticism of individual plays arranged in the order of their approximate critical importance, and concludes with a brief summary of the current state of criticism. The third section treats canon (including apocrypha), dates, and the state of the standard and other editions of the plays and nondramatic works. The arrangement of this section is chronological, following the preferred performance dates given in the *Annals of English Drama* and its *Supplements*; the play titles are cited as they appear in the *Annals*. At the contributor's discretion, items are either discussed in the commentary or listed in the See Also section. Contributors were free to modify these general guidelines to better accommodate the specific published material on a given author. Essays on the anonymous plays are organized independently according to the nature of the published studies; anonymous plays are discussed in the order of their performance date in the *Annals*. The section on minor named dramatists uses an annotated bibliography format arranged according to the date of publication of the criticism. Series titles are included only when they indicate the nature of the work or are useful as finding tools.

The use of chronological guidelines to determine the dramatists and plays included here resulted in a less homogeneous grouping than that in each of the three previous volumes in the series. The diversity of the plays discussed and of the critical response to them reflects a fragmentation which is a fact of the history of Jacobean and Caroline drama. Fletcher, Beaumont, and their associates provide a tenuous unity to some of this material, but the accident of time, rather than distinct schools, movements, or dominant figures, determined this volume's contents.

The series owes a special debt to the librarians of more than a dozen colleges and universities and to the staffs of the Folger Shakespeare Library, Widener Library of Harvard University, and the Library of Congress, who located especially rare items. Professors Alfred Harbage and Samuel Schoenbaum gave permission to use information from the revised *Annals of English Drama* and the *Supplements to the Revised Edition* and to follow those works as principles of organization. Permission to use the Master List and Table of Abbreviations of the *MLA International Bibliography* was granted by the Bibliographer of the Association, Harrison T. Meserole. Our list of journal and series abbreviations conforms to the MLA list except that we include several older titles not in the current MLA tables.

The University of Nebraska Press has generously supported this series for more than a decade. The editors gratefully acknowledge the Press's consistent response in the best traditions of academic publishing.

Alfred Harbage, the series advisory editor, was our constant guide and best critic. He made changes in the earliest plans prior to their submission to the Press and at the time of his death, in May, 1976, most of the material for this final volume was in draft form. He generously gave of his learning and his humanity; we are in his debt. This volume and the series are dedicated to his memory.

Terence P. Logan
Denzell S. Smith

LIST OF ABBREVIATIONS

AION-SG	*Annali Istituto Universitario Orientale, Napoli, Sezione Germanica*
AN&Q	*American Notes and Queries*
Archiv	*Archiv für das Studium der Neueren Sprachen und Literaturen*
ASNSP	*Annali della Scuola Normale Superiore de Pisa*
AUMLA	*Journal of the Australasian Universities Language and Literature Association*
AUR	*Aberdeen University Review*
BBr	*Books at Brown*
BFLS	*Bulletin de la Faculté des Lettres de Strasbourg*
BHR	*Bibliothéque d'Humanisme et Renaissance*
BJRL	*Bulletin of the John Rylands Library*
BLM	*Bonniers Litterära Magasin*
BNYPL	*Bulletin of the New York Public Library*
Boek	*Het Boek*
BRMMLA	*Bulletin of the Rocky Mountain Modern Language Association*
BUSE	*Boston University Studies in English*
CE	*College English*
CJ	*Classical Journal*
CL	*Comparative Literature*
CLAJ	*College Language Association Journal*
ClareQ	*Claremont Quarterly*
ColQ	*Colorado Quarterly*
CompD	*Comparative Drama*
CritQ	*Critical Quarterly*
CS	*Cahiers du Sud*
DA	*Dissertation Abstracts*
Drama	*Drama: The Quarterly Theatre Review*
DramS	*Drama Survey*
DUJ	*Durham University Journal*
EA	*Etudes Anglaises*
EDH	Essays by Divers Hands
EJ	*English Journal*

ELH	*Journal of English Literary History*
ELN	*English Language Notes*
EM	*English Miscellany*
E&S	*Essays and Studies by Members of the English Association*
ES	*English Studies*
ESA	*English Studies in Africa*
ESQ	*Emerson Society Quarterly*
ESRS	*Emporia State Research Studies*
ETJ	*Educational Theatre Journal*
Expl	*Explicator*
FK	*Filológiai Közlöny*
FurmS	*Furman Studies*
HAB	*Humanities Association Bulletin*
Hispano	*Hispanófila*
HLQ	*Huntington Library Quarterly*
HTR	*Harvard Theological Review*
IER	*Irish Ecclesiastical Record*
JEGP	*Journal of English and Germanic Philology*
JHI	*Journal of the History of Ideas*
JQ	*Journalism Quarterly*
JWCI	*Journal of the Warburg and Courtauld Institute*
KR	*Kenyon Review*
L&P	*Literature and Psychology*
LCrit	*Literary Criterion*
LHR	*Lock Haven Review*
Library	*The Library*
McNR	*McNeese Review*
MLN	*Modern Language Notes*
MLQ	*Modern Language Quarterly*
MLR	*Modern Language Review*
Month	*The Month*
MP	*Modern Philology*
MSpr	*Moderna Språk*
MuK	*Maske und Kothurn*
N&Q	*Notes and Queries*
Neophil	*Neophilologus*
NM	*Neuphilologische Mitteilungen*
NS	*Die Neueren Sprachen*
NSE	Norwegian Studies in English
NTg	*De Nieuwe Taalgids*

PBA	*Proceedings of the British Academy*
PBSA	*Papers of the Bibliographical Society of America*
PLPLS-LHS	*Proceedings of the Leeds Philosophic and Literary Society, Literary and Historical Section*
PMLA	*Publications of the Modern Language Association of America*
PP	*Philologica Pragensia*
PQ	*Philological Quarterly*
PTRSC	*Proceedings and Transactions of the Royal Society of Canada*
QQ	*Queen's Quarterly*
QR	*Quarterly Review*
QRL	*Quarterly Review of Literature*
RAA	*Revue Anglo-Américaine*
RBPH	*Revue Belge de Philologie et d'Histoire*
REL	*Review of English Literature*
RenD	*Renaissance Drama*
RenP	*Renaissance Papers*
RES	*Review of English Studies*
RIP	*Rice Institute Pamphlets*
RLC	*Revue de Littérature Comparée*
RLMC	*Rivista di Letterature Moderne e Comparate*
RLV	*Revue des Langues Vivantes*
RMS	*Renaissance and Modern Studies*
RN	*Renaissance News*
RORD	*Research Opportunities in Renaissance Drama*
RRDS	Regents Renaissance Drama Series
RS	*Research Studies*
SAB	*South Atlantic Bulletin*
SAQ	*South Atlantic Quarterly*
SB	*Studies in Bibliography: Papers of the Bibliographical Society of the University of Virginia*
ScS	*Scottish Studies*
SEL	*Studies in English Literature, 1500-1900*
SELit	*Studies in English Literature* (English Literary Society of Japan)
SFQ	*Southern Folklore Quarterly*
ShAB	*Shakespeare Association Bulletin*
ShakS	*Shakespeare Studies*
ShN	*Shakespeare Newsletter*

ShS	*Shakespeare Survey*
SJ	*Shakespeare-Jahrbuch*
SJH	*Shakespeare-Jahrbuch* (Heidelberg)
SJW	*Shakespeare-Jahrbuch* (Weimar)
SOF	*Sudöst-Forschungen*
SP	*Studies in Philology*
SQ	*Shakespeare Quarterly*
SR	*Sewanee Review*
SRen	*Studies in the Renaissance*
SSF	*Studies in Short Fiction*
SuAS	Stratford-upon-Avon Studies, ed. John Russell Brown and Bernard Harris
SzEP	Studien zur Englischen Philologie
TDR	*Tulane Drama Review* (since 1968, *The Drama Review*)
TEAS	Twayne's English Author Series
TFSB	*Tennessee Folklore Society Bulletin*
TLS	[London] *Times Literary Supplement*
TSE	*Tulane Studies in English*
TSL	*Tennessee Studies in Literature*
TSLL	*Texas Studies in Literature and Language*
UDR	*University of Dayton Review*
UFMH	University of Florida Monographs, Humanities Series
UMSE	*University of Mississippi Studies in English*
UTQ	*University of Toronto Quarterly*
VUSH	Vanderbilt University Studies in the Humanities
WF	*Western Folklore*
WSt	*Word Study*
WTW	Writers and Their Work
YWES	*Year's Work in English Studies*
ZAA	*Zeitschrift für Anglistik und Amerikanistik*

THE LATER JACOBEAN AND CAROLINE DRAMATISTS

FRANCIS BEAUMONT AND
JOHN FLETCHER

Denzell S. Smith

The Dramatic Works in the Beaumont and Fletcher Canon, gen. ed. Fredson Bowers, will, when completed, be standard. Three volumes have been published (1966-76). The plays remain available in Arnold Glover and A. R. Waller, ed., *The Works of Francis Beaumont and John Fletcher*, 10 vols. (1905-12). Twenty plays may be found in the incomplete edition of A. H. Bullen and others, *The Works of Francis Beaumont and John Fletcher*, four volumes of a proposed twelve published (1904-12).

I. GENERAL

A. BIOGRAPHICAL

Aubrey's famous brief description of the bachelor lives of Beaumont and Fletcher, and Fuller's longer ones (in *Worthies of Kent* and *Worthies of Northhamptonshire*) are reprinted by G. B. Harrison, *Shakespeare's Fellows: Being a Brief Chronicle of the Shakespearean Age* (1923). Harrison also quotes all of Beaumont's letter to Jonson (first printed in the 1647 Folio), and argues against the wits' club at the Mermaid. Charles Mills Gayley's critical biography, *Beaumont the Dramatist: A Portrait, with Some Account of His Circle, Elizabethan and Jacobean, and of His Association with John Fletcher*, dates from 1914. In vol. 3 of *The Elizabethan Stage* (1923), E. K. Chambers gives the facts of Beaumont's life, together with conjectures about Beaumont's independent writing, the partnership and its dates, and Fletcher's later career. Beaumont's life is told in novel form by Winifred Bryher (Winifred Ellerman) in *The Player's Boy* (1953).

G. E. Bentley, *The Later Jacobean and Caroline Stage*, vol. 3 (1956), summarizes the facts of Fletcher's life with citations from early sources and ample illustrative quotation. He concludes by noting that he found three hundred allusions to Beaumont and Fletcher "without any particular search," thereby attesting to his observation that "with Shakespeare and Jonson, they formed the great triumvirate of the English drama in the estimate of their successors of the seventeenth and eighteenth centuries."

In *The Profession of Dramatist in Shakespeare's Time, 1590-1642* (1971), Bentley argues several important points: Fletcher's production of thirty-two and a half plays in sixteen and a half years for the King's Men is about the norm for contracted work; he wrote alone or collaborated in forty-two plays for the King's Men; he had "some non-publishing" arrangement with that company; and he began writing for them about 1609-10 (earlier Bentley had said that the King's Men secured Beaumont and Fletcher as playwrights for the newly acquired Blackfriars Theater in 1608: "Shakespeare and the Blackfriars Theatre," *ShS* 1 [1948]: 38-50). *English Literary Autographs 1550-1650*, Pt. 3 (1932), ed. W. W. Greg, contains a resumé of Fletcher's life and work prefixed to a facsimile of the undated verse letter (discovered in 1925) with prose conclusion signed "John Fletcher" and addressed to the Countess of Huntingdon. Greg's inference is that the signature, address, and one word added to the subscription are autograph. Whether the letter, also printed in J. R. Clemens, "A Recent Discovery," *University of California Chronicle* 34 (1932):335-37, is a holograph or not was debated by Greg and Samuel A. Tannenbaum.

B. GENERAL STUDIES OF THE PLAYS

Because Chambers, vol. 3 (1923), discusses plays in the canon dated before 1616 and Bentley, vol. 3 (1956), discusses those dated after 1616 but seldom includes general criticism, this section will treat significant general criticism written between 1923 and 1941.

Criticism of plays in the canon should be measured against the facts provided by Chambers in *The Elizabethan Stage* and by Bentley in *The Jacobean and Caroline Stage*. Bentley is acutely aware of the need to label hunches, guesses, or speculations as such.

The pamphlet by Ian Fletcher, *Beaumont and Fletcher* (1967), in the Writers and Their Work series, is an appreciative, informative summary of the major problems that must be confronted in dealing with the plays. It touches on biography, collaboration, reputation, staging, general effect, genre problems, briefly discusses the major plays, and contains a useful eleven-page select bibliography. Thomas Marc Parrott and Robert Hamilton Ball, *A Short View of Elizabethan Drama* (1943), remark briefly on sources, plot, style, main effects, quality, and stage history; Beaumont and Fletcher were the "creators and the great exemplars" of courtly drama. Frederick S. Boas, *An Introduction to Stuart Drama* (1946), surveys the later plays, providing printing and performance dates, plot summaries, brief critical remarks, and relevant factual information. Nancy Cotton Pearse, *John Fletcher's Chastity Plays: Mirrors of Modesty* (1973), usefully summarizes critical attitudes to the plays since Coleridge.

The bulk of criticism up to about 1940, whether appreciative or unappreciative, repeats descriptive comments made in pioneering studies. G. C. Macaulay, *Francis Beaumont: A Critical Study* (1883), observes that Beaumont is a grave genius with a regular, vigorous, ironical, and metaphorical style. Ashley H. Thorndike, *The Influence of Beaumont and Fletcher on Shakespere* (1901), notices the inventive plots, variety of emotional effects, and heroic actions, but views characterization less favorably; in his *English Comedy* (1929) he admires the "sheer immediate theatrical effectiveness" of the plays. Gayley, *Beaumont, the Dramatist* (I,A), approves of Beaumont as philosophical and earnest; his characters are true to nature. Fletcher, although without ethical insight, is a skilled dramatist who captivates through rapidity and variety. Later appreciative comments include those by A. K. McIlwraith, ed., *Five Stuart Tragedies* (1953), and Sir Thomas Beecham in his lecture *John Fletcher* (1956).

Other critics are less favorable. Allardyce Nicoll, in *British Drama: An Historical Survey from the Beginnings to the Present Time* (1929; 5th ed. 1963), says that fundamentally Beaumont and Fletcher "are theatrical rather than dramatic," a point also made by Henry W. Wells, *Elizabethan and Jacobean Playwrights* (1939), who objects to the superficiality and theatricality of the plays. William W. Appleton, *Beaumont and Fletcher: A Critical Study* (1956), believes that Fletcher had no talent for tragedy and that his comedies are not informed by a basic comic situation. His later collaborations are "literary in the worst sense of the word." More recently, John R. McElroy objects to the lack of "imaginative depth and intellectual conviction" and to the failure to "convey a serious outlook on life," in *Parody and Burlesque in the Tragicomedies of Thomas Middleton* (1972).

The general view that the plays are not serious—indeed are immoral—provided a basis for viewing them as part of the "decadent" stage of the early seventeenth century. Paul Elmer More charged that they were "simply wanton" and catered to the tastes of an immoral age, in "Beaumont and Fletcher," *With the Wits*, Shelburne Essays, Tenth Series (1919), pp. 3-40. This viewpoint remains common. L. C. Knights, *Drama and Society in the Age of Jonson* (1937), claims that moral issues are "not squarely faced" and that the plays do not "explore and express emotions, and that is decadence." L. G. Salingar, "The Decline of Tragedy in the Age of Shakespeare," in *The Age of Shakespeare* (1955; vol. 2 of the *Pelican Guide to English Literature*, ed. Boris Ford), pp. 429-40, finds the plays without "moral insight or intellectual honesty"; they also are "emotionally shallow, arbitrary, and confined," and therefore artistically decadent. These "irresponsible" and "ethically frivolous" plays, says Robert Ornstein in *The Moral Vision of Jacobean Tragedy* (1960), reveal a "decline of artistic standards and a debasement of the audience's taste." And in the section titled "The Decadence" of his study, *Elizabethan and Jacobean Tragedy* (1964), T. B. Tomlinson says: "The issue is not who wrote the plays, but what—if anything—is their worth?" His answer is that "it is a mistake to take them too seriously."

In "Le déclin de la scène 'indivisible' élisebéthaine: Beaumont, Fletcher, et Heywood," *Dramaturgie et société: rapports entre l'œuvre théâtrale, son interprétation et son public aux xvie et xviie siécles*, 2 vols. (1968), 1: 814-27, Robert Weimann argues that the supposed decline of the drama in the Beaumont and Fletcher plays cannot be explained by merely citing their characteristics; rather, the relationship of audience and society to the plays, and the social structure described in them, must be examined. Weimann claims that Elizabethan drama had "en effet un théâtre 'indivisible' avec un poésie 'illimité'"; Jacobean drama did not.

M. C. Bradbrook earlier defined the "decline." In *Growth and Structure of Elizabethan Comedy* (1955), she regards the emphasis on wit rather than on feeling in the Beaumont and Fletcher plays as a sign of a breakdown of older values and beliefs, for "beyond their own wilfulness and wit, Fletcher's heroes have nothing to rely on." Since "private affections and individual standards" provide the only means for decision, "the bonds of society are loosed, and the territory of art is circumscribed." In *Themes and Conventions of Elizabethan Tragedy* (1935), Bradbrook argues that the collapse of the poetic structure is directly related to the collapse of the moral structure, for the two are interdependent. Structural use of subplot is abandoned and there is no verbal framework: "the basis of these plays is an outrageous stimulation."

Also, the comedies are not critical, "for criticism implies a fixed standard of judgment which these dramatists did not possess." Fletcher's inability to maintain the distinction between comedy and tragedy indicates a lack of strength, a strength which the earlier drama possessed. There is a "coarsening of the feeling . . . together with an increased dexterity in the manipulation of the emotional effects of narrative and character." But the plays do show development in typical characters, in farcical narrative, in the way the mind works, and in complex manipulation of suspense.

George Herndl, *The High Design: English Renaissance Tragedy and the Natural Law* (1970), presents the thesis that changes in the conception of natural law brought a change in the conception of tragedy. Because the "inherently rational order of natural law did not exist for Beaumont and Fletcher," they contrived a "deceptive substitute." Unlike earlier tragic characters who strive to achieve their rational natures, characters in Beaumont and Fletcher are static, embodying virtues, and the conflict is between the character's virtue and outer circumstance. The resolutions of the plots are not "genuine"; rather, by introducing concealed facts, plots "dissolve" the problem which motivated action. Plots are arranged for theatrical effect rather than in causal sequence, and reversal and surprise replace tragic inevitability. This tragicomic world is unrelated to the natural world. It derives from Senecan, Platonic, courtly, and chivalric traditions, and is meant "for an audience which no longer share[s] the vision of law which had made Shakespearean tragedy possible."

Unlike several of the critics cited above who attribute the decline of the drama partly to the "coterie" audience of courtiers who favored the plays, Alfred Harbage, *Cavalier Drama: An Historical and Critical Supplement to the Study of the Elizabethan and Restoration Stage* (1936), argues that Fletcher wrote for a "popular audience with popular methods." After comparing Fletcher to the cavalier plays, he concludes that Fletcher is traditional, realistic, concerned about organic action, and resourceful in adapting sources.

Several continental critics place the changes in drama in a different perspective when they see them as reflecting the baroque movement in the arts. A. Koszul, "Beaumont et Fletcher, et le baroque," *Le théâtre élizabéthain* (a special issue of *CS*, 10 [1933]:214-16, rpt. with additions 1940, pp. 210-16), finds traces of the baroque in the plays, but notices that the dramatists also responded to the traditions of the popular theater. Koszul identifies the baroque effect as preeminently theatrical, and tied to Jesuit religious art. Giuliano Pellegrini, *Barocco Inglese* (1953), uses the plays as an example of the increasing tendency to baroque style and content in the early Jacobean era. Plot becomes all-important; conflict of passions is the real core of the plays; and dramatic situations are uncomplicated but intense. He makes some interesting comparisons to Italian literature and painting of the period, but his arguments are frequently overstated and only rarely convincing. Marco Mincoff adapts Wölfflin's pairs of opposite tendencies in Renaissance and baroque art to compare Shakespeare and Fletcher in *Baroque Literature in England* (1947). Fletcher is the first baroque dramatist either in England or Europe: the principles of his art are practically identical to those of Restoration drama. In "Shakespeare, Fletcher, and Baroque Tragedy," *ShS* 20 (1967):1–15, Mincoff argues that the center of Shakespearean tragedy (a term which includes Marlowe and Chapman) is intensely personal, "a war within the state of man himself," and in it the hero's personality disintegrates or is torn apart. But the conflict at the center of baroque tragedy (a term which includes the generation after Shakespeare) is summed up in a love-honor conflict which the hero can debate. Fletcher tends to subordinate everything to a dominant concept, to the typical, and pares away nonessential details of character.

Rolf Soellner, "Baroque Passion in Shakespeare and His Contemporaries," *ShakS* 1 (1965):294–302, centers on the tendency to boundless and ecstatic passion in the hero. Passion serves as an artistic principle which exploits all opportunities for movement and tension. The passion of the baroque hero becomes overwhelming, threatening to engulf him; it increases by its collision with an opposing principle. The resulting conflict forces the hero from one end of the emotional scale to the other, and the hero's sufferings are accompanied by violent gesture and action. Dramatic psychology is made subservient to an art which strives to go beyond probability.

Believing that the plays "were much more influenced by the political movements of the time than is usually realized," Winifred Bryher [Winifred Ellerman], "A Note on Beaumont and Fletcher," *Life and Letters Today* 36 (1943):5–9, urges readers to look up what happened the year the play was being written. In "The Social Background of Beaumont and Fletcher," *English Miscellany: A Symposium of History, Literature, and the Arts,* ed. Mario Praz et al. (1950):1–30, Marco Mincoff sees the cause for the "inexplicable popularity" of Beaumont and Fletcher in the change from a bourgeois to a courtly culture and the reaction against the extremes of satirical protest at the beginning of the century.

The fullest discussion of the effect of the social and political situation of the age on the plays is provided in the influential criticism of John F. Danby. In "Jacobean Absolutists: The Placing of Beaumont and Fletcher," *Cambridge Journal* 3 (1949-50):515-40 (rpt. in his *Poets on Fortune's Hill: Studies in Sidney, Shakespeare, Beaumont and Fletcher* [1952], reprinted and retitled as *Elizabethan and Jacobean Poets* [1964], pp. 152-83, and in R. J. Kaufmann, ed., *Elizabethan Drama: Modern Essays in Criticism* [1961], pp. 268-96), Danby proposes that the influence of the Jacobean court vulgarized both the politics and the literature of the Elizabethan "great house." Beaumont and Fletcher are "prime agents in the degeneration" of this tradition; their "work indicates the collapse of a culture." In the life of their times as in their plays, the "setting for the main actors was one in which all-or-nothing, and either-or, were continually presented as the alternatives for choice." Typical situations in the plays "turn on the divisions that such rival absolutes bring about when the central characters find themselves between two or more of them." The hero can live with one or the other; interest rises because the absolutes clash, and the plot is arranged so that opposite pulls can be exerted on the hero.

In *Elizabethan and Jacobean Poets*, Danby argues that Beaumont and Fletcher formed the attitudes of their audience rather than merely reflected them. Men in real life, like the heroes of the plays, were forced to choose one or the other of contrary, either-or alternatives, such as loyalty to the king or to an opposing party, or loyalty to the king or to a Petrarchan lover. The interest in the plays is in "those situations of conflict which rival loyalties bring along with them, which circumstances alone can manoeuvre into existence, and which choices can only perpetuate or aggravate."

Much earlier, J. St. Loe Strachey, ed., *Beaumont and Fletcher*, 2 vols. (1887), argued a view similar to Danby's. The dramatists "stand alone as representatives of the age when English manners and English literature were most affected by the life of the court." Franz Grosse, *Das englische Renaissancedrama im Spiegel zeitgenössischer Staatstheorien* (1935), describes the crassly absolutist political theory in the plays, emphasizing "das Gottesgnadentum," the state of grace (as claimed by James I) in which the inviolable monarch becomes a holy person. Grosse does not claim that the political theory of the plays otherwise reflects James's reign.

Appleton (above) follows Danby in arguing that the collaborative plays of Beaumont and Fletcher exemplify clashing absolutes. He links tragicomedy to the decay in the seventeenth century of the previous century's society and values. The genre is hybrid entertainment suitable for a dissolving society. Una Ellis-Fermor notices the explicit discussion of topics important in that age: friendship, honor, the nature of kingship, and the conduct proper to a gentleman, in *The Jacobean Tragedy: An Interpretation* (1936). These topics are debated "in all the heat of immediate experience" by characters with opposing views. However, the theater, "the effectiveness of the successive and related episodes," not the content or underlying thought, is the dramatists' main concern, Ellis-Fermor continues. They balance with "the finest theatrical tact" distinct and varied characters, speeches and "brilliance of sentiment," "delicately articulated" plots, boldly and freshly debated pertinent topics, and lively imagery and diction.

In *The Language of Tragedy* (1947), Moody E. Prior echoes earlier views, but emphasizes the poetry. He observes that the peculiar effect of the plays—their "sharpness and brilliance"—derives from verse that appears not to be verse, the design of the plays (emphasis on situation, surprise, and concealed knowledge), schematic but clear characterization, and the narrow focus on characters in a society "with codes having no very large reference beyond themselves." The poetry is not "organically related to everything else in the play," but works for verisimilitude, "ornament, and theatrical brilliance."

When Ellis-Fermor (above) speaks of the "superlatively good" structure of the plays, noting the "effectiveness of the successive and related episodes" by which the plays proceed in a "series of brilliant tableaux," she describes the structural principle but does not account for the effect. Later critics seek to explain the effect by examining the rhetorical nature of the plays. Arthur Mizener, in his seminal essay "The High Design of *A King and No King*," *MP* 38 (1949):133-54 (rpt. in Max Bluestone and Norman Rabkin, ed., *Shakespeare's Contemporaries*, 2nd ed. [1970], pp. 342-62), explains the "emotional form" of the plays. The primary aim of Beaumont and Fletcher was to order their material in an emotional or psychological form as a means to generate in the audience a patterned sequence of responses. The narrative is merely a means to his end; it is not, as earlier critics argue, the "bearer of the play's meaning and value." Mizener demonstrates in *A King and No King* how the arrangement of speeches within the scenes, the arrangement of the scenes, and the arrangement of the emotional climaxes of the acts comprise an emotional form. Speeches and scenes which are not formally ordered in terms of the narrative in fact give the play its emotional pattern. The dramatists' "primary concern is to arouse in the audience, at each step, the feeling which is a psychologically dramatic successor to the feeling aroused by the previous speech"; they use "the narrative effect of suspense to support and enrich an emotional climax, rather than using emotional effects to support and enrich a narrative climax." Thus the plots are perfectly suited to the emotional form.

Eugene M. Waith, "Characterization in John Fletcher's Tragicomedies," *RES* 19 (1943):141–64, analyzes the method and effect of characterization within scenes. He argues that Fletcher's supposed inconsistency of characterization must be considered in relation to other aspects of his technique and to the intention of his plays, which is to arouse a "middle mood," neither tragic nor comic. The audience's response to the characters is a "middle" attitude—not the continuous identification required by tragedy, but identification greater than that permitted by comedy or satire. Fletcher's characters are abstract and extreme; important scenes are based upon the conflict between a pair of them. They are given certain ethical traits and one or two others, thus creating many-sided but not well-rounded characters. Consistency or integration of character can be overlooked in the "appreciation of a series of emotions expressed by characters who are important only as elements in the design of each scene."

Lawrence B. Wallis continues the rhetorical analysis of the plays. In *Fletcher, Beaumont & Company: Entertainers to the Jacobean Gentry* (1947), he agrees with Mizener in seeing the narrative structure as only an "imposing pretense." Since the dramatists were indeed "entertainers," without seriousness, profundity, depth in philosophy of life or interpretation of human nature, or political, social, or poetic insight, moral judgments are irrelevant. Wallis finds their uniqueness in "emotional patterning," a technique of juxtaposing "in relatively swift succession . . . diverse emotional attitudes and reactions." Their main contribution to seventeenth-century drama is this new kind of tragicomedy.

Waith developed his analysis of rhetorical method in *The Pattern of Tragicomedy in Beaumont and Fletcher* (1952). Plays in the canon, early or late, of whatever genre, reveal the characteristics of the pattern under eight headings: (1) imitation of the manners of the familiar world; (2) remoteness from the familiar world; (3) intricacy of plot;

(4) the improbable hypothesis; (5) the atmosphere of evil; (6) Protean characters; (7) "lively touches of passion"; (8) the language of emotion. The effect of the pattern is to deemphasize meaning and to emphasize emotional and esthetic responses. Waith argues that the pattern is derived from a rhetorical tradition ("the material of the Senecan *Controversiae* is the essence of Fletcherian tragicomedy"), but that a combination of the conventions of satire and romance also increases formalization and decreases meaning. He discusses the pattern briefly in later plays, but looks closely at "the best examples" of Fletcher's art, the six tragicomedies written alone in his last ten years: *The Mad Lover, The Loyal Subject, The Humorous Lieutenant, Women Pleased, The Island Princess,* and *A Wife for a Month.* Each play displays at least one aspect of Fletcher's "singular technique."

Waith claims that the artistic taste of the times determined the success of Beaumont and Fletcher, not their ideas. They needed an audience which appreciated their exuberant rhetoric, and a spectator who could simultaneously appreciate his emotional response and admire the strategy of the rhetorician. The plays are compared to art forms such as ballet or opera, in which "the most powerful emotional stimuli are frankly acknowledged and admired," for those forms require the same acceptance of contrivance and declamatory passages. Waith sees the plays as deliberately "indefinite" in theme, without that "particularity" which gives meaning to "the best tragedies of this period." "For the very reason that the theme is so indefinite . . . the presentation must be varied to provide a new stimulus, and therefore the emotional effect of the plays is directly related to the important principle of variation."

In "Beaumont, Fletcher, and 'Beaumont & Fletcher': Some Distinctions," *English Literary Renaissance* 1 (1971):144–64, Philip J. Finkelpearl takes exception to Waith's view that rhetoric itself supersedes the meaning of the actions by pointing out the distanced, critical attitudes in the plays. Finkelpearl revives the argument that Beaumont was "serious" by discussing his verse epistles to Ben Jonson (they reflect the realistic and satiric social and esthetic tendencies of the Inner Temple) and his first play, *The Woman Hater* (which explains how rhetoric can mislead and experience can purify rhetoric). Regarding the collaborative plays as so "seamless" that he is "skeptical of the significance of any effort to unravel the separate strands," Finkelpearl analyzes the satiric pattern of *Philaster, A King and No King,* and *The Maid's Tragedy.* They "dramatize a moral vacuum and a hollow center. They are not signs of decadence of the Jacobean theater [but] plays which comment on the decadence of the age." The plays which appeared "after Beaumont's retirement are another kind of substance."

In a later development of his ideas, Eugene M. Waith, *Ideas of Greatness: Heroic Drama in England* (1971), states that Fletcher and his collaborators had a "keen awareness of the importance of rhetoric for heroic elevation," and that they were the "chief purveyors of heroic ideals." "Flashes of declamatory rhetoric" are one of the characteristics of Fletcher's style. Earlier heroic plays emphasized ethics; these plays emphasize etiquette. Love, honor, and refined sensibilities become important. Two formal characteristics are stressed: tragicomedy as a form served the "emphasis on human potentiality found in heroic literature," and rhetoric "helped to form the language of the Caroline and Restoration stage." The hero's "concern with the proper thing to do extends to the proper way to speak." See also James W. Tupper, "The Relation of the Heroic Play to the Romances of Beaumont and Fletcher," *PMLA* 20 (1905):584-621.

In *Jacobean Dramatic Perspectives* (1972), Arthur C. Kirsch, arguing against Danby (above), believes it a fallacy to see the plays as an expression of Jacobean *angst*. Taking his clues from Waith and Finkelpearl (above), Kirsch emphasizes the contrivance with which the choices are posed, not what the choices represent. "We are not intended to take either the absolutes or the protagonists very seriously. The choices are indeed empty of meaning, and not because they are the expression of an empty or disoriented society, but because the alternatives they pose are essentially rhetorical counters in a theatrical display." The detachment and self-consciousness of these tragedies and tragicomedies, without a vision of fortunate suffering or moral clarity, were a "damaging legacy" to seventeenth-century drama. Barbara Lauren, "John Ford: A Caroline Alternative to Beaumont and Fletcher," *Modern Language Studies* 5,i (1975):53-66, uses Kirsch's view towards Beaumont and Fletcher as a starting point to claim that Ford, who structures his plays like those of Beaumont and Fletcher, differs from them in that he upholds dignity and integrity, thereby again making tragedy possible.

Except for the very recent studies of Leech and Hoy (below), criticism of the form of the Beaumont and Fletcher plays follows the lead of Frank Humphrey Ristine, *English Tragicomedy: Its Origin and History* (1910), in summarizing their well-known characteristics (including comments on type characters, romantic story, manipulation of plot, theatricality, and so on). Madeleine Doran, *Endeavors of Art: A*

Study of Form in Elizabethan Drama (1954), declares that Fletcher's definition of tragicomedy is "the only important attempt in England"; it satisfactorily describes the form. Helen Kaufman, "The Influence of Italian Drama on Pre-Restoration English Comedy," *Italica* 31 (1954): 8–23, observes that while there is no concrete evidence of Fletcher's indebtedness to Italian comedy, his plays share the characteristics of the Italian comedy of intrigue: they are gay in tone, and combine "romantic intrigue, realistic farce, and clever dialogue."

In *Tragicomedy: Its Origin and Development in Italy, France, and England* (1955), Marvin T. Herrick shows that English tragicomedy arose gradually from a variety of sources, and that Beaumont and Fletcher came at the climax of a gradual development. Herrick agrees that Waith's eight characteristics (above) are salient, but says that they are not peculiar to Beaumont and Fletcher: they are prominent in many earlier and contemporary tragicomedies. The plays share the qualities and devices of early Italian, French, and English tragicomedy. Philip Edwards, "The Danger Not the Death: The Art of John Fletcher," in *Jacobean Theatre*, SuAS, vol. 1 (1960), pp. 159–77, isolates as "shaping elements of Fletcher's tragicomedy mystification, debate and persuasion, prurience, improbable plots with elaborate complications, and strong scenes." Joseph W. Donohue, Jr. argues that plays in the canon contain "in essence . . . the characteristics manifested by Romantic tragedy" (he cites the well-known characteristics of the plays), that the characters are "coreless," and that structure rests on withholding essential information, in *Dramatic Character in the English Romantic Age* (1970).

Clifford Leech, *The John Fletcher Plays* (1962), deals with problems of form. He distinguishes three major styles of Elizabethan drama: the highly formal style, archaic by 1600, which was straightforward in presentation of simple feelings, idea or conflict, and frank in artifice and rhetoric; the "less formal, more image-packed" style, "subtle and involuted in the expression of thought," as seen in the early Jonson and Marston just before 1600; and the more relaxed style of Beaumont and Fletcher, which put no strain on the audience's attention. (The chapter on style appeared earlier as "The Dramatic Style of John Fletcher," *English Studies Today*, ed. G. A. Bonnard, 2nd series [1961], pp. 143–57.) "Dislocation" is a characteristic trait of plays in the canon; they are "destructive in implication." Leech notices the "variety in material and temper" of Fletcher's comedies, and remarks that their comic effects arise from contrast in plots, characters, situations, and values. In tragicomedy, Fletcher develops "a situation that discharges two separate impulses operating at different speeds": this is the "characteristic contrivance of action." Guarini's description applies to the plays. Unlike other tragedies of the period, Fletcher's deals with "the peripheral things in human experience." His characters "are generally made by their experience," whereas tragedy usually sets the predetermined "process of event" against the hero's own "mode of existence." Fletcher's tragedies are without "grand scale," and they have a simpler plot line than the tragicomedies. To give them the impression of richness, Fletcher uses two devices, "formal debating of a set theme and . . . patterned repetition of action."

In *The Hyacinth Room: An Investigation into the Nature of Comedy, Tragedy, and Tragicomedy* (1964), Cyrus Hoy suggests that the tragicomedy of Beaumont and Fletcher is not "serious" because the conception of tragedy and comedy "which underlies it is so frankly arbitrary." The potentially tragic situations are absorbed by technical ingenuity; because they cannot end "tragically"—in death—they must end "comically"—in a last-minute deliverance from disaster. Hoy amplifies his views of Beaumont and Fletcher in "Renaissance and Restoration Dramatic Plotting," *RenD* 9 (1966):247-64. The Beaumont and Fletcher plays turn on ethical dilemmas in the form of a question, a "tug of war," between man's inclination to virtue or vice. Unlike earlier drama, "complications arising from misplaced love . . . provide materials for the depiction of tragic—or near-tragic—suffering." Jacobean tragicomedy has an "essentially comic design" (intrigue-ridden plots of romantic love) onto which is imposed a "burden of . . . tragic implication," of emotional intensity and mental agitation.

Only two recent general studies center on the themes of the plays. Leonora Leet Brodwin, *Elizabethan Love Tragedy 1587-1625* (1971), claims that *Cupid's Revenge*, *The Maid's Tragedy*, and *The Double Marriage* treat of "one theme, conceived in one manner: the tragedy of irresponsible involvement." The plays show an increased understanding of the nature of false romantic love. In *Cupid's Revenge*, "the denial of importance to love is a tragic error; in *The Maid's Tragedy* this initial denial causes any love relationship that is based upon it to be vulnerable." In *The Double Marriage*, Fletcher "discerns that the initial denial of importance to love . . . is . . . the result of a lack of integration in the lover." These plays mark a return to the norm of courtly love. Pearse (I,B) argues that the authors of the 1647 Folio commendatory verses were correct in praising Fletcher for his morality. In "play after play,

Fletcher created exemplary chaste heroines"; designated as "saints," they are contrasted with characters who are "devils," frequently producing a morality-play structure. The identifying feature of a "chastity play" is the set speech praising that virtue after it has survived a test. Conventional situations meant to elicit the set speech include the chastity test, the pretense of wantonness, and the summons to court. These situations comprise the "prurient" episodes moralistic critics objected to. But the situations were not meant to be true to life; Fletcher's aim was conventionally to denounce lust and defend chastity. Pearse treats sixteenth-century religious and social attitudes toward chastity, classical models of chaste and unchaste women, English heroines historical and legendary, and classical and native models in prose fiction. The most successful plays on the theme are *The Loyal Subject*, *The Custom of the Country*, *A Wife for a Month*, and *The Humorous Lieutenant*.

For each of the thirteen plays with extant music, Edwin S. Lindsey, "The Music of the Songs in Fletcher's Plays," *SP* 21 (1924):325-55, quotes the songs, cites the source of the music (but prints only representative selections), discusses the song's function and the authenticity of the extant music, and describes the music. In "The Original Music for Beaumont's Play *The Knight of the Burning Pestle*," *SP* 26 (1929): 425-43, Lindsey observes that the surviving authentic original music for thirteen of the forty songs in the play gives a clear idea of the overall style of its music. Ten are ballad tunes, one a catch, one a fragment of a madrigal, and one a composer's air; these are the chief types of Elizabethan secular music. For each of the thirteen songs, Lindsey gives words and their sources, explains the nature, source, and authenticity of the music, shows how the music fits the words, and explains how the song as a whole contributes to the scene. He argues that the songs "are an integral part of the artistic plan of the play." E. H. Fellowes, ed., *Songs and Lyrics from the Plays of Beaumont and Fletcher: With Contemporary Musical Settings* (1928), prints the lyrics from the 1679 Folio but only "certain seventeenth century settings to the songs." J. P. Cutts, ed., *La musique de scène de la troupe de Shakespeare* (1959), prints fifty-three contemporary settings for songs from plays in the repertoire of the King's Men during James's reign, including representative songs from eighteen Beaumont and Fletcher plays. R. W. Ingram, "Patterns of Music and Action in Fletcherian Drama," in *Music in English Renaissance Drama*, ed. John H. Long (1968), pp. 75-95, says that "most of the musical passages are found either in those plays by [Fletcher] alone or in scenes from collaborative plays generally allowed to be his." Fletcher used music to "sharpen the reversals of expectation and the clashes of emotion on which he . . . relied for theatrical effect." He also used music to achieve transitions between otherwise clashing or disconnected scenes or moods. There is a similar variety of effects in the use of song, but Fletcher's "most exciting achievements occur when the pattern of action over an entire play is echoed by the musical pattern." Ingram discusses *The Prophetess*, *The Little French Lawyer*, *The Double Marriage*, and *Valentinian*.

Various dramatic devices are the subject of several articles. Joseph T. McCullen, Jr., "Madness and the Isolation of Characters in Elizabethan and Early Stuart Drama," *SP* 48 (1951):206-18, maintains that the dramatists used madness to isolate their characters. Fletcher repeatedly makes unavailing the sympathy friends proffer mad folk "so their folly will provide entertainment." Dieter Mehl, *The Elizabethan Dumb Show: The History of a Dramatic Convention* (1966; German ed. 1964), explains how Fletcher's tragicomedies use the dumb show experimentally to mark a particular climax (*The Prophetess*), to contain as much incident as the play itself (*Four Plays*), or to present a turning point in the plot (*Queen of Corinth*, *The Faithful Friends*). Donald K. Anderson, Jr., discusses "The Banquet of Love in English Drama (1595-1642)," *JEGP* 63 (1964):422-32. Fletcher (with or without Beaumont and Massinger) uses this set scene five times. In none of his three longest banquet scenes (*Custom of the Country*, *The Captain*, *The Bloody Brother*) is the love consummated. These scenes reveal Fletcher's typical titillating suspense and quick turn of action.

In "'These Pretty Devices': A Study of Masques in Plays," *A Book of Masques in Honour of Allardyce Nicoll*, ed. T. J. B. Spencer and Stanley W. Wells (1967), pp. 407-48, Inga-Stina Ewbank surveys inserted masks in plays to show "that playwrights were attracted to the masque not just as a means to 'bumbaste out a play' by spectacle, but as a functional dramatic device—a way of starting, furthering and resolving plots, and of adding meanings to plots." Suzanne Gossett, "Masque Influence on the Dramaturgy of Beaumont and Fletcher," *MP* 69 (1972): 199-208, notices the simultaneous emergence in 1605-8 of the "romantic, even antirealistic" forms of the mask and tragicomedy. Beaumont and Fletcher's use of masks had an "aesthetic logic," for the pattern of the mask resembles that of tragicomedy: a "virtuous force . . . will prove stronger than the evil," as well as other resemblances. Masks in the plays also "destroy[ed] conventional comic and tragic expectations," and thereby "proved a major asset in the search for the difficult balance which creates tragicomedy." For a record of places and dates of performance and a summary of the relationship of the texts to the playhouses, see T. J. King, *Shakespearean Staging, 1599–1642* (1971).

Archer Taylor lists proverbial comparisons, proverbial phrases, and proverbs: "Proverbial Comparisons in the Plays of Beaumont and Fletcher," *Journal of American Folklore* 70 (1957):25–36 (250 comparisons); "Proverbial Phrases in the Plays of Beaumont and Fletcher," *Bulletin of the Tennessee Folklore Society* 23 (1957):39–59 (ca. 300 phrases); "Proverbs in the Plays of Beaumont and Fletcher," *Southern Folklore Quarterly* 24 (1960):77–100 (ca. 325 proverbs).

The conclusion reached by Ashley H. Thorndike in 1901 (above), that Shakespeare's change from tragedy to romance is accounted for by the contemporary production of the Beaumont and Fletcher romances, and that these plays influenced *Cymbeline*, *The Winter's Tale*, and *The Tempest*, generally has been rejected. However, E. C. Pettet, *Shakespeare and the Romance Tradition* (1949), and E. M. W. Tillyard, *Shakespeare's Last Plays* (1938), agree with Thorndike, Pettet qualifiedly, Tillyard less so. Donald Joseph McGinn, *Shakespeare's Influence on the Drama of His Age, Studied in "Hamlet"* (1938), discovers resemblances to *Hamlet* in situation, character, and attitude in *Four Plays*, *Philaster*, and *The Maid's Tragedy*. In *The Debt to Shakespeare in the Beaumont and Fletcher Plays* (1938), Daniel Morley MacKeithan finds that in seven plays Beaumont is indebted to Shakespeare for verbal echoes, characters, and details of plot, and that in twenty-eight plays Fletcher is similarly indebted, as well as for songs, scenes, and reworking of plays. Murray Abend, "Shakespeare's Influences in Beaumont and Fletcher," *N&Q* 197 (1952):272–74, 360–63, cites borrowings not included in C. M. Ingleby, et al., *The Shakspere Allusion Book*, 2 vols. (1908), and MacKeithan (above). About forty-eight percent of the borrowings are from *Hamlet*. He continues the list in "More Allusions to Shakespeare in Beaumont and Fletcher," *N&Q* 198 (1953):191–92.

Current critical opinion is well summarized by J. M. Nosworthy in his New Arden edition of *Cymbeline* (1955). He suggests that Thorndike (above) is in error for several reasons. A seasoned dramatist probably would not slavishly imitate novices; much of *Cymbeline* evolved naturally from Shakespeare's earlier work; Beaumont and Fletcher (like Shakespeare) "were following a rehabilitated dramatic convention";

and the "fairly numerous" parallels between *Philaster* and *Cymbeline* remain "ambiguous evidence." That Shakespeare wrote a new kind of play for a new theater, the Blackfriars, acquired in 1608 by the King's Men, and for its new audience, is the point made by Gerald Eades Bentley in *Shakespeare and His Theatre* (1964) to account for Shakespeare's romances and late collaborative work.

John E. Cunningham, *Elizabethan and Early Stuart Drama* (1965), holds that *Cymbeline* has all the qualities and elicits the reactions of tragicomedy; thus Shakespeare is the leader. In "Shakespeare and the New Dramatists of the King's Men, 1606-1613," *Later Shakespeare*, SuAS, vol. 8 (1966), pp. 235-61, Richard Proudfoot sees little Shakespearean influence in Beaumont's unaided work, while Fletcher's unaided work shows a pervasive influence. In their collaborative work, Shakespearean situations and characters are borrowed and simplified, with frequent verbal echoes in the tragedies. The "polite tone" of Beaumont and Fletcher is their "really new" contribution. David L. Frost, *The School of Shakespeare: The Influence of Shakespeare on English Drama 1600-42* (1968), points out that the Beaumont and Fletcher canon is full of unimportant borrowings from Shakespeare. These, and the early date of *Pericles* (1607 or before), suggest that Shakespeare was the leader. Shakespeare satisfied the expectation of his audience in romance for unusual narrative full of excitement and surprise, but Beaumont and Fletcher "resist customary expectation." Frost finds that Shakespeare supplies elevated sentiment and intellectual point, but Beaumont and Fletcher do not. The evidence in the canon suggests how hard it was for Shakespeare's followers to avoid reminiscence.

The Beaumont and Fletcher plays influenced later dramatists and remained great favorites on the Restoration stage. Allardyce Nicoll, *A History of Restoration Drama 1660-1700* (1923), briefly treats their influence, adaptations, and revivals, remarking that Fletcher's *Wild Goose Chase* "might almost be mistaken for the work of one of the writers of the manners school." Arthur C. Sprague describes the theatrical history of the plays from 1660 to 1710 and twenty adaptations of them, *Beaumont and Fletcher on the Restoration Stage* (1962). John Harold Wilson, *The Influence of Beaumont and Fletcher on Restoration Drama* (1928), traces the frequency of Beaumont and Fletcher, Shakespeare, and Jonson revivals during the Restoration; while their plays were most frequently produced, Beaumont and Fletcher were not judged as highly as Jonson. Alteration of plays in the canon increased towards the end of the century, and by 1700, sixteen plays had been altered and thirty-nine had been produced. John James Elson, ed., *The Wits, or Sport upon Sport* (1932), includes drolls derived from fourteen plays in the canon. For Beaumont and Fletcher, Georg Frohberg, "Das Fortleben des elisabethanischen Dramas im Zeitalter der Restauration," *SJ* 69 (1933):61–86, cites revivals, dates, theaters, drolls taken from the plays, and contemporary reception. In *Shakespeare and Jonson: Their Reputations in the Seventeenth Century Compared* (1945), Gerald E. Bentley lists allusions to Beaumont and Fletcher from 1633 to 1700. William W. Appleton (above) describes the characteristics common to tragicomedy and to heroic drama, arguing that Beaumont and Fletcher prepared the ground for the new genre. He also discusses their influence on the comedy of manners. See also Gunnar Sorelius, *"The Giant Race Before the Flood": Pre-Restoration Drama on the Stage and in the Criticism of the Restoration* (1966).

Donald J. Rulfs, "Beaumont and Fletcher on the London Stage 1776-1833," *PMLA* 63 (1948):1245-64, remarks on the decline of Beaumont and Fletcher during the eighteenth century until Garrick's retirement from the stage in 1776, a revival of interest shortly afterwards, and a continued degree of interest until the retirement of Kean in 1833. *Rule a Wife and Have a Wife* remained a stock piece from 1776 to 1833, and *The Chances* from 1777 to 1808. Joseph W. Donohue, Jr. (above), makes a case for a homogenous dramatic tradition from Fletcher and his collaborators to Romantic writers, a tradition he calls the "affective drama of situation."

C. THE WORKS AT LARGE

Beaumont's poems have elicited little critical response, and the canon remains in doubt. Norman Ault argues that "On the Tombs in Westminster Abbey" is not by Beaumont, but in likelihood by William Basse, in "A Memento for Mortalitie," *TLS*, 12 Jan. 1933, p. 24. The lines in that poem, "Here are sands, ignoble things/ Dropt from the ruined sides of kings," says John Robert Moore in "Beaumont's 'On the Tombs in Westminster Abbey,'" *Expl* 1 (1943): Item 27, "refer to the effigies over the royal graves, visibly crumbling into sand where the stone is breaking." Mark Eccles, "Francis Beaumont's *Grammar Lecture*," *RES* 16 (1940):402–14, explains that Beaumont delivered a mock lecture at the Christmas revels of the Inner Temple between 1601 and 1605. Eccles prints it for the first time, with a brief description of the witty and satiric tone of the revels.

Percy Simpson provides a printing history, lists manuscripts, and reviews the evidence for the date (1608-10) in his note "Francis Beaumont's Verse-letter to Ben Jonson: 'The sun, which doth the greatest comfort bring . . .,'" *MLR* 46 (1951):435-36. I. A. Shapiro, "'The Mermaid Club': An Answer and a Rejoinder," *MLR* 46 (1951):58-63, urges that a collation of all versions of the poem before 1640 and an examination of the ascriptions of authorship be done before Beaumont's authorship is taken for granted. Philip J. Finkelpearl, "'Wit' in Francis Beaumont's Poems," *MLQ* 28 (1967):33-44, asserts that Beaumont's "wit" in his early poems is satiric and bright, revealing a distrust of the seeming certainties of life and literary convention. The verse-letter to Jonson criticizes "wit" and favors "judgment." It reveals what Jonson taught Beaumont, that "true wit is based upon maturity and an awareness of the 'good.'" Beaumont rejects false rhetoric just as he does false wit.

Douglas Bush, *Mythology and the Renaissance Tradition in English Poetry* (1932; rev. ed. 1963), says that the evidence of Beaumont's authorship of *Salmacis and Hermaphroditus* is "inconclusive." Ovid's story is inventively expanded, phrases from Golding's translation are reproduced (suggesting that a foreign redaction was not used), and Marlowe's influence is strong while Shakespeare's is weak. In *Elizabethan Poetry: A Study in Conventions, Meaning and Expression* (1952), Hallett Smith contrasts *Salmacis and Hermaphroditus* to Arthur Golding's and Thomas Peend's versions (both 1565) to provide a framework for his study of Elizabethan mythological-erotic poetry. He describes Ovid's treatment of the story, the medieval tradition which allegorized the tale, and explains in detail how Beaumont (if Beaumont it is) "elaborate[s] Ovid in an Ovidian way" by interpolating myths and involving the gods in the action. Nigel Alexander, ed., *Elizabethan Narrative Verse* (1967), says that "wit and passion" distinguish the Ovidian tradition; Beaumont's poem exemplifies these qualities as well as comic irony. The details and digressions of the poem reveal the author's purpose: to tell a "story of purposes mistook which fall upon the inventors' heads." Philip J. Finkelpearl addresses the question of "The Authorship of *Salmacis and Hermaphroditus*" in *N&Q* 16 (1969): 367-68. Close verbal parallels occur between the poem and *The Metamorphosis of Tabacco*, probably by John Beaumont, Francis's brother; both poems were probably written when the brothers were in residence at the Inner Temple, at which time they composed Ovidian poems, wrote dedications to each other, and published their poems anonymously, like gentlemen. Roger Sell, "The Authorship of *The Metamorphosis of Tobacco*," *N&Q* 19 (1972): 10-14, believes that the attribution of the work to Francis is firmer than it is to John. Contemporary evidence suggests it, and the attribution "creates no awkwardness about reconciling the poem with the known character of the poet." Elizabeth Story Donno, ed., *Elizabethan Minor Epics* (1963), includes *Salmacis* in her text and brief critical introduction.

Samuel A. Tannenbaum's *Beaumont and Fletcher: A Concise Bibliography* (1938) and the *Supplement* with Dorothy R. Tannenbaum (1946) were reprinted in *Elizabethan Bibliographies*, vol. 1 (1967), and continued to 1965 by Charles A. Pennel and William P. Williams, *Elizabethan Bibliographies Supplements VIII: Francis Beaumont, John Fletcher, Philip Massinger, John Ford, James Shirley* (1968). A selected list is in Irving Ribner, *Tudor and Stuart Drama*, Goldentree Bibliographies (1966), continued by Clifford Charles Huffman, "Tudor and Stuart Drama: A Bibliography 1966-1971," *ETJ* 24 (1972): 169-78. A brief survey of texts, critical studies, and commentary is in Michael Taylor, "Beaumont and Fletcher, Heywood, and Dekker," in *English Drama (Excluding Shakespeare): Select Bibliographical Guides*, ed. Stanley Wells (1975), pp. 100-112. Hans Walter Gabler, *English Renaissance Studies in German 1945-1967* (1971), provides a check list of 406 items, excluding articles in journals or festschriften.

II. CRITICISM OF INDIVIDUAL PLAYS AND STATE OF SCHOLARSHIP

A. INDIVIDUAL PLAYS

Useful studies published between 1923 and 1941 are included for those plays discussed by Chambers and thus not by Bentley.

The Knight of the Burning Pestle

Alfred Harbage's comment in *Shakespeare and the Rival Traditions* (1952), that the play "provides the most thorough as well as the most amusing parody of popular drama and caricature of citizen auditors," is echoed in the introductions to several recent single-volume editions of the play. John Doebler, in his edition for RRDS (1967), attributes the play's initial failure to too fine irony and too genial satire of the middle class. The private theater audience was accustomed to sardonic plays. Since satire in *The Knight* depends on the reaction of literal-minded

Nell and George to what they see, the frame cannot be separated from the play. Their interruptions "reveal the many connections between Beaumont's satire and his burlesque," and their inability to follow the plot reveals their "lack of sophistication about art and their moral obliquity." They prefer a series of episodes which thrill or flatter them. Their "resistance to corrective satire" and "partiality for the literature of flattery . . . or fantasy . . . are the expressions of self-satisfaction and pride resisting self-evaluation," and thus their "tastes in literature are an ironic comment upon their own values." Like Jonson, Beaumont believes that "morality demands looking squarely at commonplace reality."

In the Fountainwell Drama Texts edition, Andrew Gurr regards the basic play, its satire, and the comments of the citizens as three plays, with different satirical lines of attack. The titles suggested for the three plays in the course of the action exemplify their point: *The London Merchant* hints at satire in the conflict of the values of the merchant and the humor of the prodigal; *The Grocers' Honour* burlesques the pretension to courtly honor in the grocery; and *The Burning Pestle* hits at the Citizen's pretensions to honor and his ingenuousness. The bawdy ambiguities in the title exemplify the "guying of citizen taste," and the play lays bare the citizens' "favorite kinds of play, their hearty naivete, and their comically complacent insensitivity to their own ignorance" so that it "can deny everything [the citizens] stand for." M. T. Jones-Davies, ed., *Le chevalier de l'ardent pilon* (1958), gives extended consideration to diction, syntax, and poetic technique. He also discusses the play's genre, satire, realism, and stage history.

The play rejects older modes of realistic presentation and the subsequent identification with the characters, according to Inge Leimberg, "Das Spiel mit der dramatischen Illusion in Beaumonts *The Knight of the Burning Pestle*," *Anglia* 81 (1963): 142-74. It satirizes these modes while creating a taste for distance and illusion which was exploited by Beaumont and Fletcher in later plays. Robert Weimann, *Drama und Wirklichkeit in der Shakespearezeit* (1958), discusses the rise of political absolutism, analyzing from this viewpoint the play's form and themes, its reflection of the new theatrical milieu, and in general the new political reality in the treatment of politics, family, morality, religion, and war in the plays of Beaumont and Fletcher and Heywood. Marion A. Taylor, "Lady Arabella Stuart and Beaumont and Fletcher," *Papers on Language and Literature* 8 (1972): 252-60, reports that in 1610 Lady Arabella felt herself slandered by a comedy, which has for some time been identified as *Epicoene* because of a seventeen-line passage about the Prince of Moldavia and his mistress. But *The Knight* contains 114 lines about a "farcical romance in Moldavia"; the Princess of Moldavia in the play is described as resembling Arabella.

Thelma N. Greenfield, *The Induction in Elizabethan Drama* (1969), asserts that the play has the "most magnificent frame in Elizabethan drama." The induction uses techniques from earlier plays and develops them fully, including "a contrast in the imaginative levels of the frame and the play proper; frame characters realistically portrayed as 'censuring' spectators of the play; the entrance of a frame character into the play proper; a representation—comically treated—of the confusion of art with life; a satiric handling of the frame; a reflection of at least part of the actual audience; and a presentation of the problem of taste in drama." The skillful use of these techniques sustains three imaginative levels simultaneously and becomes the "means of a full character portrayal . . . of the personages of the frame." Dramatic technique is also examined by John Doebler in "The Tone of the Jasper and Luce Scenes in Beaumont's *The Knight of the Burning Pestle*," *ES* 56(1975): 108-13. The Jasper-Luce scenes invite interpretation as either "touching sentiment or overblown sentimentality"; other plays of the period with similarities in structure, style, and point of view are analyzed, especially *Wily Beguiled* and *The Shoemaker's Holiday*. Doebler concludes that Beaumont "intends us to take Jasper and Luce seriously and to respond to their speeches as touching sentiment"; the play is in the tradition of *The Shoemaker's Holiday* "where romantic love is posed against a mildly satirized society."

In "Beaumont's *The Knight of the Burning Pestle* and the Prodigal Son Plays," *SEL* 5 (1965): 333-44, Doebler demonstrates how "one of the major lines of action" contains most of the elements of the many prodigal son plays that preceded Beaumont's play, but "none of the elements are in the right place as far as the tradition goes." A comparison of *The Knight* to *Eastward Hoe* helps explain the parody which "satirizes the middle class identifying of material and moral values which created the stock pattern of the prodigal son play." Beaumont "satirizes easy middle-class morality through a ridicule of the Citizen and his wife, in turn a satire on stock responses through the parody of a stock dramatic form." Baldwin Maxwell, " 'Twenty Good Nights'— *The Knight of the Burning Pestle* and Middleton's *Family of Love*," *MLN* 63 (1948): 233-37, argues that Beaumont parodies Middleton's play. W. J. Olive, however, in " 'Twenty Good Nights'—*The Knight of the Burning Pestle, The Family of Love,* and *Romeo and Juliet,*" *SP* 47 (1950: 182-89, reasserts the earlier critical view that Shakespeare is Beaumont's chief target here as he is elsewhere, but adds that Beaumont may have Middleton's play in mind.

The Maid's Tragedy

In *Masters of the Drama* (1940; 3rd rev. ed., 1954), John Gassner writes that "to reveal the insipidity of the plot, its execrable motivation or the want of it, and the tastelessness of many of the lines one would have to reprint the play. It is incredible that *The Maid's Tragedy* should be ranked among the best Elizabethan tragedies by many writers. . . . Here, as in so much of Beaumont and Fletcher's work, shallow showmanship usurps the place of honest craftsmanship." Cunningham, *Elizabethan and Early Stuart Drama* (I,B), condemns the play for its treatment of cruelty and violence ("perverse"), and the imbecilic behavior of the characters. But the play has an impact in spite of its faults because of its strong scenes, its down-to-earth comedy, and its conventional theme (the conflict between human affection and official duty), which requires that we respond to the characters' struggles even though the situations are unrealistic and extraordinary.

Robert Ornstein, *Moral Vision* (I,B), agrees with Danby, *Poets on Fortune's Hill* (I,B), that there is a "metaphysical" unity in the play. Each scene is a "variation on a central Petrarchan theme of love and honor," and each scene acts out the "contrarieties of love and hate, desire and death . . . ." But Ornstein's discussion emphasizes character, especially Evadne's perversion. Aspatia's devotion and innocence, juxtaposed to Evadne's lust, "points to the unconscious morbid sexuality of Aspatia's death wish." Robert R. Reed, Jr., *Bedlam on the Jacobean Stage* (1952), believes that Fletcher's mad folk differ from other pathological studies in not being shown against a background of Machiavellian evil and in locating their trouble as much in their hearts as in their minds. Aspatia, however, differs from Fletcher's general treatment; she is a study in melancholy.

Amintor's fault, claims Finkelpearl ("Beaumont, Fletcher, and 'Beaumont and Fletcher,' " I,B), is his uncritical acceptance of the standards and language of the court; his notion of "honor" is the pretense that the myth celebrated by the mask is true (that women are ideally beautiful and chaste, men brave and noble). When Amintor learns the truth about Evadne, he has nothing to cling to but the myth. Only one character, Melantius, akin to the Country Fellow in

Philaster, is "canny" enough to comprehend it and use it for his own purpose. Evadne does not subscribe to it. Following Hoy's ascription of authorship (below, III,A), Brodwin claims that Beaumont controls Amintor's characterization, incorporating the conflicting attitudes in Amintor into a unified portrayal of character. The "double attitude" seen by Danby, *Poets on Fortune's Hill* (I,B), is Beaumont's creation. The ending does not evade moral responsibility but favors "redemptive forgiveness." Wallis, *Fletcher, Beaumont & Company* (I,B), observes that the characters are puppets, controlled by event and emotional conflict. Characters normally take two opposing views towards a situation, and emotional patterning can be discerned in situation, scene, act, and play.

Less attention has been paid to the plot than to character, but Andrew Gurr, editing the play for the Fountainwell Drama Series, notices that it "has that anomaly amongst Elizabethan tragedies, an original plot." The collaborative plays of Beaumont and Fletcher owe little to literary sources. Their "ingenuity was spent on laying down a strong story-line within which exist complexities . . . where a question could be posed and resolved." There is little complexity of characterization in the play because the "starting point . . . is a moral problem, private and political, [which] involves a construction of attitudes to the King's crime and a pair of alternative resolutions for the problem thus presented. For this purpose only attitudes are needed, not characters."

Two studies center on theme. Fredson Bowers, *Elizabethan Revenge Tragedy, 1587–1642* (1940), explains that the play introduces the strain of romance into revenge tragedy, emphasizes theatrical situations, and popularizes the clash of blood-revenge with the divine right of kings. Bowers discusses the nature and extent of the idea of divine right as a prelude to pointing out the "fluid morality" in the play which enabled the dramatists to present a subject's personal revenge on a king and yet not give offense. The ending, with its hint of vengeance from Heaven, is a statement of what was always implicit in Kydian tragedy, a theme which was to assume greater importance in the work of later dramatists. The play is the first tragic development of a question suggested but not elaborated in such chronicle histories as *Richard II*, *Edward II*, and *The Revenge of Bussy D'Ambois*. Howard B. Norland, editing the play for RRDS (1968), argues that the play turns on the two issues of love and honor, not as clear-cut virtues or opposites, but as "multi-faceted social ideals that are subject to perversion and are potentially self-destructive." The "paradoxical mores" of Jacobean society are thus exposed, and the "contending values" placed in relief. Norland points out the correspondences between King James's debate with Parliament over the king's rights, and the similar issue in the play. Aspatia's "association of love and death becomes the dominant note of the tragedy," and thus the "contemporary mores of love" are exposed to the coterie audience. Similarly, the value of honor is seen as "not only paradoxical but also subject to perversion and ultimately self-destructive"; an analysis of the plot points out how the code of honor "proves both self-contradictory and self-destructive." These problems are developed but not resolved in the play.

Several essays discuss dramatic technique. Michael Neill, "'The Simetry, which Gives a Poem Grace': Masque, Imagery, and the Fancy of *The Maid's Tragedy*," *RenD* 3 (1970): 111-35, views the mask in Act I as "part of a carefully worked out dramatic scheme" involving imagery which links the mask to the play. Neill analyzes the "disturbing ambiguities" of the mask and its night-day antithesis, arguing that the verbal and dramatic ironies elsewhere in the play are similarly structured in opposites. "The wedding mask justifies its formal prominence by the way in which its fundamental oppositions and ambiguities prefigure the development of the whole elaborate edifice of structural and rhetorical conceits." The play turns familiar situations inside out, and its language goes through a "corresponding series of inversions." The play exemplifies Fletcher's characteristic plot features: "paradoxical perversions of familiar social situations . . . the working out of these paradoxes . . . and the elaborate tissues of deception, dissimulation, and error . . . which serve to keep up the audience's interest."

While most critics agree the mask is only a "piéce de circonstance" (Paul Reyher, *Les masques anglais* [1909]), Ewbank, "'These Pretty Devices,'" (I,B), argues that it has a "strongly ironical bearing on the action of the play. Its highly conventional themes are "used as a foil to the actual marriage-night in II i"; mask imagery reappears in this scene. The play presents the assumptions of the traditional marriage mask (pre-nuptial chastity, bridal bliss, and royal integrity), and contrasts them with corrupt reality. The praise of the king at the end of the mask is ironic. The mask is "artistically finished: its exposition is conducted by dialogue rather than by the simpler device of the presenter; it has a full mythological plot . . . and a complimentary climax; it has two songs and two 'measures.' "

Other studies treat various topics. A. Bronson Feldman, "The Yellow Malady: Short Studies of Five Tragedies of Jealousy," *L&P* 6 (1956):

38-52, finds that the play corroborates his view that jealous lovers are yellow of face, "a sickness of lust and cowardice," which springs "from a long ingrown contempt for the opposite sex"—and worse, each of the dramatists who wrote the play "suffered from these primitive passions." Leech, *The John Fletcher Plays* (I,B), notices the echoes of *Hamlet*. For Harry Levin, "An Echo from *The Spanish Tragedy*," *MLN* 64 (1949): 297-302, is found in the Painter's scene in II. ii. Webster was indebted to *The Maid's Tragedy* in his *Duchess of Malfi* for general subject, tricks of characterization, and phrasing, according to Mario Praz, "John Webster and *The Maid's Tragedy*," *ES* 37 (1956): 252-58. Percy Simpson, "King Charles the First as Dramatic Critic," *Bodleian Quarterly Record* 8 (1937): 257-62 (rpt. in his *Studies in Elizabethan Drama* [1955], pp. 131-37), reports that Charles's annotations in his copy of the play correct what he felt were weaknesses in IV. ii, especially the easy duping of the court by Melantius. Finally, David George, "Early Cast Lists for Two Beaumont and Fletcher Plays," *Theatre Notebook* 28 (1974): 9-11, describes what he believes to be a 1663 cast list written in a seventeenth-century hand in the margin of a leaf of Q6 (1650; probably really 1660); the names are those of three members of the King's Men who continued acting into the Restoration.

Philaster

Andrew Gurr's Revels edition (1969) considers many earlier critical topics. While there is no single source, the play's aim is to translate the literary and educational designs of Sidney's *Arcadia* into drama. The conventions of the prose romance provide the materials for the play. Its success was not due to a difference in taste in the Blackfriars and Globe audiences (as G. E. Bentley argues in "Shakespeare and the Blackfriars Theatre," I,A), but to a renewal of interest in romantic drama by the dramatists themselves, who created a taste for which they were appreciated. Gurr disagrees with Danby in *Poets on Fortune's Hill* (I,B), who claims Beaumont is confused in the clash of absolutes. The play is "an idyllically complete version of the Henry V legend," and supports and reflects Elizabethan political beliefs. Bellario's service as the platonically loving servant of Philaster and the princess "makes her the exemplification of the twin ideals of service in love and government, honest love and duty without lust or self-interest." *Philaster* is the "precise opposite" of Middleton's and Webster's tragedies, "where earthly corruption is the only datum"; it is the literature of the golden world.

Dora Jean Ashe, editing the play for RRDS (1974), makes extensive use of the best previous scholarship to provide a useful overview of the pastoral, tragicomic, declamatory, and satiric traditions which influenced the play. Its relationship to the pastoral romances of Montemayor and Sidney is developed, as is its dependence on *The Faithful Shepherdess* and Guarini's description of the genre. The two Sicilies of the play reflect on the one hand recent political events and on the other Theocritus and the myths of Ovid. The survey of influences on the play "does not lead to an acceptable valuation." But the play will never again be popular; its "principal lure will continue to lie in its fascination for critics."

In "The Citizens in *Philaster*: Their Function and Significance," *SP* 43 (1946): 203-12, Mary G. M. Adkins argues that *Philaster* is an exception to the rule that Beaumont and Fletcher are sympathetic to the aristocracy because of their birth and the demands of royal patronage, for in it "the citizens are the dominant force." They depose the usurper, send the interloper back to Spain, and restore Philaster—plot developments that are somewhat surprising, for the reigning king claims absolute authority and divine right. Philaster treats the citizens with respect. If 1609/10 is the date of composition, it accords with James's attempts to reach a compromise with his first parliament before he dissolved it in February 1611. John F. Danby, "Jacobean Absolutists: The Placing of Beaumont and Fletcher" (I,B), claims that in the "person of Philaster the embryonic Cavalier could live through in pantomime what he would later have to live through in fact." Situations in real life were rooted in the Petrarchan "core" of the play, "the central love-triangle, conflict, and self-contortion," which "fate" and "cut off" the hero.

Peter Davison, "The Serious Concerns of *Philaster*," *ELH* 30 (1963): 1-15, argues that Beaumont and Fletcher reflect and comment on contemporary political thought. *Philaster* does more than provide theatrical thrills for a sophisticated audience; it gives serious consideration to contemporary political problems. He notices many parallels in political ideas between the play and James's political writings before 1610, and suggests that the play not only mirrors contemporary political thought but even presents James's statements on the stage. Davison concludes that the dramatists attempted to reconcile the irreconcilable; they would form opinion so the developing split between King and Parliament could reasonably be reconciled.

In "*Philaster* and *Cymbeline*," *English Institute Essays* (1951), pp. 146-67 (rpt. in *Shakespeare's Contemporaries*, ed. Max Bluestone and

Norman Rabkin [1961], pp. 250-62; 2nd ed. [1970], pp. 330-42), Harold S. Wilson notices that the dramatic methods, and therefore the effects, of the plays differ: *Philaster* depends for its effects on excitement and surprise, *Cymbeline* on preparation and gratified expectation, so that irony functions. Joseph W. Donohue, Jr., *Dramatic Character in the English Romantic Age* (I,B), finds in *Philaster* the characteristics of Romantic tragedy, especially emotional manipulation of the audience and "skillful alternation of tendencies toward action and countertendencies toward the . . . emblematic embodiment of impassioned stance." The first act establishes Philaster's character: "his passionate responsiveness within the carefully prescribed limits of a scene, . . . his perversion from some posited norm of reasoned conduct under pressure of extreme circumstances, and his apparent psychological inconsistency." Characters resist rapidly changing conditions by adopting absolute and extreme positions which are often emblematic. Such pictorial tendencies "anticipate the *paysage interieur* which, in Romantic art, leads the beholder from the contemplation of external surroundings into the mental state of the figure in the landscape."

The effect of the play is also discussed by Clifford Leech, *The John Fletcher Plays* (I,B), who notices the "critical impulse" which "comments on human pretenses." Some complexity of feeling emerges, and the laughter "contributes powerfully to the total effect." Ornstein, *Moral Vision* (I,B), says that *Philaster*, like *The Maid's Tragedy*, is constructed like an optical illusion: the plays "literally change shape when viewed from different perspectives." In *Philaster*, Beaumont is not concerned with social realities, but with literary postures. The play invites us to be amused by its hero, and many situations suggest a "subtle comedy of incongruity." Cunningham, *Elizabethan and Early Stuart Drama* (I,B), objects to the rant, posturing, triteness of the moral, and irresponsibility of the characters, but claims that single scenes and an undercurrent of humor impress the reader. Finkelpearl, "Beaumont, Fletcher, and 'Beaumont and Fletcher,' " (I,B), calls the play a "satirical comedy." Because devotion to Philaster continues in spite of his enormities, the effect is to require us to question the values of everyone in the play. His conduct is absurd and his character unchangeable; he is a comic fool. Finkelpearl argues against Waith (I,B, *Pattern of Tragicomedy*) by suggesting that Philaster's "tirades" are "excessive within the pattern of relationships in the play. The prose of the citizens and of the conniving courtiers has more validity than the poetical outbursts by the courtly world whose 'recreations' are shown to be foolish, unreasonable, and ultimately contemptible."

Several articles discover sources. T. P. Harrison, Jr., "A Probable Source of Beaumont and Fletcher's *Philaster*," *PMLA* 41 (1926): 294–303, traces indebtedness for the main outline to Perez's continuation of Montemayor's *Diana*. James E. Savage, "Beaumont and Fletcher's *Philaster* and Sidney's *Arcadia*," *ELH* 14 (1947): 194–206, claims that "not Montemayor, but Sidney, furnished the materials," these being transmitted through *Cupid's Revenge* (below). *Philaster* is the later of the two plays.

David George, "Early Cast Lists" (above, *Maid's Tragedy*), describes what he believes to be a 1630's cast list for *Philaster* written in a seventeenth-century hand in the margin of a leaf of Q4 (1634); the names are those of members of the King's Men in the later 1630s. The date of the list is about 1640.

The Faithful Shepherdess

Both Ashe (above, *Philaster*), and Wallis (I,B) explain how the play anticipates *Philaster* in plot, effects, atmosphere, and emotional patterning. But Marco Mincoff, "*The Faithful Shepherdess*: A Fletcherian Experiment," *RenD* 9 (1966): 163–77, observes that the play differs from many of Fletcher's later plays in its action, which slowly rises and falls rather than being spread out over a series of peaks; in having intersecting actions rather than two lines of action; and in its poetry, the integrating element which sets this play apart from Fletcher's other work.

About Italian influences, Mincoff claims that Guarini's play did not affect Fletcher's ending, nor the structure as a whole, but it did provide a model for the "artificial, sentimental, romantic atmosphere" and a pattern for grouping the characters, a point overlooked by Waith ("Characterization in John Fletcher's Tragicomedies," I,B). Mincoff follows the lead in *Pastoral Poetry and Pastoral Drama* (1906), by W. W. Greg, who said that the play was an adaptation, not a mere imitation, of Italian models. David Orr, *Italian Renaissance Drama in England Before 1625* (1970), merely quotes Greg's observations about Fletcher's independence (in Greg's edition of the play in vol. 3 of *The Works of Francis Beaumont and John Fletcher*, ed. A. H. Bullen [1908]). But V. M. Jeffery, "Italian Influence in Fletcher's *Faithful Shepherdess*," *MLR* 21 (1926): 147–58, describes Fletcher's debt to Italian pastoral drama—*Mirzia* by Marsi in particular—in characterization and treatment of episode. Herrick, *Tragicomedy* (I,B), explains how Fletcher both follows and departs from Guarini's theory of pastoral tragicomedy.

Willard Thorp, *The Triumph of Realism in Elizabethan Drama 1558–1612* (1916), calls *The Faithful Shepherdess* the "most striking example of all Elizabethan plays with chastity as their subject." But it "is not a play to be taken seriously," because it presents a literary view of its subject and therefore is "not to be judged by realistic standards." Pearse, *John Fletcher's Chastity Plays* (I,B) holds that Fletcher glorifies chaste womanhood in a Spenser-like faery atmosphere. Chastity is given mystical and magical powers; it is glorified by means of exhortation, precept, and example. The play is an esthetic, not a moral failure, with lack of plot as its basic fault. Fletcher found it difficult to dramatize a "virtue that in life is essentially passive."

A King and No King

Mizener's well-known article is discussed above (I,B). Ornstein, *Moral Vision* (I,B), finds the play morally "delicate," with its "central theme of incestuous love . . . handled with . . . restraint." But Fletcher does not seek a "genuine ethical solution"; rather he "falls back on the ever-useful trumpery of romance." Robert K. Turner, Jr., "The Morality of a *A King and No King*," *RenP* 1958, 1959, 1960 (1961), pp. 93–103, identifies Arbaces's internal conflict as between Will and Reason. The morality figures of Mardonius and Bessus are his good and evil angels (as Mizener claimed). But in this play, unlike the morally stronger Elizabethan tragedy, "Will has its way while Reason stands by and nods approvingly." Sin is not paid for, "punishment for surrender to the passions vanishes," and the play is morally shabby. The outcome suited the tastes of an audience which was morally indulgent and lax. Turner echoes these views in his edition of the play for RRDS (1963).

Finkelpearl, "Beaumont, Fletcher, and 'Beaumont and Fletcher'" (I,B), objects to Turner's statement that the ending is a "moral blur." The comic device of Arbaces-no-king and Panthea-not-his-sister does not point out, as Turner claims, that "punishment for surrender to the passions vanishes, [which is] a subversion of the moral and intellectual code which had formed the basis for tragedy." This reading, Finkelpearl says, results from "miscalculating the tone and hence the genre of the play." Our response to Arbaces is regulated by other characters who respond to passion-provoking situations—Prince Tigranes and Ligones, who admit and master intemperance, and Captain Bessus, the coward in whom Arbaces sees his own moral state. In this play as in others, Beaumont and Fletcher "control our attitudes, [but] the spectator must put the pieces together." The play does not center on incest, but on a portrait of radical intemperance and vainglory.

In *Ideas of Greatness* (I,B), Waith discusses the hero, whose rant is "finally understandable as the speech of a pseudo-hero." The inner torment he suffers when he thinks he loves his sister is brought into focus by a "modulation of [his] style, which is always declamatory." Arbaces believes in the nobility of man, and although he is no king, his "values are not mocked." Leech, *John Fletcher Plays*, (I,B), observes that *A King and No King* is carefully structured, but unlike Waith (above), who regards Penthra's love for Arbaces as "inexplicable," Leech believes it is psychologically plausible, because of Arbaces' changed behavior.

Ulrich Broich, "Beaumont and Fletcher: *A King and No King*," in *Das Englische Drama vom Mittelalter bis zur Gegenwart*, ed. Dieter Mehl, vol. 1 (1970), pp. 274-90, emphasizes the ambivalence of the play's title, the characters' true natures, and the alternation of serious and comic passages. Animal and disease imagery points up the tragic conflict. M. R. Toynbee, "Le Capitaine Bessus," *TLS*, 14 July 1950, p. 437, explains that the allusion in a letter from Henrietta Maria to Charles I on 25 Feb. 1642/43 is to Captain Bessus in *A King and No King*, a play acted before the king and queen early in 1637.

Valentinian

In *The Irresistible Theatre: Volume I, From the Conquest to the Commonwealth* (1957), W. Bridges-Adams praises the play as "an exemplary work for any dramatist who values craftsmanship." He admires its economy of construction, its restrained handling of climactic scenes, and the "opposition, suspense, and surprise" in nearly every scene. R. W. Ingram believes that *Valentinian* best displays Fletcher's art with music, in "Patterns of Music and Action in Fletcherian Drama," (I,B).

Other critics are less favorable. Waith, *Ideas of Greatness* (I,B), says that the play emphasizes the "importance of a code of behavior" in its action, and that "solemn considerations of conduct" give the play whatever elevation it has. Leech, *John Fletcher Plays* (I,B), calls the play "cold" because of the set debates and frequent references to the gods. Geoffrey Aggeler, "Irony and Honour in Jacobean Tragedy," *HAB* 18, ii (1967): 8-19, believes that Leech is in error when he says the play is "a study of how suffering and loss, for Maximus does suffer in Lucina's loss, can corrupt." Maximus rather becomes more despicable because he "considers honour to be ample compensation for all his losses. For him, friendship, love, and the well-being of Rome weigh little against 'honour.' " The play is a "bitter satire on honour as reputation," and indicates the contemporary tendency to follow Aristotle and Cicero in regard to honor.

Marco Mincoff, "Fletcher's Early Tragedies," *RenD* 7 (1964): 70-94, argues that Fletcher's concept of honor looks forward to the Restoration, as does the principle on which his conflicts are based: the collision of the desires of men with a code imposed by society. Mincoff suggests that the bridge between Fletcher and French neoclassical tragedy is to be found in their shared "coherent, logical flow of argument, strongly tinged by emotion," an argument which draws out the clash of person with code. The play harshly satirizes corrupt courtiers, and opposes to them the honesty and virtue of the camp. Lucyle Hook, *"The Rape of Europa by Jupiter,"* in *On Stage and Off: Eight Essays in English Literature*, ed. John W. Ehrstine, et al. (1968), pp. 56-62, discusses Rochester's neoclassical version of *Valentinian*, performed in 1684. Rochester criticized corruption in government in his own time, and rearranged Fletcher's scenes (eliminating the last act) to concentrate upon Lucina's violation and the subsequent revenge by Maximus. Lucina is made the center of the play rather than a pawn.

Wallis, *Fletcher, Beaumont & Company* (I,B), analyzes the play as a typical example of Fletcher's control of structural features by emotional form; thus the traditional criticism of the play for its disunity of plot, structural faults, and support of tyranny is circumvented. Bowers, *Elizabethan Revenge Tragedy* (above, *Maid's Tragedy*), explains how the play follows the pattern of the Kydian revenge play up to the point when Maximus, a successful revenger, abandons suicide and "turns ambitious villain." Bowers takes Fletcher to task for inconsistent characterization.

The remaining plays will follow in alphabetical order.

Beggars' Bush

John H. Dorenkamp edited the play in 1967. He observes that the plots are closely integrated and skillfully handled. They unify the play and increase its tempo; it is a play of action. But characterization is weak, and time is confused. The play is distinct from typical Beaumont and Fletcher tragicomedies (the elements of tragicomedy are subdued) and comedies (in its handling of romantic material). Murray Abend, "Moslem Generosity and Beaumont and Fletcher," *N&Q* 196 (1951):7, annotates a line in IV. iii which reveals the general low opinion of Turks and Moslems in the decades following Elizabeth's death. John P. Cutts, "A Newly Discovered Musical Setting from Fletcher's *Beggars' Bush*," *CompD* 5 (1971): 101-5, gives a hitherto unknown version of the music for the song "Bring out your cony-skins" as extant in a manuscript part-book compiled about 1637 by Thomas Smith. See Bentley (vol. 3) for a discussion of dating (undetermined), source, the manuscript, and Restoration allusions.

The Bloody Brother

In *Elizabethan Revenge Tragedy* (I,B), Bowers says that the play "presents the strongest possible evidence for the taint which by this time explicitly clung to the Kydian revenger of blood, no matter how strong and relatively pure his motives." The revenger, Edith, "appears contaminated by the essentially dishonorable means she has employed to trick Rollo to his death." In his edition of the play (1948), J. D. Jump cites the sources known since Langbaine: Herodian, chiefly, and also Dio's *Roman History* and Seneca's *Thebais*. Jump lists performances to 1708. Bertha Hensman, *The Shares of Fletcher, Field, and Massinger in Twelve Plays of the Beaumont and Fletcher Canon*, 2 vols. (1974), vol. 2, expands the list of sources.

Bonduca

Arthur Sherbo, "Fletcher 'In Flagrante Delicto,' " *N&Q* 193 (1949): 92-93, lists several parallel passages in *Bonduca* and *Tamburlaine* Part 1. S. W. Brossman, "Dryden's *Cleomenes* and Fletcher's *Bonduca*," *N&Q* 4 (1957): 66-68, claims that parallel passages exemplify Dryden's "reliance on Fletcher for words, expressions, situations, and basic characterization." Irving Ribner, *The English History Play in the Age of Shakespeare* (1957; rev. ed. 1965), calls the play a "historical romance" rather than a history. It weaves two stories together and in them embodies romantic themes invented by the dramatist. The play does not explore the political implications of its subject, but uses history "as a background for romantic themes." Fletcher was not concerned about the serious functions of history. Mincoff, "Fletcher's Early Tragedies," (above, *Valentinian*), says that the play has the main themes of *Valentinian*: praise of the army, virtues and hardship of the soldier, and a new concept of honor. Fletcher spreads out the "points of high tension throughout the play," and gives every character a big scene. "The contrasts are not so much of characters as of philosophies and attitudes that lead to dramatic conflicts and emotionally tinged debates designed to underline accepted codes of behavior." Waith, *Ideas of Greatness* (I,B), claims that like *Barnavelt* and *The False One*, this play "presents heroic behavior with less trickery and more serious concern" than *The Knight of Malta* and *A King and No King*. In the strife of honor, the contrast between a right and a wrong way of attaining honor recurs in the play; the contrast is repeated comically in two minor characters, Petillius and Junius. Other characters are contrasted to reveal variations on the theme of honor. Even victory seems less important to the warriors than behaving nobly. The play is close to the heroic tragedy of Davenant.

The Captain

Ornstein, *Moral Vision* (I,B), objects to the "disgusting prurience" of the incest scene.

The Chances

William C. Powell, "A Note on the Stage History of Beaumont and Fletcher's *Love's Pilgrimage* and *The Chances*," *MLN* 56 (1940): 122-27, corrects the error in the stage history of the two plays which assumes a revival of each between 1623 and 1625. The error arises from incorrect identification of actors whose names appear in the stage directions of the first folio texts. Bentley (vol. 3) observes that *The Chances* is "one of the most successful of Fletcher's comedies," frequently performed and reprinted in the eighteenth and nineteenth centuries.

The Coxcomb

Charles E. Ward, "A Note on Beaumont and Fletcher's *Coxcomb*," *PQ* 9 (1930): 73-76, discusses changes in the traditional story, concluding that the play is an original variation on an old tale. Suzanne Gossett, "The Term 'Masque' in Shakespeare and Fletcher, and *The Coxcomb*," *SEL* 14 (1974): 285-95, believes that a "confused critical tradition holds that a masque is missing" from the play; the evidence is inconclusive. Shakespeare always used the word to refer to an "Elizabethan type of masque, consisting of an entrance and a dance," but perhaps the confusion in *The Coxcomb* derives from Fletcher's use of the word to mean "any form of show, in this case a dance."

Cupid's Revenge

James E. Savage suggests that the play uses material from Sidney's *Arcadia*, and analyzes similarities in plot and characterization between the play and *Philaster* in "Beaumont and Fletcher's *Philaster* and Sidney's *Arcadia*" (above, *Philaster*). In "The Date of Beaumont and Fletcher's *Cupid's Revenge*," *ELH* 15 (1948): 286-94, Savage dates the play 1607 or early 1608 from allusions to contemporary events. Thus the play is earlier than *Philaster*, which is "a more skillful exploitation" of materials freely drawn from the *Arcadia*. Brodwin, *Elizabethan Love Tragedy* (I,B), analyzes the action to show that the "denial of seriousness to love leads to impermanent involvements and to the further misery of their consequences." Michael C. Andrews, "The Sources of *Andromana*," *RES* 19 (1968): 295-300, says that W. W. Greg's claim in *Pastoral Poetry* (above, *Faithful Shepherdess*) that the *Arcadia* is the sole source of *Andromana, or the Merchant's Wife* (1642, unknown author) has not been questioned. Andrews argues from resemblances in plot and character that *Cupid's Revenge*, which appeared in three editions by 1635, is the more important source. John P. Cutts, "William Lawes' Writing for the Theatre and the Court," *Library* 7 (1950): 225-34, identifies the setting for the song "Lovers Rejoice" in I. i in Lawes's autograph manuscript.

The Custom of the Country

W. D. Howarth, "Cervantes and Fletcher: A Theme with Variations," *MLR* 56 (1961): 563-66, finds that Cervantes presents the episode of the ritual defloration of the bride as a barbarous outrage which really happens, while Fletcher and Massinger are concerned not with the moral implications but with the "romanesque possibilities" of the episode. Both Bond and Bentley had previously noticed the source, *Los trabajos de Persiles y Sigismunda*, English translation 1619; Bentley uses the date as an anterior limit for the play. J. L. Cardozo, *The Contemporary Jew in Elizabethan Drama* (1925), points out that Fletcher follows his source in his treatment of Jews.

To Leech, the play "illustrates Fletcher's love of the rare situation," and the effect of some scenes suggests that his dramatic methods are "running out of control" (*John Fletcher Plays*, I,B). Ewbank, "These Pretty Devices" (I,B), says that the "masque devices emphasize violent emotional contrasts," and the mask functions purely for emotional heightening. Pearse, *John Fletcher's Chastity Plays* (I,B) believes that while the play often has been denounced as lewd, it in fact is "one of the most lively and amusing" of Fletcher's chastity plays. It presents a "series of conversions and tests enclosed within the large frame of the ordeals" of the hero and heroine. The bawdy humor of the scenes showing the hero's brother as a male prostitute are "clearly pointed satire on the age-old theme of the insatiable lust of women." Hensman, *The Shares of Fletcher*, vol. 2 (above, *Bloody Brother*), is less favorable; she cites "failures in craftsmanship and artistic perceptiveness," especially in the breach of the decorum of comedy.

The Double Marriage

E. M. Waith, "The Sources of *The Double Marriage* by Fletcher and Massinger," *MLN* 64 (1949): 505-10, finds the historical background and names of characters to be from Thomas Danett's translation of *The Historie of Philip De Commines* (1596) and the plot from two stories in Lazarus Pyott's *The Orator* (1596). In "John Fletcher and the Art of Declamation," *PMLA* 66 (1951): 226-34, Waith presents evidence for the indebtedness of this play, *The Laws of Candy*, and *The Queen of Corinth* to the *Controversiae* of Seneca the Elder for improbable situations or preposterous hypotheses, irreconcilable oppositions of chief characters, and concern with oratorical eloquence. Waith sees a tradition of declamation as a major influence on Beaumont and Fletcher, in addition to the earlier recognized influences of satirical drama and romance. Brodwin, *Elizabethan Love Tragedy* (I,B), claims Fletcher saw in this play that the "initial denial of importance to love, which causes the vulnerability of false romantic love, is itself the result of a lack of integration in the lover." The ideal of love itself fails, and despair is the final state.

The Fair Maid of the Inn

Baldwin Maxwell, "The Source of the Principal Plot of *The Fair Maid of the Inn*," *MLN* 59 (1944): 122-27, corrects the view that Cervantes' *La ilustre Fregona* is the source; the family feud of the

Neri and Bianchi in Florence, available in several accounts, provided the main plot of friendship, feud, and reconciliation, while Cervantes' novel may have provided certain situations which promoted the happy ending. Hensman, *The Shares of Fletcher* (above, *Bloody Brother*), believes that the source of the original play is Cervantes' novel, but finds other sources to be Machiavelli's *Florentine History* and the Elder Seneca's *Excerpta Controversarium*, Bk. VI, no. 3.

The False One

Fletcher shares the view of his time that Egyptians were, like other Africans, black; the Cleopatra in the play is a Grecian, a foreigner to Egypt, surrounded by Egyptians, according to Eldred Jones, *Othello's Countrymen: The African in English Renaissance Drama* (1965). Ewbank, "These Pretty Devices" (I,B), believes that the mask achieves its "intrigue purpose" of dazzling Caesar. Waith, *Ideas of Greatness* (I,B), holds that the nobility of Caesar is contrasted to the falseness of Septimius, whose motives are purely materialistic. The values of the heroic romance are revealed in Cleopatra's reasons for luring Caesar to reject a bribe. Her character—stern and courageous—is different from that of Shakespeare's Cleopatra, who is "slippery and 'riggish.'" She is the equal in honor of Caesar.

Four Plays, or Moral Representations, in One

Enid Welsford, *The Court Masque: A Study in the Relationship between Poetry and the Revels* (1927) admires the framework of the induction and asserts that the play is a "triumph of constructive skill." The tendency to fuse mask and drama is illustrated in the play. Each play presents an idea relevant to the newlywedded pair for whom it was presented. Allardyce Nicoll, *Stuart Masques and the Renaissance Stage* (1938), claims the play is the "most interesting scenically of all seventeenth century dramas," but unfortunately information about its original performance is lacking. Stage directions suggest performance in a public playhouse. Greenfield, *The Induction in Elizabethan Drama* (above, *Knight of the Burning Pestle*), thinks that the actual audience was treated as part of the imaginary situation of the frame. The induction unifies the four plays by providing a context for them and offering an excuse for their artificial representations. Each of the four plays, which successively become more elaborate and artificial, has a specific theme. "They are arranged in a progressive order according to theme, beginning with a virtue men can achieve—honor—proceeding to the great powers that control men's lives—love, death, and time." About *The Triumph of Honor*, Pearse, *John Fletcher's Chastity Plays* (I,B), observes that Fletcher changes the emphasis of his source (Chaucer's *Franklin's Tale*) from a trial of courtesy to a trial of chastity. Fletcher's *Triumph of Death* is a moral allegory in which the opposing forces of chastity and lechery contend for the soul; the source is Painter's *Palace of Pleasure*, tome 1, novella 42.

Henry VIII

The extensive criticism on this play since 1923 lies outside the scope of this chapter. See Walther Ebisch and Levin L. Schücking, *A Shakespeare Bibliography* (1930) and *Supplement* for 1930-1935 (1936); Gordon Ross Smith, *A Classified Shakespeare Bibliography 1936-1958* (1963); and for 1959 following, the annual listing "Shakespeare: An Annotated Bibliography," in *Shakespeare Quarterly*. Also see James G. McManaway and Jeanne Addison Roberts, *A Selective Bibliography of Shakespeare: Editions, Textual Studies, Commentary* (1975), and the survey of texts, critical studies, and commentary in G. R. Proudfoot, *"Henry VIII, The Two Noble Kinsmen*, and the Apocryphal Plays," in *Shakespeare: Select Bibliographical Guides*, ed. Stanley Wells (1973), pp. 284-97.

The Honest Man's Fortune

Montague's temptation of the Lady of Orleans is really a chastity test; both characters are cleared of suspicion by it, and Montague is characterized as an "honest man," according to Pearse, *John Fletcher's Chastity Plays* (I,B).

The Humorous Lieutenant

While both romance and satire are evident in Fletcher's handling of character, plot, and theme, according to Waith, *The Pattern of Tragicomedy* (I,B), the play's emotional tautness suggests the predominance of romance. Celia, the heroine, is versatile, witty, and eloquent, but "like the entire play, [she] is stunningly, unashamedly factitious." The antithesis of lover and warrior generates the humor. Leech, *The John Fletcher Plays* (I,B), claims this is Fletcher's best comedy. The essential idea of the play is found in the "dislocation between [Fletcher's] strange central situations on the one hand and the semi-naturalistic surroundings on the other." Pearse, *John Fletcher's Chastity Plays* (I,B), also admires this play. It is the "most delightful" of the chastity plays; "the conventional testing of the heroine is here handled with a naturalness and good humor not found elsewhere in Fletcher." Bentley (vol. 3) observes that the play has no known source.

The Mask of the Inner Temple and Gray's Inn

Nicoll, *Stuart Masques* (above, *Four Plays*), dates its performance 20 February 1613 in the Banqueting House, briefly describes the machinery and properties needed to stage it, and observes that "no vital experimentation was indulged in for the performance." In *Songs and Dances for the Stuart Masque: An Edition of Sixty-Three Items of Music for the English Court Masque from 1604 to 1641* (1959), Andrew J. Sabol includes music by Giovanni Coperario probably used for two dances in the mask. The introduction to Philip Edwards's edition in *A Book of Masques in Honour of Allardyce Nicoll*, ed. T. J. B. Spencer and Stanley W. Wells (1967), pp. 125-48, supplements Chambers's information (*Elizabethan Stage*, vol. 3) about date, authorship, cost, and circumstances of performance. The second antimask is of interest as a "parody of the traditional country dances at the ancient May-games."

The Island Princess

Waith, *Pattern of Tragicomedy* (I,B), claims that the apparent religious theme is "dilated to the point where it gives a hazy impression of seriousness," but the "true theme" of the play is "the vindication of honor." This play demonstrates "that the structure of Fletcherian tragicomedy is a series of variations on a theme."

The Knight of Malta

Arthur Sherbo, "*The Knight of Malta* and Boccaccio's *Filocolo*," *ES* 33 (1952): 254-57, supports with positive evidence Waith's assertion (in *Pattern of Tragicomedy*) that Fletcherian drama was influenced by the tradition of declamation and also possibly by the "medieval *jeu parti* with its descendants in those *novelle* which were arranged to illustrate the different sides of an argument, such as those in Boccaccio's *Filocolo*." The source is not Painter's *Palace of Pleasure* but that part of the *Filicolo* called *The Thirteen Questions of Love*. Jones, *Othello's Countrymen* (above, *The False One*), identifies the theme as the conflict between love and honor. Oiana's maid, the black Zanthia, "represents lust and a complete absence of honor"; on the symbolic level she is the devil, the agent of evil. Waith, *Ideas of Greatness* (I,B), uses the play to illustrate how heroic ideals function in many of the Beaumont and Fletcher plays. It presents a "world of powerful moral contrasts where the lofty ideals of the good characters are . . . completely formulated in terms of chivalry." Rhetoric is deliberately used to heighten the significance of the conflicts. The emotional exploitation of heroic values is carried to an extreme, and character and theme are subordinated to emotional effect.

The Laws of Candy

Bentley (vol. 3) says that dramatic records "suggest that this was one of the least popular of the Fletcher plays—and deservedly so." Hensman, *The Shares of Fletcher*, vol. 2 (above, *Bloody Brother*) discusses sources, dramatic techniques, and versification. *The Laws* is a fragmented romantic play in a Senecan context. See *The Double Marriage* (above).

The Little French Lawyer

Hensmen, *The Shares of Fletcher*, vol. 2 (above, *Bloody Brother*), follows Bentley (vol. 3) in believing Acts I-III to be dependent on Mateo Aleman's novel *Guzman de Alfarache*, but adds that Acts IV and V perhaps are from Painter or Boccaccio.

The Lovers' Progress (The Wandering Lovers)

Hensmen, *The Shares of Fletcher*, vol. 2 (above, *Bloody Brother*), claims that Massinger's revision provided a "new rhetorical context" containing arguments on the "Platonic themes of Love and Friendship versus Love and Honour at the levels of the ideal, the realistic, the comic, the fantastic, and the lewd."

Love's Cure

Martin E. Erickson, "A Review of Scholarship Dealing with the Problem of a Spanish Source for *Love's Cure*," in *Studies in Comparative Literature*, ed. Waldo F. McNeir (1962), pp. 102-19, believes the source is *La fuerza de la costumbre* (1625), by Guillén de Castro y

Bellvis, a view held as early as 1897 by A. L. Stiefel. Bentley (vol. 3) summarizes discussions of the sources.

Love's Pilgrimage

Bentley (vol. 3) discusses the play's relationship to Jonson's *The New Inn*. See *The Chances*, above.

The Loyal Subject

Eugene M. Waith, "A Tragicomedy of Humors: Fletcher's *The Loyal Subject*," *MLQ* 6 (1945): 299-311, reprinted without the Jonson information in *The Pattern of Tragicomedy* (I,B), treats Fletcher's changes in his sources (he simplifies and unifies them), compares Fletcher's treatment of humor characters to Jonson's, and examines the structure. In this as in other Fletcherian tragicomedies, a group of characters defends the popular concept of honor; the clash of materialists with this group offers a simplified treatment of the problem of good and evil; "the ethical contrast is made explicit by continual . . . verbalization"; and Fletcher's ethical contrasts are not always fused with character and plot. The serious theme of materialistic corruption remains undeveloped. While the "theme is moral, the variations exploit this moral content for the sake of the emotional tensions implicit in it." Frederick S. Boas remarked about this article in *YWES* for 1945 (1947) that "Waith attaches somewhat excessive importance to his detailed discussion of this play."

C. F. Tucker Brooke, "The Royal Fletcher and the Loyal Heywood," in *Elizabethan Studies and Other Essays in Honor of George F. Reynolds*, Univ. of Colorado Studies, Ser. B, Studies in Humanities, vol. 2, no. 4 (1945), pp. 192-94, finds that Heywood's *The Royal King* contains old-fashioned truth in which wrongs are righted and actions nobly done, while Fletcher's *Loyal Subject* is deft, dazzling, and hollow—a fantasy of Heywood's simple truths. He finds it remarkable that the kings in Fletcherian plays are of such "abnormally low quality" in drama "written of, by, and for cavaliers." Brooke's observations are further developed by Norman Rabkin, "The Double Plot: Notes on the History of a Convention," *RenD* 7 (1964): 55-69. The use of the double plot in Heywood's play is in accord with the older view that "the world [was] a unified whole whose parts . . . were subject to an embracing universal law," but Fletcher's use of Heywood's plots reveals "the dichotomized, narrowly focused, and essentially meaningless spiritual universe" of the later decade. Fletcher makes the plot more sensational, sets good against evil in a simpler fashion, and patterns the plots more symmetrically than Heywood.

Ervin C. Brody, *The Demetrius Legend and Its Literary Treatment in the Age of the Baroque* (1972), claims that the play is really a "veiled" history of Demetrius, son of Ivan the Terrible. *The Loyal Subject* is a history play dependent on contemporary histories and Lope de Vega's *El gran duque de Moscovia* (ca. 1613), not a tragicomedy derived from a story by Matteo Bandello. Another view of what the play is "really" about is suggested by Pearse, *John Fletcher's Chastity Plays* (I,B). Fletcher changed his sources to portray the beneficent effects of exemplary chastity; tales of courtesy and generosity are transformed into plays of chastity.

The Mad Lover

In "Music and *The Mad Lover*," *SRen* 8 (1961): 236-48, John P. Cutts claims this play "affords perhaps the most extensive example within a single play of the use of musical sound and imagery in the depiction and cure of madness." Because the music has survived, "it is possible to reconstruct the effect of performance with exceptional precision." Inga-Stina Ewbank compares the mask in IV.i, which is put on to cure a lover of his melancholy, to others which attempt similarly a "psycho-pathological cure of some character," in "'These Pretty Devices,'" (I,B). Waith, *Pattern of Tragicomedy* (I,B), finds that the "overblown language" of the mad lover Memnon makes him ridiculous at the play's opening; through a series of tricks the plot is advanced so that at the end Memnon is broadly comic rather than farcical. "Fletcher achieves a beautifully articulated piece of fooling with the material of romance and tragedy." Bentley (vol. 3) cites references to the play by contemporary writers.

The Maid in the Mill

The play follows closely the well known source of the Florimel plot (in Painter's *Palace of Pleasure*), but some of the changes in the plot are due to the authors' recollection of the Perdita plot in *The Winter's Tale*, according to Daniel M. McKeithan, "Shakespearian Echoes in the Florimel Plot of Fletcher and Rowley's *The Maid in the Mill*," *PQ* 17 (1938): 396-98. Bentley (vol. 3) thinks the echoes of *Winter's Tale* "by no means certain." In "'May a Man Be Caught with Faces?': The

Convention of 'Heart' and 'Face' in Fletcher and Rowley's *The Maid in the Mill*," *E&S* 20 (1967): 47-63, Klaus Peter Steiger concludes that "heart" (or "breast") and "face" (or "tongue" or "lip") are used conventionally to express the difference between the outward cover and the inner value of a character. A character's outward beauty, seen with the eye, is subject to misapprehension by others, but his inward beauty is subject only to emotional perception. Steiger extends these observations to Elizabethan drama in general.

Monsieur Thomas

Leech, *John Fletcher Plays* (I,B), notices that the inverted values of the Thomas-Sebastian plot (in which the father decries his son's virtuous behavior) are set off against those of the Valentine-Francesco plot (in which virtue triumphs). Fletcher links "two variations on his basic theme"—the war between the sexes—by several plot devices, and the scenes show a "mastery of the comic situation and a shrewd probing into human responses." Waith, *Ideas of Greatness* (I,B), argues that the determination of the three central characters to live up to heroic ideals creates the situations of the play: Francisco's dilemma comes from his being "caught between love for the girl and gratitude to a generous friend." The sensitivity, delicacy, and courtesy of the three central characters is attributed to Fletcher's source, Honoré d'Urfé's *L'astrée*.

The Nice Valour

Ewbank, "'These Pretty Devices,'" (I,B), observes that much of the play is taken up with the continuation of the mask in II.i, which intends to restore to sanity a passionate madman. But like the therapeutic mask in *The Mad Lover* (above), the effort fails. C. Harold Hurley, "The Discovery of Beaumont and Fletcher's *Nice Valour* as a Source for Milton's 'Il Penseroso,'" *N&Q* 20 (1973): 166-67, says that Thomas Seward, not J. Sympson, should be credited with the discovery, made in the 1750 edition of Beaumont and Fletcher's *Works*.

The Night Walker

Allan Stevenson reports his amusing literary detective work which identifies the Restoration actors at Smock Alley Theater, Dublin, who performed in Fletcher's play in "The Case of the Decapitated Cast or *The Night-walker* at Smock Alley," *SQ* 6 (1955): 275-96. The Folger copy of the play contains on the outer margin of the leaf with "The Actor's Names" a seventeenth-century handwritten list of the actors— but a binder cut off first names and part of each last name.

The Pilgrim

Bentley (vol. 3) summarizes the debate about indebtedness to Lope de Vega. Reed, *Bedlam on the Jacobean Stage* (I,B), believes Fletcher's mad characters are more "theatrical" than the madmen of his fellow dramatists, but like them the madmen are part of the satire that informs many of plays. Leo Hughes and A. H. Scouten, "The Penzance Promptbook of *The Pilgrim*," *MP* 73 (1975): 33-53, discuss the several eighteenth-century prompters' markings in this prompt copy of the 1700 quarto.

The Prophetess

Ingram, "Patterns of Music and Action in Fletcherian Drama," (I,B), points out that the abundant use of song, dance, and music helps carry the plot. The play strains at the limits of drama in its kinship to an opera libretto.

The Queen of Corinth

Baldwin Maxwell, *Studies in Beaumont, Fletcher, and Massinger* (1939), seeks clues for dates of composition in the two attitudes that the Beaumont and Fletcher plays show towards duelling. Plays previous to 1620 make no objection to it; those known to be written after 1620 eloquently plead against it. This play, ca. 1616-17, appears to be the first to reflect the change, which accords with growing opposition to duelling by King James.

Rule a Wife and Have a Wife

In "Cervantes' *El casamiento engañoso* and Fletcher's *Rule a Wife and Have a Wife*," *Hispanic Review* 12 (1944): 330-38, R. Patricia Grant establishes that Cervantes' novel, published in 1613, is Fletcher's source for the minor plot. Edward M. Wilson, "*Rule a Wife and Have a Wife* and *El sagaz estacio*," *RES* 24 (1948): 189-94, claims that Fletcher is indebted to Salas Barbadillo's novel (published 1620, French translation 1634, no seventeenth-century English translation) for part of his main plot. Richard Levin, *The Multiple Plot in English Renaissance*

Drama (1971), finds that the main plot and the subplot are "direct contrast plots," and that the farce of the wealthy fool trying to buy the favors of the heroine is an example of a "three level hierarchy" in plot. This third set of actions and characters produces effects unlike those of the double plots.

Sir John van Olden Barnavelt

The criticism in Wilhelmina P. Frijlinck's edition (1922) is negative. Waith, *Ideas of Greatness* (I,B), compares the once-great hero to Chapman's Byron: he "clings obstinately to the illusion that nothing he does can alter that greatness." The motive for Barnavelt's actions is spite, although in his self-estimate he is an honorable man; "he clothes himself in rhetoric." Bentley, *Profession of Dramatist* (I,A), reports the play's prohibition in 1619, when the manuscript was allowed by the censor, forbidden by the Bishop of London, but finally permitted performance. Bentley attributes the lack of records and publication to the religious controversy which made everyone "uneasy."

Thierry and Theodoret

Bowers, *Elizabethan Revenge Tragedy* (I,B), views the play as a "pure villain tragedy," even though traditional revenge characters appear in it, and many actions are begun which normally lead to revenge. The unfulfilled promise of revenge makes for an unintegrated and confused plot. "Pure villainy entireiy usurp[s] the normal interest in revenge as a motivation for tragic action." Clifford Leech traces the resemblances between this play and *King Lear* in *The John Fletcher Plays* (I,B). He suggests that the "series of tragic events is wholly rooted in a particular character, not in a situation or event."

The Two Noble Kinsmen

The criticism on this play since 1923 lies outside the scope of this chapter. See the bibliographies cited under *Henry VIII*, above.

A Very Woman

Hensman, *The Shares of Fletcher*, vol. 2 (above, *Bloody Brother*), attempts to identify the authors and sources of the play (the chief source is Cervantes' *El amante liberal*), and the sources used by Massinger when he revised it in 1635 (chiefly Burton's *Anatomy of Melancholy*).

A Wife for a Month

Waith, "Characterization in John Fletcher's Tragicomedies" (I,B), analyzes Fletcher's technique. In *The Pattern of Tragicomedy* (I,B), Waith's analysis emphasizes variations on antithetical patterns, and the conflicts of honor with dishonor. The characteristics of the tragicomic pattern are shown fully in the play. Leech, *The John Fletcher Plays* (I,B), emphasizes the unusual situation and the oppressiveness of the play. He discusses the "ironic fusing of situation and character." While imperfect, the play exhibits Fletcher's characteristic disturbing element, vital characters, variety of interest, skill in planning, and sense of the actual. Ewbank, "'These Pretty Devices'" (I,B), discusses the mask. The marriage mask in II.i lacks an intrinsic connection with the plot, but it has thematic relevance. The maskers are personified vices, as suited to the macabre marriage they celebrate. "Some of them are the emotions and vices which lie behind the harrowing twists of the plot, and so the masque is used . . . to comment on the intrigue and anticipate some of its developments." The maskers as personified abstractions anticipate the moral masks of the 1630's.

Pearse, *John Fletcher's Chastity Plays* (I,B), treats the theme of the play. While it is considered one of Fletcher's "lewdest" plays, *Wife for a Month* nonetheless is a chastity play which "uses the theme of impotence to build elaborately to a test of chastity within marriage." The high point of the famous wedding night scene (III.i) is not Valerio's pretense of impotence, but Evanthe's resolution to live in continence with him, though she earlier is portrayed as having strong physical desires. Four other encounters in the plot prove the chastity of the pair, who are permitted to consummate their marriage only after their trials by "devilish villains"—in keeping with the morality-play grouping of characters in Fletcher's chastity plays.

The Wild Goose Chase

Leech suggests that the play's pre-Restoration popularity is probably accounted for by its portrayal of a woman as a relentless wooer, in *The John Fletcher Plays* (I,B). While the central male character in both this play and Congreve's *Way of the World* is named Mirabel, Fletcher favors "the strange situation, the strong passion," whereas Congreve sought "society's norm . . . and . . . common impulses." See Bentley (vol. 3) for scholarship about the play's relationship to George Farquhar's *The Inconstant* (1702).

Wit at Several Weapons

Archer Taylor, "The Nursery Rhyme of Solomon Grundy," *Journal of American Folklore* 69 (1956): 356, notices its presence in IV.i; this antecedes the earliest date (1842) cited by Iona and Peter Opie, *The Oxford Dictionary of Nursery Rhymes*, for Grundy's "melancholy career." James E. Savage, "The Effects of Revision in the Beaumont and Fletcher Play, *Wit at Several Weapons*," *UMSE* 1 (1960): 32-50, suggests that inconsistency of dialogue and action and contemporary allusions are probably the result of revision. Other consequences of revision are "irregularities in the meter, shifts from prose to verse, or verse to prose, completely irrelevant speeches, [and] notable inconsistencies in character and action." The reviser sought to make the play more timely, not to improve it.

Wit without Money

The source of the third epigraph to Melville's "Barrington Isle and the Buccaneers" in *The Encantadas* is from *Wit Without Money*, I.i, and is a passage Melville marked in his copy of the 1679 folio, claims D. Mathis Eddy, "Melville's Response to Beaumont and Fletcher: A New Source for *The Encantadas*," *American Literature* 40 (1968): 374-80. In "*Wit Without Money*: A Fletcherian Antecedent to *Keep the Widow Waking*," *CompD* 8 (1974): 172-83, Charles R. Forker notices that the widow-baiting of the hero Valentine in Fletcher's play parallels the story told in a broadside ballad and a satirical pamphlet about the duping of a widow in outline, details, and theme; the lost *Keep the Widow Waking* perhaps was influenced by Fletcher's play.

The Woman Hater

In "Allusions to James I and His Court in Marston's *Fawn* and Beaumont's *Woman Hater*," *PMLA* 44 (1929): 1048-65, Albert W. Upton claims that the Duke is the object of remarks aimed at James and his court (capriciousness in preferment, a timorous nature, addiction to the cockpit, favoritism, elevation for the wife's sake, and others). Levin, *The Multiple Plot* (above, *Rule a Wife*), uses the play as an example of an "equivalence plot" (in the main plot Gondarino would avoid all females as in the subplot Lazarello would find a choice fish). The plots never make contact on the causal level, yet are continuously juxtaposed. No one has yet explained the combination. Diction reinforces similarities in topic, and the comic aberrations of the protagonists are balanced in representing opposite extreme responses.

The Woman's Prize

Baldwin Maxwell, "*The Woman's Prize, or the Tamer Tamed,*" *MP* 32 (1934-35): 353-63, rpt. in his *Studies in Beaumont, Fletcher, and Massinger* (1939), pp. 29-45, urges that the play is not a sequel or adaptation of Shakespeare's *The Taming of the Shrew*. Fletcher liked the theme of a struggle for governance, and sought to associate his play with the earlier comedy by using a few remembered names and by superimposing a number of allusions to *The Shrew*. However, both George B. Ferguson and Clifford Leech view the play as a sequel to Shakespeare's. In his edition of *The Woman's Prize* (1966), Ferguson describes the way in which it "continues" *The Shrew*. Ferguson objects to Fletcher's plotting, motivation, and treatment of conflict in the play, but views the comic situation, wit, and language favorably. Leech, *John Fletcher Plays* (I,B), calls it an "ironic" sequel. Petruchio is subdued, since he appeared to be victorious in Shakespeare; Fletcher insists that "encounters between men and women should be on equal terms."

Women Pleased

Bentley (vol. 3) thinks the play "ill constructed," and possibly a revision by Fletcher of an earlier play. But Barbara Matulka, *The Novels of Juan de Flores and Their European Diffusion* (1931), corroborates Willy Kiepert, *Fletcher's "Women Pleased" und seine Quellen* (1903, summarized in Bentley), that the source for the first part of the main plot is de Flores' *Grisel y Mirabella* and "not some intermediary source." Helen Kaufman, "The Influence of Italian Drama on Pre-Restoration English Comedy" (I,B), also corroborates Kiepert's conclusions that the *Decameron* is a source, noting that to those tales are added stock characters and situations from Italian intrigue comedy. In *Pattern of Tragicomedy* (I,B), Waith calls the play a failure. The fault lies in Claudio's role: it cannot be seen as distorted and his unmasking as a revelation of the truth; the relationship of the revelation to the plot is "flimsy"; and Claudio's behavior is only weakly related to the theme that women should have mastery.

B. OVER-ALL STATE OF CRITICISM

The bulk of criticism of the Beaumont and Fletcher canon in the last hundred years is tediously repetitive. The "characteristics" of the plays are described nearly identically by critic after critic, followed by a favorable or unfavorable assessment depending on the critic's sensitivity to the "morality" of the plays, or to the critic's attachment to the idea of "decadence" in Jacobean drama. Tomlinson's dismissal of the plays as worthless (I,B), and Appleton's judgment that Fletcher was untalented in both tragedy and comedy (I,B), are not extreme considering the weight of the critical tradition. Yet as Bentley remarks (vol. 3), in the view of men of the seventeenth and eighteenth centuries, Beaumont and Fletcher were one of the great triumvirate of English dramatists. A reader of modern criticism does not find that judgment confirmed. There is not a recent full-scale biography, or a detailed "life and works" (like M. T. Jones-Davies's two-volume study of Dekker), or a critical study that could be called "standard."

Much effort has been expended in attempts to determine the shares of different dramatists in the plays, presumably on the assumption—among others—that if shares could be assigned, then the dramatic practice of Beaumont could be distinguished from that of Fletcher, or that of Fletcher from that of Field, Rowley, or Massinger. Cyrus Hoy's determination of portions (below, III,A) has been generally accepted for fifteen years, but no body of criticism built on his assignments has materialized (and he in general confirms earlier assignments). An exception is the study of the chastity theme in Fletcher's portions by Nancy Cotton Pearse (I,B), which also reveals much about Fletcher's dramatic practice. Many critics even state that while they are aware that portions of plays have been reliably assigned, they will ignore the fact of collaboration. Perhaps problems of critical method in dealing with collaborative plays need to be reconsidered.

Two recent critical viewpoints have been especially useful—Danby's emphasis on the social and political perspectives of the plays, and Waith's on their rhetorical method. Each critic has fully developed his views, and other recent critics, either agreeing or disagreeing, demonstrate that the plays are amenable to thoughtful analysis. As the previous summary of criticism of individual plays reveals, little has been done with most of them. In the final assessment, there is but a handful of memorable essays on plays in the canon.

III. CANON

A. PLAYS IN CHRONOLOGICAL ORDER

The source for the order in which the plays are listed, the title, ascription, type of play, date of first performance (in italics preceding the semicolon), and date of seventeenth-century publication is Alfred Harbage, *Annals of English Drama, 975-1700*, rev. S. Schoenbaum (1964), and the *Supplements* by Schoenbaum (1966, 1970). Only plays assigned or possibly assigned to Beaumont or Fletcher in the *Annals* are listed below, and Restoration adaptations of plays in the canon are not discussed. W. W. Greg, *A Bibliography of the English Printed Drama to the Restoration*, 4 vols. (1939-59), describes the quartos in vols. 1 and 2, and the 1647 and 1679 folios in vol. 3. A useful list of editions from the first to 1966 is found in the compilation by Carl J. Stratman, *Bibliography of English Printed Tragedy 1565-1900* (1966). The reader should consult the discussions of issues relating to the canon in E. K. Chambers, *The Elizabethan Stage*, 4 vols. (1923) for pre-1616 plays, and G. E. Bentley, *The Jacobean and Caroline Stage*, 7 vols. (1941-68) for plays dated 1616 and later. Bentley's discussion of the Fletcher canon is in vol. 3 (1956).

Since that date, two reassessments have appeared. The first and most important is by Cyrus Hoy, "The Shares of Fletcher and His Collaborators in the Beaumont and Fletcher Canon," *SB* 8 (1956): 129-46; 9 (1957): 143-62; 11 (1958): 85-106; 12 (1959): 91-116; 13 (1960): 77-108; 14 (1961): 45-67; 15 (1962): 71-90. Hoy finds Beaumont's hand in fourteen and Fletcher's in fifty-one plays in the canon. He summarizes his findings in the last article (pp. 85-86). Bertha Hensman, *Shares of Fletcher* (II,A, *Bloody Brother*) studies twelve plays of the canon in detail, and, in vol. 2, lists sixty plays by Fletcher and his collaborators (named, dated, sources identified).

Hoy's assignments, based on linguistic preferences, have been well received. Leech, *The John Fletcher Plays* (I,B), finds that the tests "serve reasonably well for distinguishing Fletcher from Massinger but prove far less convincing when they are used in an attempt to break up the original partnership." The interested reader should examine Part I of Hoy's series and the introductory pages to each of the subsequent parts, for a discussion of his method and its application. Schoenbaum (*Internal Evidence*, below) observes that Hoy's findings are generally "solid," although he has reservations about the tests when they are applied to writers whose preferences are not distinctive and when several writers work in "intimate collaboration." Hoy's ascriptions are reviewed in the textual introductions to the plays in Bowers's *Dramatic Works*. Hensman, *Shares of Fletcher* (II,A, *Bloody Brother*), applies some of the traditional tests (theatrical expertise, moral earnestness, quality of verse) and also considers the characteristic ways in which the dramatists make use of their sources as a means of assigning shares.

The textual introductions to each play in the ongoing *Dramatic Works* under the general editorship of Fredson Bowers provide full discussions. R. C. Bald, "Bibliographical Studies in the Beaumont and Fletcher Folio of 1647," *Transactions of the Bibliographical Society*, Suppl. 13 (1938), pp. 1-114, treats three major topics: Moseley's publishing venture (the collection of copy, the printers, and the printing process); five manuscripts that exist for plays in the 1647 folio and their relationship to the text; and the nature of printer's copy (which was prompt copy for all but eight of thirty-four plays).

David V. Erdman and Ephim G. Fogel, ed., *Evidence for Authorship: Essays on Problems of Attribution, with an Annotated Bibliography of Selected Readings* (1966), include an annotated bibliography of general studies of attribution problems in Elizabethan drama, and representative listings for the major dramatists. Important for this chapter is the survey and summary of studies in the canon of *Henry VIII* from 1733 through 1962, and *The Two Noble Kinsmen* from 1780-1963. Erdman and Fogel also summarize other important general studies of attribution problems in Elizabethan drama: E. H. C. Oliphant, "How Not to Play the Game of Parallels," *JEGP* 28 (1929): 1-15; M. St. Clare Byrne, "Bibliographical Clues in Collaborate Plays," *Library* 12 (1932): 21-48; R. C. Bald, "The *Locrine* and *George-a-Greene* Title-Page Inscriptions," *Library* 15 (1934): 293-305; Giles E. Dawson, "Authenticity and Attribution of Written Matter," *English Institute Annual, 1942* (1943); pp. 77-100; James G. McManaway, "Latin Title-Page Mottoes as a Clue to Dramatic Authorship," *Library* 26 (1945): 28-36; W. W. Greg, "Authorship Attributions in the Early Play-Lists, 1656-71," *Edinburgh Bibliographical Society Transactions*, 2, Pt. 4 (1946): 305-29; and R. C. Bald, "Bibliographical Studies in the Beaumont and Fletcher Folio of 1647," above.

An enlightening history of the many failures and few successes of attribution studies in Elizabethan drama, and a discussion and evaluation of methods, is S. Schoenbaum's *Internal Evidence and Elizabethan Dramatic Authorship: An Essay in Literary History and Method* (1966).

The methods, and thus much of the work, of the early canonical investigators is discredited convincingly by Schoenbaum, who, for example, calls H. Dugdale Sykes and E. H. C. Oliphant "the impressionists" (their studies are dated 1924 and 1929 respectively). Schoenbaum lays down principles to be observed by those who assign shares: external evidence cannot be ignored; if stylistic criteria are to have meaning, the play must be written in a style; work with reliable tests; textual analysis precedes canonical analysis; a reasonable amount of unquestioned dramatic writing, apart from collaboration, must be extant; intuitions carry no weight as evidence; and stylistic evidence should be supplemented by textual evidence.

Schoenbaum's principles reinforce those stated by Bentley in "Authenticity and Attribution in the Jacobean and Caroline Drama," *English Institute Annual, 1942* (1943), pp. 101–18 (rpt. in Erdman and Fogel, ed., *Evidence for Authorship*, above, pp. 179–87). Bentley remarks that Collier, Fleay, Sykes, Lawrence, and Wilson "have flitted about" among plays of disputed authorship, "assigning parents here and putative parents there," but that "such mock-judicial activities are . . . reminiscent of Gilbert and Sullivan . . . and entertaining though they may be . . . they create havoc for the literary historian." He concludes that "the dramatic historian must label most of the attempts at disintegrating the Beaumont and Fletcher canon 'Not Proved.'" This chapter will not summarize the work of investigators before Hoy.

W. M. Baillie discusses the use of computers in assigning shares in "Authorship Attribution in Jacobean Dramatic Texts," *Computers in the Humanities*, ed. J. L. Mitchell (1974), pp. 73–81. The paper describes the methodology used to make a computer-assisted analysis of verbal style in *Cymbeline* and *The Winter's Tale*, and in Fletcher's *The Woman's Prize* and *Valentinian*. Baillie comes to the conclusion that "the range of grammatical variance among different scenes and different speakers within single plays, and between two plays by the same writer, is not so wide as to preclude us from distinguishing one writer from another." Baillie proposes that a study of *Henry VIII* "can now proceed with confidence," and that the methodology appears to be useful for other plays of disputed authorship.

The Woman Hater, Beaumont, with Fletcher; comedy (*1606;* 1607)

The ascription to Beaumont with Fletcher has remained firm. Hoy, Part 3, assigns Beaumont I, II, III.ii–iv, IV.i, V.i, iii–iv, and Beaumont and Fletcher III.i, IV.ii–iii, V.ii, v. Hoy believes that this, the first

Beaumont and Fletcher play to appear in print, "is essentially Beaumont's [in this Hoy echoes Chambers], and in all probability represents an early work of his unaided authorship." Only five scenes were revised by Fletcher, as shown by his preference for *ye* rather than *you*. George Walton Williams, editing the play for the new *Dramatic Works*, vol. 1 (1966), modifies Hoy's assignment of scenes to Fletcher. Originally Fletcher's or completely rewritten by him are III.i.1-153, III.ii, IV.ii.1-271, and V.ii, iv. Less assuredly Fletcher's are III.iii, IV.ii.272-361, and V.i. The collaboration left few discrepancies in the play. Date of first performance was 1606, by the Children of Paul's. Williams also establishes the authority of the seventeenth-century editions. Wilfred T. Jewkes, *Act Division in Elizabethan and Jacobean Plays, 1583-1616* (1958), believes the stage and marginal directions are authorial; there is no trace of the playhouse in them. Copy was probably a holograph. Pearse, *John Fletcher's Chastity Plays* (I,B) observes that Fletcher's hand is found in the scenes that present the chastity test.

The Knight of the Burning Pestle, Beaumont (with Fletcher?); burlesque romance (*1607;* 1613)

Schoenbaum advances a firm performance date of 1607 in the first *Supplement* in place of the 1607-ca. 1610 limits given in the revised *Annals.* Hoy, Part 3, asserts that "in all essentials, the play is the product of a single dramatist." There is "no shred of evidence" for Fletcher's presence in linguistic, metrical, or syntactic evidence. The *Annals* recalls earlier investigators in querying whether Fletcher is part author. Hoy also edited the play for Bowers's *Dramatic Works*, and in the textual introduction identifies and determines the shares of the two compositors of Q1 (1613) in the shop of Nicholas Okes. The manuscript from which the play was set was a "good" one, either Beaumont's or a transcript. Hoy observes that act endings are designated in the first quartos of plays in the canon in which Beaumont's presence is dominant. Q2 and Q3 are briefly described; the play in the folio of 1679 derives from Q3. Jewkes (above) believes that printer's copy was "an author's manuscript . . . prepared for the stage." Chambers (vol. 3) discusses at length evidence for the date, preferring 1607, a date supported by Maxwell in *Studies in Beaumont* (II,A, *Woman's Prize*).

The Faithful Shepherdess, Fletcher; pastoral (*1608-9;* ca. 1609)

Hoy, Part 1, excluded the play from his study because "its language is that of pastoral poetry, uncolloquial and somewhat archaic. It abounds in linguistic forms . . . which Fletcher seldom or never uses in his other unaided plays." The play is "undoubtedly Fletcher's own." Chambers (vol. 3) assigns the play to Fletcher, to the Queen's Revels as producers, and to the date of 1608-9. Jewkes, *Act Division* (above, *Woman Hater*) finds "no evidence of the playhouse" in the text. The "unusually slovenly" printing suggests foul papers as printer's copy. Hoy edited the play for vol. 3 of the new *Dramatic Works* (1976). He establishes the undated first quarto as his copy text, limiting its publication to December 1608–January 1610, the traceable dates of the partnership of its publishers. Copy text was a carefully prepared manuscript, either holograph or a transcript; the play was set by four compositors, whose characteristics are described. Punctuation is the "most formidable" problem for the editor.

Cupid's Revenge, Fletcher, with Beaumont; tragedy (ca. *1607-12; 1615*)

Hoy, Part 3, says there is no clear linguistic evidence for their respective shares, but what evidence there is suggests a revision by Beaumont. He gives to Beaumont I.i, iii, II.i–ii, iv–v, III.i–ii, IV.i, v, and V.i; to Fletcher I.ii, iv, II.iii, vi, III.iii–iv, and V.ii–iii. Fredson Bowers edited the play for his *Dramatic Works*, vol. 2 (1970). He establishes the shares of the two compositors who set it, concluding that assignment on the basis of "spelling and typographical evidence is rarely in doubt." Printer's copy probably was authorial papers (made by Beaumont) with notes by the bookkeeper. Only Q1 (1615) has textual authority. Hans Walter Gabler, "*Cupid's Revenge* (Q1) and Its Compositors. Part I: Composition and Printing," *SB* 24 (1971): 69-90, supports Bowers's statement of the authority of Q1, but says its reliability is "less than assured." Gabler establishes the conditions and order of composition as preliminary to a second study of copy spellings and authorial characteristics. Chambers (vol. 3) says that known performances fix the anterior date of composition as no later than 1611-12; "no close inferior limit can be fixed." Bowers (above) suggests a date of composition "about" 1607-8. Jewkes, *Act Division* (above, *Woman Hater*) finds the stage directions unlike those in other Beaumont and Fletcher plays: "they are infrequent . . . very brief . . . abrupt, and not clear to the reader." There are many traces of performance, and "copy may possibly have been a prompt-book."

Philaster, or Love Lies a-Bleeding, Beaumont, with Fletcher; tragi-comedy (*1608–10;* 1620)

Early investigators as well as Hoy, Part 3, give more of the play to Beaumont than to Fletcher. Hoy assigns to Beaumont I.ii, II.i, iii–iva (to Pharamond's entrance), III, IV.iii–vi, V.i–ii, iiia (to King's exit), v; to Fletcher I.i, II.ii, ivb (from Pharamond's entrance to end), IV.i–ii, V.iiib (from King's exit to end), iv. Hoy believes that Beaumont's is the controlling hand, although Fletcher's share is greater than in either *The Maid's Tragedy* or *A King and No King.* Only traces of Fletcher's linguistic preferences are present. In his edition for the *Dramatic Works,* vol. 1 (1966), Robert K. Turner cites Hoy's assignments. Turner thinks the text of Q1 inferior to Q2, and reconstructs the printing of each. Copy for Q2 was composite; the beginning and end, differing from Q1, was set from manuscript, the middle from an annotated copy of Q1. The annotator worked from authoritative papers. Q1 probably was in the same hand throughout ("a poorly written manuscript which came into being through some kind of reporting"), but the beginning and ending appear not to be authorial. Q1 is a "bad text"; copy text for Turner's edition is Q2. Turner had earlier described "The Printing of *Philaster* Q1 and Q2" in *Library* 15 (1960): 21–32. Leo Kirschbaum, "A Census of Bad Quartos," *RES* 14 (1938): 20–43 believes Q1 was a memorially reconstructed text. J. E. Savage, "The 'Gaping Wounds' in the Text of *Philaster,*" *PQ* 28 (1949): 443–57, claims that censorship accounts for the "wounds"; Q1 represents the play as actually performed, while Q2 is a literary version of the play as originally written. Jewkes, *Act Division* (above, *Woman Hater*), agrees. Davison, "The Serious Concerns of *Philaster*" (II,A, *Philaster*), notices that Q1 omits references to Spain in accord with King James's wish for peace. Chambers (vol. 3) suggests 1608–10 as a composition date, observing that it is not "possible to be more precise." Savage cites four allusions which help establish the date as the latter part of 1610.

The Coxcomb, Fletcher, with Beaumont (revised by Massinger or W. Rowley?); comedy (*1608–10;* 1647)

Jewkes, *Act Division* (above, *Woman Hater*) disagrees with R. C. Bald, "Bibliographical Studies" (above, headnote), that printer's copy for the 1647 folio text was a prompt copy. Irby B. Cauthen, Jr., editing the play for Bowers's *Dramatic Works,* vol. 1 (1966), believes copy was a promptbook or a transcript of it. Cauthen cites Hoy's assignment of parts, but adds that the play was revised by another. Hoy, Part 3, says that Fletcher's usual language preferences are not noticeably found in the extant text, and to determine shares he used metrical tests. He also regarded Viola's scenes as Beaumont's, and the main plot as Fletcher's. (Samuel C. Chew once attributed the subplot to Beaumont because he is consistently hostile to drunkenness: "Beaumont on Drunkenness," *MLN* 36 [1921]: 53-55.) Hoy concludes that the play is a revised collaboration. He assigns shares to Beaumont, I.iv, II.iv, IV.i, iii, vii, and V; to Fletcher, I.i-iii, v, II.i, iii, III.i-ii, IV.ii, iv-vi, viii; and to joint authorship, I.vi, II.ii, and III.iii. Chambers, vol. 3, dates the original version between 1608 and 1610.

Wit at Several Weapons, Fletcher (with Middleton? W. Rowley?); comedy (ca. *1609-20;* 1647)

The *Annals* reports that the play has recently been assigned almost entirely to Middleton and Rowley. Hoy, Part 5, gives the play entirely to them, stating that while the comic intrigue and the clown have suggested Middleton and Rowley as collaborators since Fleay, the linguistic pattern of the 1647 folio text provides sufficient evidence for a firm attribution. "The extant text represents, in all essential respects," their work. Richard Hindry Barker, *Thomas Middleton* (1958), says that the external evidence for Beaumont and Fletcher is "fairly strong" (the play is in the first folio; was later entered as theirs in the Stationers' Register; was ascribed to them in Archer's play list; and the folio epilogue mentions Fletcher as one of the authors). But after considering characteristics of style, Barker suggests the play is by Middleton and Rowley. Savage, "The Effects of Revision" (II,A, *Wit at Several Weapons*), thinks that inconsistency of dialogue and action and contemporary allusions are probably the result of revision; the play appears to date from 1608 on internal evidence, with revision about 1620. Stanley W. Wells, "The Lady and the Stable Groome," *N&Q* 7 (1960): 31, suggests Rowley as a collaborator on the basis of one parallel passage, possibly a topical allusion.

The Maid's Tragedy, Beaumont, with Fletcher; tragedy (ca. *1608-11;* 1619)

Hoy, Part 3, says the play is "essentially Beaumont's work," with Fletcher's contribution confined to four scenes, although one (IV.i) is the climax of the play. Linguistic evidence tells little about their shares. He assigns to Beaumont I, II.i, III.i, IV.ii, and V.iii; to Fletcher II.ii, IV.i, and V.i–ii. In his edition for Bowers's *Dramatic Works*, vol. 2 (1966), Robert K. Turner, Jr., explains that of the nine seventeenth-century editions, only the first two (Q1, 1619, and Q2, 1622) are basic to establishing the text. Q1 lacks about eighty authoritative lines found in Q2, and Q1 has omissions, substitutions, mislineation, and misreadings; it shows vague signs of theatrical cutting. Turner favors rough foul papers as the cause. Q2 was not printed independently, but it introduces four hundred substantive changes. Behind the superiority of Q2 probably lies a transcript made by Beaumont of the foul papers, although other possibilities exist. Turner had established Q1 as the copy text in "The Relationship of *The Maid's Tragedy* Q1 and Q2," *PBSA* 51 (1957): 322–27, and described its printing history in detail in "The Printing of Beaumont and Fletcher's *The Maid's Tragedy* Q1 (1619)," *SB* 13 (1960): 199–220.

In his edition, Turner also examines Howard Norland's conclusions ("The Text of *The Maid's Tragedy*," *PBSA* 61 [1967]: 173–200), suggesting that a promptbook did not supply the Q2 changes, and that other reasons account for the varying quality of copy. Norland would adopt only those readings in Q2 "which clearly correct the Q1 text or which clearly suggest authorial revision." Norland's text appeared in an RRDS edition in 1968 (II,A, *Maid's Tragedy*). In that edition, he suggests a "heavily revised and occasionally illegible" manuscript as the source of the errors for sheets B–G of Q1; sheets H–L are much cleaner. The ultimate source appears to be foul papers. Writing after Turner's edition had appeared, Norland says that Q2 "was printed from an annotated copy of Q1," in likelihood an authorial revision. In his edition for the Fountainwell Drama Series, Andrew Gurr (II,A, *Maid's Tragedy*) agrees with Turner that there is no theater influence in either Q1 or Q2. Gurr succinctly explains the textual problems. Chambers (vol. 3) says "any date within ca. 1608–11" is possible; in his edition Turner observes that the date is uncertain, but the play probably was in existence by 1611.

A King and No King, Beaumont and Fletcher; tragicomedy (*1611;*1619)

Berta Sturman, "The Second Quarto of *A King and No King,* 1625," *SB* 4 (1951–52): 166–70, provides a detailed comparison of the first and second quartos, concluding that Q2 was printed from a copy of Q1 which was the official stage copy. The text was not noticeably altered, and no appreciable additions were made. Hoy, Part 3, gives the play largely to Beaumont, who is also responsible for the final form. Beaumont's language preferences, "apart from his avoidance of *ye*," are not essentially different from Fletcher's, as this play shows. Fletcher's extra-metrical verse sets his scenes apart, although prose also occurs in his share. Beaumont's share is I, II, III, IV.iv, V.ii, iv; Fletcher's IV.i–iii, V.i, iii. In his RRDS edition (1963) Robert K. Turner, Jr., agrees with Sturman about the Q2 copy. He prefers to follow Q1 in the main as copy text. In "The Printing of *A King and No King* Q1," *SB* 18 (1965): 255-61, Turner finds the quarto interesting because it was set up seriatim rather than by formes, as was customary. This fact is important in editorial decisions about the lineation of verse and prose; the editor should follow the lineation of the quarto when he is "uncertain whether to print verse or prose." The history of the printing is reconstructed in detail. George Walton Williams, editing the play for Bowers's *Dramatic Works*, vol. 2 (1966), follows Turner's view that an exemplum of Q1 was compared to some authoritative manuscript. Williams believes that most of the Q2 contractions of linguistic forms are without authority; Q1 is his copy text. Copy for it was a scribal transcript. Hans Walter Gabler, "John Beale's Compositors in *A King and No King*," *SB* 24 (1971): 138-43, argues from compositorial spellings that four compositors set Q1, whereas Turner (*SB*) claimed only two.

The Night Walker, or The Little Thief, Fletcher (revised by Shirley and licensed 11 May 1633); comedy (ca. *1611*?, 1640)

An entry in Herbert's Office-Book for 1633 gives the original play entirely to Fletcher. Hoy says the manuscript behind the substantive 1640 quarto edition represents Shirley's revision, and that while Fletcher's characteristic linguistic forms are present, other forms not his, but occurring regularly in Shirley's unaided work, are also found. Shirley's revision, which extended over the whole play, went beyond stylistic details. Hoy gives Fletcher I.vii–viii and II.i; Fletcher and Shirley I.i–vi, II.ii–iv, and III–V. Maxwell, *Studies in Beaumont* (II,A, *Woman's Prize*), observing that earlier editors assigned a date of 1608 to 1613, uses allusions as evidence to argue for 1611.

The Woman's Prize, or the Tamer Tamed, Fletcher; comedy (*1604*-ca. *1617;* 1647 & MS)

Hoy, Part 1, assigns the play entirely to Fletcher. Baldwin Maxwell, "The Woman's Prize" (II,A, *Woman's Prize*), believes an early date cannot be argued on the basis of the play being an answer to Shakespeare's *Taming of the Shrew* (as Chambers, vol. 3, had argued). However, topical allusions point to early 1611. R. Warwick Bond, "On Six Plays in Beaumont and Fletcher, 1679," *RES* 11 (1935): 257-75, finds that double endings and run-on lines suggest a date late in Fletcher's career, 1618-22; T. W. Baldwin early had assigned 1621, the date of its first recorded performance at court, in "A Note on John Fletcher," *MLN* 38 (1923): 377-78. E. H. C. Oliphant, "Three Beaumont and Fletcher Plays," *RES* 12 (1936): 197-202, holds to an early date; the play we have might be a rewriting of an early play; verse tests which suggest 1618-22 to Bond (above) do not preclude an early date; Chambers observes that if the play is an answer to *Shrew*, then it "would have more point the nearer it came to the date of the original"; and arguments for it having been performed by the King's Men are strong. Jewkes, *Act Division* (above, *Woman Hater*), responding to Bald's useful discussion of the two texts of *Woman's Prize* (above, headnote), believes it unlikely that the folio text was printed from a promptbook.

The Captain, Fletcher (with Beaumont?); comedy (*1609-12;* 1647)

Hoy, Part 6, assigns Beaumont IV.iv, Fletcher I–IV.iii and V.i–ii, and both writers V.iii–v. It is certain that Fletcher is not the sole author and that his share has been altered. Only in IV.iv are we "in the presence of a second dramatist"; the scene is long, important, and masterfully done. The verse and linguistic preferences are not Fletcher's. Oliphant thought it was Beaumont's, and Gayley (I,A) thought that if Beaumont was in the play at all it was here; Beaumont seems to have given final form to the play. L. A. Beaurline, editing the play for the new *Dramatic Works*, vol. 1, suggests that perhaps Fletcher "wrote the whole play for the early performances," or that Beaumont "collaborated on later scenes." It was later revised by another, perhaps Massinger. Beaurline follows Chambers's dating for composition, 1609-12, with an acting date of 1612-13 by the King's Men at court. Beaurline supports and amplifies

Bald (above, headnote) in regard to printer's copy not being prompt copy, and summarizes Robert K. Turner, Jr., "The Printers and the Beaumont and Fletcher Folio of 1647, Section 2," *SB* 20 (1967): 35–59, in regard to the printing history.

Four Plays, or Moral Representations, in One, Fletcher (with Beaumont? or Field?); moral (ca. *1608–13;* 1647)

Hoy, Part 4, says the last two plays are "undoubtedly" Fletcher's, but that the induction and first two plays with their connecting link are the work of another dramatist. Hoy regards the linguistic pattern as well as other nonlinguistic characteristics in them as Field's. Thus he assigns Field the *Induction, The Triumph of Honour,* and *The Triumph of Love,* and Fletcher *The Triumph of Death* and *The Triumph of Time.* Chambers (vol. 3) says "there is no clear indication of date."

The Mask of the Inner Temple and Gray's Inn, Beaumont; mask (*20 Feb. 1613;* ca. 1613)

The *Annals* assigns the play to Beaumont alone. Hoy says its poetic diction precludes use of the linguistic forms which provide evidence for his study; he regards it as Beaumont's unaided work. In his edition for vol. 1 of the *Dramatic Works,* Fredson Bowers discusses the cancellation of the original quarto title-page assignment to Beaumont, the location of the mask in the 1647 folio, differences between the quarto and the Folio text which suggest that the manuscript behind F1 is of "a different tradition" from that behind the quarto. The quarto "represents a reading edition especially prepared for the press . . . the F1 text may closely reflect the original form of the manuscript prepared for the Inns." Philip Edwards, in his edition (II, A, *Mask of the Inner Temple*), argues that both the 1613 quarto and the 1647 folio editions derive from the same manuscript, and that this manuscript was copied by someone connected with the performance who "greatly amplified its brief notes on the dancing and action." This transcript provided copy for the quarto. The folio was set from a late transcript of the original manuscript; the copy is nearly useless, "except for its preservation of the original stage-directions."

Bonduca, Fletcher; tragedy (*1611–14;* 1647 & MS)

Chambers, the *Annals,* and Hoy give the play entirely to Fletcher. In *Dramatic Documents from the Elizabethan Playhouses,* vol. 1

(1931), W. W. Greg describes the manuscript, which evidently is a "transcript prepared in the playhouse for a private collector." The scribe states that his copy was made "from the fowle papers of the Authors." Comparison of the 1647 folio text and the manuscript reveals that the stage directions differ widely but the entrances are nearly identical. Greg later edited the manuscript for the Malone Society (1951), with an introduction. Bald, "Bibliographical Studies" (above, headnote), and Jewkes, *Act Division* (above, *The Woman Hater*), agree that the folio text derives from copy connected with production.

The Scornful Lady, Fletcher, with Beaumont; comedy (*1613–16;* 1616)

Hoy, Part 3, gives Beaumont I.i, II.i, and V.ii; Fletcher I.ii, II.ii–iii, III, IV, and V.i, iii–iv, observing that Fletcher's linguistic preferences are clearer than in most of their collaborations, although Beaumont is responsible for the final form of the text. Hoy also edited the play for vol. 2 of the *Dramatic Works.* Only the first quarto (1616) is substantive. It was probably prepared from a scribal copy of the author's papers; problems arising from the typesetting by two compositors are discussed and the history of seventeenth-century editions is traced. On the basis of the long and descriptive stage directions, Jewkes, *Act Division* (above, *Woman Hater*), believes that "copy must have been the author's manuscript or a non-theatrical transcript." Maxwell, *Studies in Beaumont* (II, A, *Woman's Prize*) reconsiders the evidence of allusions (see Chambers, vol. 3) for a composition date early in 1610.

The Honest Man's Fortune, Fletcher; tragicomedy, with Field? Massinger? Tourneur? (*1613;* 1647 & MS)

Hoy, Part 4, clarifies a long series of complex arguments about assignment of parts, observing that a scribal transcript (ed. by Gerritsen, below) and the folio provide two tests for the play. Both present linguistic evidence "very much of a piece." Of the usual candidates—Fletcher, Massinger, Field, Tourneur, and Webster—Hoy dismisses Tourneur and Webster on the basis of linguistic evidence present in their unaided work. While the play is "very largely" Field's, the "collaboration [here is] of a more closely integrated sort than the division by act and scene." Massinger's share has been much debated; Hoy cites the scholarship. Hoy assigns Field I, II, III.ib (from the entrance of

Montague to the end), ii, IV; Field and Fletcher V.i, iv; Field and Massinger III.iii; Fletcher V.ii–iii; Massinger III.ia (to the entrance of Montague).

In the introduction to his edition of *"The Honest Man's Fortune": A Critical Edition of MS Dyce 9, 1625* (1952), Johan Gerritsen discusses in detail the texts, their relationship, the manuscript, its scribe (Edward Knight) and his handwriting, and problems of authorship and sources. He believes that the Dyce manuscript, a promptbook, was copied out for prompting in 1625 at the Blackfriars, and the second version, the 1647 folio, was edited for the reader. Greg, *Dramatic Documents*, vol. 1 (above, *Bonduca*) describes the manuscript and the hand of the playhouse scribe. Greg discusses that scribe in his Malone Society edition of *Bonduca* (above, *Bonduca*) and his known copies, observing that there were two Knights. Questions of text and manuscript are also discussed by C. J. Sisson, "Bibliographical Aspects of Some Stuart Dramatic Manuscripts," *RES* 1 (1925): 421-30; W. W. Greg, "A Question of Plus or Minus," *RES* 6 (1930): 300-304; Bald, "Bibliographical Studies" (above, headnote); and Jewkes, *Act Division* (above, *Woman Hater*). Also see the discussion of the authorial problems of this play in the essay by Charles Forker on Tourneur in vol. 3 of this series, *The New Intellectuals*.

The Two Noble Kinsmen, Shakespeare, Fletcher (and Beaumont?); tragicomedy (*1613-16;* 1634)

The *Annals* assigns this play in the Shakespeare apocrypha to Shakespeare and Fletcher, and queries Beaumont as part-author. Hoy, Part 7, assigns to Shakespeare I, II.i, III.i–ii, V.ib (from exit of Palamon and Knights to end), iii–iv; to Fletcher II.ii–vi, III.iii–vi, IV, V.ia (to exit of Palamon and Knights), ii. The traditional assignment gives IV.iii and all of V.i to Shakespeare. Hoy says there is "no real difficulty" about Fletcher's share; "the linguistic evidence is sufficient to point with reasonable clarity to the specific scenes of his authorship." Shakespeare's presence is argued from nonlinguistic grounds. The linguistic patterns in the non-Fletcherian scenes are "not inconsistent" with Shakespeare's acknowledged late work: Hoy observes that printer's copy for the quarto was probably an intermediate scribal transcript rather than the annotated foul papers suggested by Frederick O. Waller, "Printer's Copy for *The Two Noble Kinsmen*," *SB* 11 (1958): 61-84.

Kenneth Muir summarizes the arguments for Shakespeare in "Shakespeare's Hand in *The Two Noble Kinsmen*," *ShS* 11 (1958): 50-59, and presents fuller arguments in his *Shakespeare as Collaborator* (1960). Erdman and Fogel (above, headnote) summarize the problems and selected studies from 1780 to 1963 (pp. 486-94). Recent studies are cited in the standard lists (cited in II,A, *Henry VIII*).

Cardenio, Shakespeare, Fletcher; tragicomedy? (acted *1612-13;* lost)

John Freehafer, "*Cardenio,* by Shakespeare and Fletcher," *PMLA* 84 (1969): 501-13, reports the scholarly consensus that Lewis Theobald's *The Double Falsehood* (1728) "is not a forgery but is based on the *Cardenio* of 1612-13; that the original authors of *Cardenio* were Fletcher and probably Shakespeare; and that Moseley's attribution of the play to them derives from an authentic manuscript." Freehafer presents new verbal parallels with early translations of *Don Quixote,* argues for Theobald's possession of the *Cardenio* manuscript as he claimed, accounts for *Cardenio* not having been published with the plays of Shakespeare or Fletcher and for Theobald's omission of it from his edition of Shakespeare, describes Theobald's deletions and changes, and cites extensive scholarly opinion, based on internal evidence, inclining to the view that Shakespeare wrote the first half of the original play, Fletcher the second. Freehafer believes, however, that proof for joint authorship comes from external evidence: chronological facts, mention of Shakespeare and Fletcher by the three commentators who examined the manuscript, and Theobald's "Preface" and royal patent. Freehafer concludes that new external evidence supports the assertions that Theobald possessed three *Cardenio* manuscripts, that the play was by Shakespeare and Fletcher, based on a 1612 translation of *Don Quixote,* that *Cardenio* was cut and perhaps altered during the Restoration, that Theobald was not forthright in dealing with the authorship problem, and that he destroyed no manuscripts.

One strong opposing voice, that of Harriet C. Frazier, has been raised against this consensus in three articles: "Theobald's *The Double Falsehood*: A Revision of Shakespeare's *Cardenio?*" *CompD* 1 (1967): 219-33; "The Rifling of Beauty's Stores: Theobald and Shakespeare," *NM* 69 (1968): 232-56; and in "Speculations on the Motives of a Forger: Theobald's *The Double Falsehood,*" *NM* 72 (1971): 287-96. Nigel Alexander observed, in *ShS* 25 (1972): 187, that Frazier argues the case for forgery "cogently and convincingly." Her main points are that Theobald forged the play from his extensive knowledge of Shakespeare's sources, vocabulary, versification, grammar, and subject matter, and that numerous additional factors—Theobald's other adaptations and imitations, his editing of Shakespeare, Shakespeare's popularity in the eighteenth century, Theobald's play of acknowledged authorship based on *Don Quixote*, the popularity of the Cardenio story and the Cervantic vogue, the absence of references to *The Double Falsehood* in Theobald's edition of Shakespeare—all help point the finger at Theobald as a forger. His motives were need for money and, far more important, "his fervent desire to connect the two greatest authors of the Spanish and English Renaissance." Both Freehafer and Frazier ("Speculations on the Motives") provide citations and summaries of earlier scholarship; the interested reader also should consult the standard Shakespeare bibliographies (cited in II,A, *Henry VIII*).

Valentinian, Fletcher; tragedy (*1610–14;* 1647)

Hoy, Part 1, gives the play entirely to Fletcher. James P. Hammersmith, "The Printers and the Beaumont and Fletcher Folio of 1647, Section 7," *PBSA* 69 (1975): 206-25, provides a full bibliographical analysis by quire for *Valentinian*, describing press work and composition. Jewkes, *Act Division* (above, *Woman Hater*), says that "the text was probably obtained from the company." Chambers (vol. 3) establishes the dates 1610-18.

Wit without Money, Fletcher (revised by another?); comedy (*1614–20;* 1639)

The *Annals* says the play was probably revised in 1620. Hoy, Part 4, gives all acts to Fletcher and an unidentified reviser, explaining that all previous studies assign it to Fletcher unaided, yet *ye* is used only once. Except for the absence of *ye*, it contains Fletcher's linguistic preferences and no trace of a second dramatist's work. The play was not relicensed when restaged. Thus, "the final form of the extant substantive edition (the 1639 quarto) is the work of a non-Fletcherian hand," and the revision was not extensive. Jewkes, *Act Division* (above, *Woman Hater*) fixes a date of 1613 by two allusions, but Maxwell, *Studies in Beaumont* (II,A, *Woman's Prize*), noting that the accepted date is 1614 (see Chambers, vol. 3), finds that allusions to contemporary events suggest either composition or revision in 1619.

A Right Woman, Beaumont and Fletcher; comedy (ca. *1608-25;* lost?)

Citing the 1660 Stationers' Register entry for *A Right Woman*, the *Annals* notes that this title is given as the alternative title for *Women Beware Women* in the Stationers' Register, 1653.

Monsieur Thomas, Fletcher; comedy (*1610*-ca. *1616;* 1639)

Chambers, the *Annals*, and Hoy give the play to Fletcher. Chambers notes that the Restoration title page identifies it as the same play as *Father's Own Son*, played at the Cockpit in 1639, and discusses its date—not earlier than its source, 1610, and probably written by 1616. Jewkes, *Act Division* (above *Woman Hater*), finds that printer's copy probably "had not been connected with actual performance."

Love's Pilgrimage, Fletcher (with Beaumont?); tragicomedy (*1616? revised 1635;* 1647)

The *Annals* states that passages from Jonson's *New Inn* (1629) were incorporated in I.i. Hoy, Part 3, is more specific, finding linguistic evidence for Beaumont in I.ia (lines 1-23), Ic (line 75 to entrance of Lazaro), IV, and V; for Fletcher in I.ii, II, and III, and with I.ib (lines 24-74) and Id (from Lazaro's entrance to the end) adapted from Jonson. He regards the play as an original Beaumont and Fletcher collaboration which has undergone alteration. Hoy summarizes the controversy over the Jonson passages by pointing out that either the King's Men salvaged what they could from Jonson's disastrous comedy, or Jonson lifted the passages from Beaumont and Fletcher's original version. C. H. Herford and Percy Simpson, ed., *Ben Jonson*, vol. 2 (1925), claim the passages for Jonson. Editing *Love's Pilgrimage* for Bower's *Dramatic Works*, vol. 2, L. A. Beaurline suggests a date of composition of 1615 or 1616 from source (Cervantes) and allusions; Maxwell, *Studies in Beaumont* (II,A, *Woman's Prize*), suggests 1616. Beaurline thinks the manuscript copy used by the printer was a prompt copy, and the play as we have it is revised. Johan Gerritsen, "The Printing of the Beaumont and Fletcher Folio of 1647," *Library* 3 (1948-49): 233-64, describes the printing history.

The Nice Valour, or the Passionate Madman, Fletcher (revised by Middleton or another?); comedy (ca. *1615-25;* 1647)

Hoy, Part 5, assigns Fletcher and Middleton I.i, II.i, IV.i, V.ii–iii, and Middleton alone III and V.i. He agrees with E. H. C. Oliphant, *The Plays of Beaumont and Fletcher* (1927), that "the play is almost entirely Middleton's," but linguistic evidence does not establish Middleton's claim. No external evidence links the play to him, but the themes and their treatment suggest him: "whether or not it is Middleton's is beyond final proof." Hoy assigns Middleton all the scenes which have no trace of Fletcher, and to both dramatists the scenes which have "Fletcherian lines in a non-Fletcherian context." He concludes that "Middleton's hand in the extant text is decidedly the predominant one." Richard Hindry Barker, *Thomas Middleton* (1958), notices the external and internal evidence, suggesting that both types point to Beaumont, or Fletcher, or both, yet the style is like Middleton's. He feels there is not enough evidence to support the theory of revision. The date is probably 1616; Maxwell, *Studies in Beaumont* (II,A, *Woman's Prize*), also suggests an early date of 1615-16 from allusions and the attitudes towards duelling.

The Mad Lover, Fletcher; tragicomedy (*acted 5 Jan. 1617;* 1647)

Hoy, Part 1, gives the play to Fletcher alone. W. J. Lawrence, "The Date of *The Mad Lover,*" *TLS,* 24 Nov. 1927, p. 888, reports that *The Diary of Lady Anne Clifford,* published in 1923, records a performance on 5 January 1616/17.

The Queen of Corinth, Fletcher (and Massinger? Field?); tragicomedy (*1616-*ca. *1618;* 1647)

Hoy, Part 4, assigns Field III and IV, Fletcher II, and Massinger I and V, from three distinct linguistic patterns. Fletcher's and Massinger's are easily identified, Hoy says, and other evidence as well as the linguistic pattern identifies the third collaborator as Field. Hensman, *Shares of Fletcher* (II,A, *Bloody Brother*), surveys previous ascriptions and argues from the use of sources for its plot structure and from idiom and versification that Massinger in 1626 revised a Fletcher-Field collaboration of 1617.

The Jeweller of Amsterdam, or The Hague, Fletcher, Field, Massinger; tragedy (*1616-19;* lost)

Bentley (vol. 3) records the Stationers' Register entry of 1654 which cites Fletcher, Field, and Massinger as authors, and gives the title of a 1616 Stationers' Register entry for a pamphlet about the jeweller's murder that year. The play is known only from this SR entry, and in likelihood was the property of the King's Men. Andrew Clark, "An Annotated List of Lost Domestic Plays, 1578-1624," *RORD* 18 (1975): 29-44, arguing that the composition date was soon after the crime, suggests 1616-17.

Thierry and Theodoret, Fletcher, Massinger (and Beaumont?); tragedy (*1607-21;* 1621)

Hoy, Part 3, gives Beaumont III, V.i, Fletcher I.i, II.ii-iii, IV.i, V.ii, and Massinger I.ii, II.i, iv, and IV.ii, asserting that there are three linguistically distinct parts which distinguish the shares. In "Notes on the Text of *Thierry and Theodoret* Q1," *SB* 14 (1961): 218-31, Robert K. Turner, Jr., observes that Q1 is of interest since it was printed (1621) in the four-year period (1619-22) which saw the publication of other King's Men plays, *Philaster, The Maid's Tragedy,* and *A King and No King,* but unlike those plays, it was not followed shortly "by a second edition containing a corrected . . . materially different text." Turner presents the bibliographical evidence for the order of printing of formes, number of compositors, delays in printing, method and speed of composition, identity of compositors, proofing, and the nature of the printer's copy (a legible, nontheatrical manuscript, probably an authorial fair copy reviewed and slightly revised by Fletcher). Turner also edited the play for vol. 3 of the *Dramatic Works.* He cites Hoy's ascriptions, assigns no date, and reviews his examination of the printing. The first quarto is copy text.

The Loyal Subject, Fletcher; tragicomedy (*licensed 16 Nov. 1618, revised 1633?;* 1647)

Earlier investigations had assigned the play to Fletcher alone, as does Hoy, Part 1. Bentley (vol. 3) discusses the extent of revision, hesitating, in spite of the phrasing of Sir Henry Herbert's relicensing entry in 1633, to assume revision.

The Knight of Malta, Fletcher, Field, Massinger; tragicomedy (*1616–19;* 1647)

Hoy, Part 4, gives Field I and V, Fletcher II, III.i, iv, and IV.ii, and Massinger III.ii–iii, IV.i, iii–iv, stating that of the three linguistic patterns in the play, two are readily distinguished as Fletcher's and Massinger's. He finds Field in I and V, as had Oliphant and others. Copy for the folio text was a promptbook manuscript by Ralph Crane. Hensman, *Shares of Fletcher* (II,A, *Bloody Brother*), concurs with the assignment of shares (the only differences in all the ascriptions is over Massinger's shares of IV). Dating the play 1619, she observes that this is the earliest play in which Massinger collaborated, and the last of Field's.

The Humorous Lieutenant, Fletcher; tragicomedy (*1619?;* 1647 & MS)

By consensus, the play is assigned to Fletcher alone. Bentley (vol. 3) discusses the various titles by which the play is known, the date (1619), and the literary manuscript prepared for Sir Kenelm Digby by Ralph Crane. Greg, *Dramatic Documents* (above, *Bonduca*), explains that the manuscript has minor omissions, including the two songs at the conjuring scene (IV.iii). The 1647 folio gives a censored and cut text which omits about seventy lines. In "Ralph Crane, Scrivener to the King's Players," *Library* 7 (1926): 194–215, rpt. in *The Seventeenth Century Stage: A Collection of Critical Essays,* ed. Gerald Eades Bentley (1968), pp. 137–55, F. P. Wilson earlier had discussed these topics. He also observed that the manuscript is "the most beautiful example of Crane's calligraphy that we have." The manuscript was printed by Dyce in 1830, but his text departed from the original in spelling and punctuation. Margaret McLaren Cook and F. P. Wilson edited the manuscript for the Malone Society with the alternate title *Demetrius and Enanthe* (1951).

The Bloody Brother (Rollo, Duke of Normandy), Fletcher (with Massinger? Jonson? and another? revised 1627–30, by Massinger?); tragedy (*1616–24;* 1639)

In Part 6, Hoy divides the play among Chapman, Fletcher, Jonson, and Massinger: Chapman, III.ia (to Edith's "O stay there Duke"), ic (from entrance of Citizens to end), IV.iii; Fletcher II, III.ib (from Edith's "O stay there Duke" to entrance of Citizens), ii, V.iib (from stage direction "Sophia, Matilda, Aubrey, and Lords at the doore" to end); Jonson IV.i–ii; Massinger I, V.ia (to exit of Hamond); Fletcher and Massinger V.ib (from exit of Hamond to end), iia (to stage direction "Sophia, Matilda, Aubrey, and Lords at the doore"). Hoy reports some of the historical facts: the 1639 quarto was titled *The Bloody Brother* and ascribed to B.J.F.; the second quarto, 1640, was titled *The Tragœdy of Rollo Duke of Normandy*, and attributed to Fletcher. Each derives from an independent manuscript, Q1 from a "literary" and Q2 from a promptbook manuscript. The authoritative text is "clearly" Q2.

Linguistic evidence enables Hoy to assign Fletcher's and Massinger's shares with no difficulty. The remaining part of the play (part of III and all of IV) "cannot be the work of a single dramatist," since regular blank verse contrasts with rhyming pentameter couplets. While "the linguistic evidence for Jonson's share in *Rollo* . . . is pitifully slight," yet it and other evidence strengthen the argument for Jonson's authorship of the scenes noted above. C. H. Herford and Percy and Evelyn Simpson, *Ben Jonson*, vol. 10 (1950), conclude that "only one scene (IV.i) shows any affinity with Jonson's work." William Wells argued for Chapman's presence. Hoy is persuaded by the aggregate of his argument (in *N&Q* 154 [1928]: 6–9); linguistic evidence from Chapman's style in tragedy (barren of contracted forms) supports Wells's view (verbal parallels and general qualities of style).

W. W. Greg, "Some Notes on the Stationers' Registers," *Library* 7 (1926–27): 376–86, explains that the Oct. 1639 SR entry assigns the play to "J.B." This is a slip for "J.F.", the "B.J.F." of the title page is a "muddled correction."

In "*Rollo, Duke of Normandy:* Some Bibliographical Notes on the Seventeenth-Century Editions," *Library* 18 (1938): 279–86, J. D. Jump establishes that Q2 (1640) differs from Q1 (1639) and is not a reprint of it; both texts are imperfect. Q2 conforms to the promptbook type, while Q1 is a more "literary" text; because of the special authority attached to a promptbook, Q2 should form the basis of an edition, with emendations from Q1. In his edition of the play in 1948 (II,A, *Bloody Brother*), Jump bases his text on Q2, dates the play either during or before 1625, and assigns parts to Massinger, Fletcher, Chapman, and Jonson. He uses parallel passages and metrical statistics for the assignments, and claims that the evidence of the metrical texts never clashed with the evidence of the parallel passages. His assignments accord nearly with Hoy's.

Hensman, *Shares of Fletcher* (II,A, *Bloody Brother*), says that Massinger, not Jonson, wrote the disputed passages in II.ii, that III.ii is

Nathan Field's, and that IV.ii is Fletcher's, who also wrote the second
stanza of the song in V.ii. She reviews scholarship on the authorship
question, arguing that the use of hitherto unidentified sources and the
techniques of their use identifies Fletcher, Massinger, and another
author. The play was first written in 1617 and revised 1627-30. Bentley (vol. 3) calls her study "by far the most solid and illuminating discussion which [he] has seen of the date and authorship of the play."

The Little French Lawyer, Fletcher, Massinger; comedy (*1619-23;*
1647)

Hoy says that while this play is a collaboration, Massinger gave final
form to the text. He assigns Fletcher II, III.i-ii, iv, IV.i-iv.vib (from
entrance of La Writ to the end), V.ia (to second entrance of Cleremont), ii; and Massinger I, III.iii, IV.v-via (to entrance of La Writ), vii,
V.ib (from second entrance of Cleremont to end), iii. Hoy believes that
the manuscript behind the first folio derives from a promptbook, since
the text "abounds" with stage directions; Massinger prepared the
promptbook manuscript. Bentley (vol. 3) dates the play 1619-23 from
the cast list in the 1679 folio; "no other reliable dating evidence for
the play has been cited."

Hensman, *The Shares of Fletcher* (II,A, *Bloody Brother*), says that
Fletcher used plot materials for their theatrical and comic possibilities,
while, in contrast, Massinger "dramatizes the rhetorical and . . . logical
materials" in the source. Thus Massinger's shares are I, III.i and iii, IV.
via and vii, V.ib and ii; Fletcher's are II.i, III.ii, iv-v, IV.i, v, vib, V.ia, ii.

Sir John van Olden Barnavelt, Fletcher, Massinger; tragedy (*Aug. 1619;*
MS)

Hoy, Part 2, follows the customary assignment to the two dramatists.
He divides the play between Fletcher I.iii, II.ii-vi, III.i, iii-iv, IV.i-iii,
V.ib (from exit of Ambassadors to exit of Provost), ii-iii, and Massinger
I.i-ii, II.i, III.ii, v-vi, IV.iv-v, V.ia (to exit of Ambassadors), ic (from
exit of Provost to end). F. P. Wilson, "Ralph Crane" (above, *Humorous
Lieutenant*), describes the extant prompt copy in Crane's hand with additions by two other persons, one a member of the acting company, the
other the Master of the Revels, Sir George Buc. (Also see Greg, *Dramatic Documents*, vol. 1 above, *Bonduca*.) Hoy notices Crane's care in
reproducing the Fletcherian *ye* form; "nowhere are the linguistic patterns of Fletcher and Massinger more sharply differentiated within the
same play than in Crane's manuscript of *Barnavelt*."

The Laws of Candy, Fletcher (revised by another? recently assigned entirely to John Ford); tragicomedy (*1619-23;* 1647)

Hoy, Part 5, finds that linguistic and other features in the play are easily discerned in Ford's unaided work. William Wells and Oliphant attribute it to Ford, but assign the concluding dialogue of I.ii to Fletcher; Hoy says there is "nothing particularly Fletcherian" in the scene. Given "the state of our present knowledge, it seems best to regard the play as wholly" Ford's. S. Schoenbaum, *Internal Evidence* (above, headnote), regards the linguistic evidence for this play as "inconclusive." Hensman, *Shares of Fletcher,* vol. 2 (II,A, *Bloody Brother*), holds that around 1626 Massinger "abortively" revised a Fletcher-Field collaboration of about 1619. She sees the plot as a fragmented romantic play in a Senecan context.

Bentley (vol. 3) remarks that the "disintegrators are pitifully uncertain in their attempts to assign authors." He evaluates evidence for date, and suggests any year from 1619 to 1622 as possible.

Women Pleased, Fletcher; tragicomedy (*1619-23;* 1647)

The *Annals* queries whether this might not be a revision of an earlier play. Hoy, Part 1, assigns it all to Fletcher, as had earlier investigators. Bentley (vol. 3) remarks that "it is unusual that a Beaumont and Fletcher play should leave no records at all before the closing of the theaters, not even in the list of the plays of the King's Men in 1641. Apparently *Women Pleased* had little or no vogue."

The Custom of the Country, Fletcher, Massinger; comedy (*1619-23;* 1647)

Bentley (vol. 3) provides historical and other information to support a date of composition of 1619 or later. Hoy, Part 2, assigns shares to Fletcher and Massinger by the use of *ye, hath,* and *'em;* Fletcher has I, III.i-iii, IV.iii-v, V.va (to entrance of Hypollita to end). The evidence suggests to Hoy that Act III and Acts I, II, IV, and V derive from two different manuscript sources. Hensman, *The Shares of Fletcher* (II,A, *Bloody Brother*) examines the use of sources and distinctive techniques to support the assignment of shares on which "all editors agree."

The Double Marriage, Fletcher, Massinger; tragedy (*1619-23;* 1647)

Hoy, Part 2, says that a systematic suppression of the *ye* form through Fletcher's portion suggests that Massinger is responsible for the final

form of the text. The play is a collaboration, not a revision of a Flet-
cherian original. Hoy assigns Fletcher II, III.ii–iii, IV.i, iii–iv, and V.i–ii;
Massinger I, III.i, IV.ii, and V.iii–iv. Earlier investigators (Fleay, Oliphant,
and Bond—who edited the play for a volume of Bullen's *Variorum* that
was never published) also divide the play between the two dramatists.
Hensman, *Shares of Fletcher*, vol. 1 (II,A, *Bloody Brother*), agrees with
Hoy except that she assigns V.i–ii to Massinger and V.iii to Fletcher.
Hensman believes that the problems of authorship dissolve when the
use of sources is examined, because Massinger interweaves ideas and
their analogues, while Fletcher expresses ideas loosely in succession.
She dates the composition of the play about 1620-21. Bentley (vol. 3)
argues for a date after 1619 and before 1623.

The False One, Fletcher, Massinger; classical history (*1619-23;* 1647)

The distribution of *ye* indicates the shares to Hoy, Part 2: Fletcher
has II, III, and IV; Massinger I and V. Like *Barnavelt*, Hoy continues,
this play "is preserved in a text which has carefully preserved the respective linguistic preferences of the two dramatists." Hoy argues that
the folio texts of this play, *The Prophetess*, and *The Spanish Curate*
"were printed from manuscripts prepared by" Ralph Crane. Hensman,
Shares of Fletcher (II, A, *Bloody Brother*) uses "hitherto unidentified"
sources—in Lucan's *Pharsalia*—to distinguish the shares, assigning
Fletcher I.ii but otherwise following Hoy. Her arguments support the
traditional date of 1619-20 (see Bentley, vol. 3, and Maxwell, *Studies
in Beaumont*, II,A, *Woman's Prize*).

The Island Princess, Fletcher; tragicomedy (*1619-21;* 1647)

Hoy's analysis, Part 1, of linguistic preferences supports the accepted
attribution to Fletcher alone. Bentley's discussion of date (vol. 3) supports the *Annals* dates.

The Pilgrim, Fletcher; comedy (*1621?;* 1647)

Earlier investigators and Hoy give the play to Fletcher. Bentley (vol.
3) presents the controversy over date, concluding that 1621 is probably
the date of first performance.

The Wild Goose Chase, Fletcher; comedy (*1621?* 1652)

Earlier investigators and Hoy give the play to Fletcher. "In the absence of evidence to the contrary," says Bentley (vol. 3), "the year

1621 is a plausible date." He also discusses the elaborate cast list of the 1652 edition. Greg, "Some Notes on the Stationers' Registers" (above, *Bloody Brother*), remarks that the SR entry for 4 September 1646 lists the play. Evidently a book could be registered without producing a copy, since Moseley's preface to the folio says the play was at that time lost.

Beggars' Bush, Fletcher (with Massinger?); comedy (ca. *1615-22;* 1647 & MS)

Hoy, Part 3, reports that the linguistic patterns of Fletcher and Massinger are clearly present. He assigns Beaumont II, V.i, iib (from entrance of Hubert to end); Fletcher III, IV; Massinger I, V.iia (to entrance of Hubert). In his edition of the play, Dorenkamp (II,A, *Beggars' Bush*) disagrees with Hoy's Beaumont assignment. He reexamines the linguistic evidence, concluding that Massinger wrote acts I, II, and V, and Fletcher III and IV. The date of composition is between 1613 and 1622. Dorenkamp also summarizes earlier assignments from F. G. Fleay's metrical analysis (1874) on. The Introduction to the edition treats the copy text (1647 folio), its printing, printer's copy, the manuscript (a transcript of a prompt copy), and later editions and adaptations.

In "*Beggars Bush*: A Reconstructed Prompt-Book and Its Copy," *SB* 27 (1974): 113-36, Fredson Bowers analyzes the bibliographical evidence to support the conclusion that the 1647 folio text was set from Massinger's fair copy of the play. This copy had previously been copied by a scribe to make a promptbook, and the promptbook was copied to make the Lambarde manuscript. Thus Bowers's comparison of a promptbook with its original source (both at one remove) leads him to observe that "normal theatrical procedure was to use an author's fair copy as the basis for the transcript of a prompt-book, not to mark it so that it became the prompt-book itself." In likelihood the company did not make suggestions for revision of the play, although there are two additions; the scribe generally copied what he found. Thus "unresolved tangles in the action and even in the casting could be transferred to print from a prompt-book or transcript."

Bowers also edited the play for vol. 3 of the *Dramatic Works*. In the Textual Introduction, Bowers mentions the play's popularity, lists the four early documents which preserve the text, and concurs with Hoy's assignments as "a working hypothesis" (he dismisses Dorenkamp's objections to Hoy as "vitiated by his attempts to assign Hoy's Beaumont sections to Massinger"). After analyzing the evidence, Bowers finds the evidence for "the nature of Massinger's participation" conflicting; thus the original date of composition is uncertain. Bowers discusses at length variant readings among the four early documents, and analyzes the second folio. The first folio is his copy text.

The Prophetess, Fletcher, Massinger; tragicomedy (*licensed 14 May 1622;* 1647)

Early investigators assigned the play to the two dramatists, but differed from Hoy, Part 2, who assigns Fletcher I, III, V.iii, and Massinger II, IV, and V.i–ii. Hoy says that the assignment of shares on linguistic evidence is clear. Hensman, *The Shares of Fletcher* (II,A, *Bloody Brother*), argues from the use of sources that Fletcher blocked out the action as a whole from Vopiscus's *History of Carinus,* and used the prophetess to unify the historical and invented episodes. Massinger revised the play in 1629, augmenting Act II, and subordinating the role of the Prophetess. Hensman assigns Fletcher I.i–iii, III.i–iii, and V.iii; Massinger abridged Fletcher in II.iii, IV.i–vi; and Massinger added to the original play II.i–iiib and V.i–ii.

The Sea Voyage, Fletcher, Massinger; comedy (*licensed 22 June 1622;* 1647)

Earlier investigators had divided the play between Fletcher and Massinger, as does Hoy, Part 2, who assigns Fletcher I and IV and Massinger II, III, and V. Hoy observes that the linguistic evidence does not clearly establish whether the present text is a Fletcher original revised in part by Massinger, or a Fletcher-Massinger collaboration which received its final form from Fletcher. Hoy favors the latter view, which accounts for Fletcher's *ye* in II, V, and the last half of III, sections which exhibit some of Massinger's most characteristic vocabulary and syntax. However, others have thought Massinger revised Fletcher; see Bentley (vol. 3).

The Spanish Curate, Fletcher, Massinger; comedy (*licensed 24 Oct. 1622;* 1647)

Saying that this is one of the clearest examples of Fletcher-Massinger collaboration in the canon, Hoy, Part 2, assigns Fletcher II, III.i–ii, IV. iii, v–vii, and V.ii, and Massinger I, III.iii, IV.i–ii, iv, and V.i, iii. Bentley concludes that composition took place no earlier than the summer before the licensing date. See Bald, "Bibliographical Studies" (above, headnote), for a discussion of the printer's copy, in likelihood a promptcopy made by Ralph Crane.

The Devil of Dowgate, or Usury Put to Use, Fletcher; comedy? (*licensed 17 Oct. 1623;* lost)

See Bentley (vol. 3) for a just dismissal of surmises about what extant play this might possibly be.

The Wandering Lovers, Fletcher (and Massinger?), revised 1634 by Massinger; tragicomedy (*licensed 6 Dec. 1623;* 1647)

Bentley (vol. 3) argues from documentary entries, historical facts, and the Epilogue and Prologue that Fletcher's *The Wandering Lovers* was revised by Massinger as *Cleander,* and later titled *The Lovers' Progress.* Hoy, Part 2, says that the linguistic evidence supports the statements in the Epilogue and Prologue which declare that the play is a revision of one by Fletcher. Massinger was the reviser; he is assigned I.i–iia (to entrance of Dorilaus), III.i, iv, IV, and V; Fletcher I.iib (from entrance of Dorilaus to end), II.i, III.ii–iii, v–vi.

The Maid in the Mill, Fletcher, W. Rowley; revised 1 Nov. 1623; comedy (*licensed 29 Aug. 1623;* 1647)

Hoy, Part 5, reports that the attribution recorded in Sir Henry Herbert's Office Book in 1623 has not been challenged. Fletcher's linguistic preferences easily distinguish his parts, which contrast to Rowley's preferences. Thus Fletcher is assigned I, III.ii–iii, V.iia (to entrance of Antonio); Rowley, II, III.i, IV, V.i, iib (from entrance of Antonio to end), assignments corresponding to those of earlier investigators.

Rule a Wife and Have a Wife, Fletcher; comedy (*licensed 19 Oct. 1624;* 1640)

This popular comedy is assigned by all to Fletcher alone; the date is fixed by its licensing. Bentley (vol. 3) briefly discusses the 1640 quarto.

A Wife for A Month, Fletcher; tragicomedy (*licensed 27 May 1624;* 1647)

By consensus, the play is Fletcher's. Bentley (vol. 3) discusses the second folio cast list, which he calls "clearly confused." He dismisses the possibility of revision.

The Chances, Fletcher; comedy (*1613-25;* 1647)

The play is Fletcher's. Hensman, *Shares of Fletcher* (II,A, *Bloody Brother*), dates the play 1625. Bentley (vol. 3) thinks that the 1615 French translation of Cervantes' *Novelas Exemplares* "provides a *terminus a quo* for the play," arguing that topical allusions point to a revival in 1627 rather than a first performance. An allusion to Jonson's *The Devil Is An Ass* (1616) suggests a date of 1617.

The Elder Brother, Fletcher (revised by Massinger?); comedy (*1625?;* 1637 & MS)

Hoy, Part 2, concludes from Fletcher's linguistic forms appearing in Massinger's scenes that the play is originally by Fletcher, but the first and last acts were rewritten by Massinger. Fletcher is assigned II, III, and IV, Massinger I and V. Bentley (vol. 3) argues that the Prologue and Epilogue indicate a first performance after Fletcher's death in August 1625; the date of composition was probably that year. Greg, *Dramatic Documents*, vol. 1 (above, *Bonduca*), describes the manuscript and the hand of the scribe. The manuscript was not used in the playhouse, and it is not a copy of a prompt copy. Poems at the end suggest a "purely literary origin." The text of the 1637 quarto and the manuscript "do not differ widely either in the dialogue or the stage-directions." Greg supplies principal variants for the 1637 and 1651 quartos.

The Noble Gentleman, Fletcher (possibly completed or revised by another); comedy (*licensed 3 Feb. 1626;* 1647)

The *Annals'* suggestion about revision reflects a view held by some investigators but rejected by others. Robert F. Willson, Jr., "Francis Beaumont and *The Noble Gentleman*," *ES* 49 (1968): 523-29, summarizes previous scholarship and supports Hoy and Oliphant in their view that the early version of the play was Beaumont's with Fletcher as reviser by offering evidence about "the presence of a burlesque character, a humour scheme, and . . . satirical allusions to various fashionable vices and popular plays," all of which occupied Beaumont in later plays. Hoy, Part 3, assigns Beaumont I.iv, II.ii, III.i, iii–iv, IV. iii–v, and Beaumont and Fletcher I.i–iii, II.i, III.ii, IV.i–ii, and V. He assigns the scenes extensively revised by Fletcher to both authors, although in those assigned to Beaumont alone, stylistic revision by Fletcher is also possible.

Bentley (vol. 3) reviews the arguments for date (which bear on Beaumont's authorship), concluding that "in such a welter of inadequately supported conclusions and dubious evidence, it seems . . . best to rely on the only piece of external evidence concerning the play which we have—Herbert's license. Possibly the play he licensed was not new, but it seems . . . sensible to assume that it was, until better evidence to the contrary is forthcoming." He also states that "the disintegrators are completely at odds about the play," and, keeping his eye on solid fact, concludes that "one can only assume that Sir Henry Herbert knew what he was talking about when he licensed the play as Fletcher's, but that he would not necessarily have known of a collaborator or reviser." Bentley discusses Oliphant on date and authorship, Maxwell on date and allusions, Bond on date, and reviews ascription arguments.

Editing the play for the new *Dramatic Works*, vol. 3 (1976), L. A. Beaurline concurs with Bentley on the inadequacy of evidence, suggesting that "composition in 1624–25 and a revival in the 1630's are just as probable" as composition in 1606. Allusions to events in court lead Beaurline to conclude that 1623 is the *terminus a quo* for the entire play. Reviewing Hoy's linguistic evidence and interpretation of it, he believes that Hoy "slipped." Because "the 'ye/you' evidence is slight," and because of the post-1619 allusions, Beaurline agrees with Bentley that in 1626 Herbert knew what he was talking about: the play "was new, possibly finished by someone else." Beaurline largely follows Turner's bibliographical analysis (above, *The Captain*).

The Fair Maid of the Inn, Fletcher (with Massinger? W. Rowley? and Ford?) comedy (*licensed 22 Jan. 1626;* 1647)

Bentley (vol. 3) says that "the best of the evidence cited [for various suggested authors] seems . . . only faintly suggestive." He favors the ascription on the title page to Fletcher alone. Since "discussions of the date of the play have generally been confused with questions of authorship," confusion about date exists; Bentley favors 22 Jan. 1625/26; topical allusions reinforce the date. Hoy, Part 5, adduces linguistic evidence to corroborate the shares claimed for Massinger (by Boyle), Ford (by Wells), and Webster (by Sykes), and argues for Fletcher's presence. Three distinct linguistic patterns in the 1647 folio text represent Massinger, Webster, and Ford, but Hoy discerns Fletcher's hand in certain passages in IV.i on the basis of linguistic preferences and rhetorical pattern. He believes the play is late, the last one worked on by Fletcher. He assigns Fletcher and Ford IV.i; Ford III; Massinger I.i and V.iiia (to entrance of the Host); and Webster II.i, IV.ii, V.i-ii, iiib (from entrance of the Host to end).

Hensman, *Shares of Fletcher* (II,A, *Bloody Brother*), reviews attribution scholarship and suggests "that the original play [1625] has been incompletely revised [1628] and supplied with a new initial action." Massinger attempted to "set an abridged and excised version of Fletcher and Rowley's original . . . within the new context of a tragi-comic plot."

B. UNCERTAIN ASCRIPTIONS; APOCRYPHA

Madon, King of Britain, Beaumont?; pseudo-history (ca. *1605-16;* lost)

The *Annals* tentatively assigns this play to Beaumont. It was entered in the Stationers' Register in 1660.

Henry VIII, Shakespeare (and Fletcher?); history (*June, 1613;* 1623)

Hoy, Part 7, assigns to Fletcher I.iii-iv, III.i, V.ii-iv; to Shakespeare I.i-ii, II.iii-iv, III.iia (to exit of King), V.i; and to Fletcher and Shakespeare II.i-ii, III.iib (from exit of King to end), IV.i-ii. The usual assignment is Fletcher, Prologue, I.iii-iv, II.i-ii, III.i-ii.203 (from exit of the King to end), IV.i-ii, V.ii-v, Epilogue; Shakespeare, I.i-ii, II.iii-iv, III.ii (lines 1-203, to exit of King), V.i. Hoy argues that the case for Fletcher's presence in this generally acknowledged Shakespearean play must rest on linguistic evidence; R. A. Foakes, New Arden edition (1957), concurs. A. C. Partridge examines the linguistic evidence in *The Problem of "Henry VIII" Reopened* (1949; rpt. in *Orthography in Shakespeare and Elizabethan Drama*, 1964). He, and Hoy, find that the *ye* of the folio is not compositorial, since its distribution does not accord with the bibliographical units of the printed edition. Other evidence, Hoy argues, suggests that no scribe put the *ye* form in the manuscript printer's copy, and the argument for Fletcher is strengthened by the known fact of Compositor B's habit of changing *ye*'s to *you*'s. Hoy argues for Fletcherian interpolations and touching up in some scenes, and for others as wholly by Fletcher on the presence of the *ye* form.

Discussion and citation of the scholarship on this topic is beyond the scope of this chapter. The interested reader should consult Erdman and Fogel, ed., *Evidence for Authorship* (II,A, *Two Noble Kinsmen*), who provide an extensive overview of the problems and scholarship and summarize selected studies from 1733 through 1962 (pp. 457-78). Also see the reviews of scholarship on this topic in E. K. Chambers, *William*

Shakespeare: A Study of Facts and Problems (1930), pp. 495-98; John Munro, ed. *The London Shakespeare* (1958), vol. 6, pp. 1143-50; R. A. Foakes, ed., *Henry VIII* (1957), New Arden edition (who also ably summarizes arguments for and against Fletcher's collaboration); and J. C. Maxwell, ed., *Henry VIII* (1968), New Cambridge edition. Studies since Erdman and Fogel (1962) are listed in "Shakespeare: An Annotated Bibliography" (II,A, *Henry VIII*). Also see the selected lists by McManaway and Roberts, and the survey by Proudfoot (II,A, *Henry VIII*).

The Faithful Friends, tragicomedy (*1613*-ca. *1621;* MS)

The *Annals* notes that this anonymous play was entered in the Stationers' Register as by Francis Beaumont and John Fletcher, and queries Daborne, Massinger, and Field as possible authors. Oliphant, *The Plays of Beaumont and Fletcher* (III,A, *Nice Valour*), found Field, Massinger, Beaumont, and Fletcher in it. Hoy (III,A, headnote) does not consider it; Chambers (vol. 3) reaches no conclusion. Dieter Mehl, "Beaumont und Fletchers *The Faithful Friends*," *Anglia* 80 (1962): 417-24, says that "it appears that much in the composition and the dramatic technique very strongly hints at Fletcher, and the play in any case should be distinguished from comparable plays of Shirley. The few preserved plays of Field and Daborne offer hardly any points of comparison."

The Widow, Middleton (with Jonson and Fletcher?); comedy (ca. *1615-17;* 1652)

Bentley (vol. 4), while summarizing ascription arguments, does not entirely dismiss Jonson and Fletcher, but reports that "there has been little disposition to find [either] in the play"; further, he concludes, "if Fletcher or Jonson had any part in *The Widow*, it must have been slight."

Love's Cure, or The Martial Maid, Massinger (revising Beaumont and Fletcher?) comedy (*1625?;* 1647)

Bentley (vol. 3) observes that "nearly everything about the play is in a state of confusion," with "the disintegrators . . . hopelessly, even ludicrously, at odds." He summarizes some of the problems about date, collaborators, and source. Hoy, Part 6, says that "the one certainty about the authorship of this play is the presence of Massinger," who is respon-

sible for nearly all of I, IV, and V in the only extant text, the 1647
folio. His portion is not in doubt; the authorship of the remaining
portion has been "the great . . . problem." There is external evidence
for revision, but no evidence for Jonson in it (as Oliphant had argued).
Hoy believes "there is no doubt at all that the reviser was Massinger,"
and that only one revision was made of a joint work of Beaumont and
Fletcher. The play was reworked from beginning to end, with I, IV, and
V virtually rewritten. Linguistic evidence supports Hoy's conjectures.
He assigns Beaumont III.i, iiib (from entrance of Malroda to Malroda's
"Do ye ask?"; Fletcher II.iia (to first exit of Bobadilla), III.iiia (to entrance of Malroda), v; Massinger I.i, iii, IV.i-iiia (to entrance of Alvarez,
Lucio, Bobadilla), iiic (from entrance of Alguazier to end), iv, V.i-ii, iiic
(final speech);Beaumont and Fletcher II.i, iic (from Clara's "No, he do's
not" to end), V.iiib (from Bobadilla's "I am not regarded" to final
speech); Fletcher and Massinger I.ii, II.iib (from first exit of Bobadilla
to Clara's "No, he do's not"), III.ii, iiic (from Malroda's "Do ye ask?"
to end), iv, IV.iiib (from entrance of Alvarez, Lucio, Bobadilla to entrance of Alguazier); and to Beaumont, Fletcher, and Massinger V.iiia
(to Bobadilla's "I am not regarded").

George Walton Williams, editing the play for the new *Dramatic
Works*, vol. 3 (1976), follows Hoy's assignments, and from them and
other evidence concludes that two of the groups of characters formed
the remains of a very early Beaumont and Fletcher collaboration
(1602-6), revised, rewritten, and reordered by Massinger from Spanish
sources after 1625. Williams does not find sufficient evidence to determine the nature of printer's copy. He describes the folio printing.

A Very Woman, or The Prince of Tarent, Massinger (reviser); tragicomedy (*licensed 6 June 1634;* 1655)

The *Annals* states that this is a possible reworking of a Fletcher and
Massinger play of ca. 1619-22. Hoy, Part 2, says that even though it
was licensed for acting as Massinger's on 6 June 1634 (9 years after
Fletcher's death), was first printed as Massinger's in *Three New Plays*
(1655), and was omitted from the 1647 folio, it is a revision by Massinger of a collaborative play. Linguistic forms determine the shares of
Fletcher and Massinger. The licensing as Massinger's is explained by the
insistence of the Master of the Revels at this time that old plays be relicensed if restaged. Fletcher is assigned II.iiib (from exit of the Duke to
end); III.i, IV.i, iii; Massinger I.i, II.i-ii, iiia (to exit of Duke), IV.ii, and
V. Roma Gill, "Collaboration and Revision in Massinger's *A Very*

Woman," *RES* 18 (1967): 136-48, concludes that our text is the result of Massinger's reworking of an old play on which he had collaborated with Fletcher. Analysis of the source suggests an intervening play by Massinger and Fletcher which probably emphasized those Fletcherian traits now only slightly discernible in the tragicomic mode of Massinger's revision.

C. CRITIQUE OF THE STANDARD EDITION

The edition of the *Works* by Arnold Glover and A. R. Waller, 10 vols. (1905-12) merely reprinted the second folio of 1679 with its spelling, and included collations of earlier printed editions. It badly needed replacing by an edition based on sound editing principles. The *Dramatic Works* under the general editorship of Fredson Bowers will, when completed, fill that need. In this critical old-spelling edition, the plays have been grouped by authors, an arrangement which, as Bowers says, "conveniently approximates the probable date of original composition for most of the works." The treatment of the copy text, silent alterations, and the apparatus of the edition are discussed in a prefatory note explaining the editorial principles which the various editors follow under the direction of the general editor. The apparatus for each play consists of a textual introduction, footnotes which list substantive departures from the copy text, a list of press-variant formes in authoritative editions, a list of emendations of accidentals, and a historical collation of substantive and semi-substantive variants in editions before 1700 and selected later editions. Robert K. Turner, Jr., supplies a description of "The Folio of 1647" in vol. 1, and reconstructs Moseley's problems in assembling copy. Appropriately, the edition has been well reviewed.

D. TEXTUAL STUDIES

Significant textual studies depend on the pioneering bibliographical work done in this century by W. W. Greg, R. B. McKerrow, and, more recently, Fredson Bowers. The interested student should consult an appropriate explanation of the relationship of a scholar's purely bibliographical studies of a text to an editor's establishment of a text. See, for example, Bowers's "Textual Criticism" in *The Aims and Methods of Scholarship in Modern Languages and Literatures*, ed. James Thorp (1963; 2nd ed. 1970), pp. 29-54, or other general discussions by Bowers. The separate introductions and appendices to the plays in the new *Dramatic Works*, ed. Bowers, provide textual information related to the editing process.

Greg contributed a preliminary study, "The Printing of the Beaumont and Fletcher Folio of 1647," *Library* 2 (1921-22): 109-15. Johan Gerritsen corrects Bald, "Bibliographical Studies" (III,A, headnote), who erroneously assigned two sections (3$ and c) of the 1647 folio to William Wilson that were printed by Susan Islip, in "The Printing of the Beaumont and Fletcher Folio of 1647" (III,A, *Love's Pilgrimage*). Gerritsen also argues for Islip as printer of section 7$, and questions the established order of imposition. Standish Henning, "The Printers and the Beaumont and Fletcher Folio of 1647, Sections 4 and 8 D-F," *SB* 22 (1969): 165-78, models his study on Charlton Hinman, *The Printing and Proof-Reading of the First Folio of Shakespeare* (1963); Hinman's study is questioned by McKenzie (below). Henning presents and discusses the evidence for the presswork, order of composition, and preferences of the two identified compositors and the possible third compositor.

Robert K. Turner, Jr., "The Printers and the Beaumont and Fletcher Folio of 1647, Section 2" (III,A, *The Captain*), calls attention to the general textual interest of the folio: it contains within its covers "eight more-or-less separate books." The publisher had the volume manufactured in sections by perhaps seven different printers. Thus it is ideal "for a comparison of the methods adopted in several contemporary houses for the printing of similar material in the same format." He discusses the order of composition and distribution, the identity of the two compositors of section 2, and the order of formes through the press. He briefly describes what is known of the printer of the section, William Wilson.

Turner studies section 1 of the folio (in *SB* 27 [1974]: 137-56), which contains *The Mad Lover*, *The Spanish Curate*, and *The Little French Lawyer*; he also identifies the printer, Thomas Warren, describes his career, and speculates on his shop. The evidence of spelling is too ambiguous to permit identification of the compositors. Turner discusses the order of printing, type recurrences, and spelling by quire (B-E).

James P. Hammersmith, "The Printers and the Beaumont and Fletcher Folio of 1647, Section 7" (III,A, *Valentinian*), identifies the printer (Susan Islip?) and the two compositors, and analyzes the two-skeleton printing and the quires containing *Valentinian* (composition, presswork, and distribution).

A few studies deal with specific bibliographical topics. Guy A. Battle, "A Bibliographical Note from the Beaumont and Fletcher First Folio,"

SB 1 (1948-49): 187-88, notices a little-used type of bibliographical evidence, progressive changes in the boxlines in the 1647 folio. These changes provide evidence for the printing order of the formes. James S. Steck, "Center Rules in Folio Printing: A New Kind of Bibliographical Evidence," *SB* 1 (1948-49): 188-91, uses section 5 of the 1647 folio as an example of center rules (separating the two columns of a double-column folio) which, when studied further, would identify the skeleton-formes. Guy A. Battle, "The Case of the Altered 'C'—A Bibliographical Problem in the Beaumont and Fletcher First Folio," *PBSA* 42 (1948): 66-70, observes that the running title in *Love's Cure* changes from a large "c" to a small "c" on 5Q4^V. The title on this sheet had to be recomposed because "there is a change-over from one play to another within the gathering." His examination of the running titles enables him to determine the order of the formes at this point.

D. F. McKenzie, "Printers of the Mind: Some Notes on Bibliographical Theories and Printing-House Practices," *SB* 22 (1969): 1-75, questions many of the assumptions—and thereby the conclusions—of textual studies of the kind summarized here and in section IIIA, conclusions on which editorial judgments about copy text and substantive emendation are based. The assumptions include the average work output for compositors and presses, the number of presses, the number and order of skeleton-formes, the number of compositors, the ratio between compositors and press-crews, the relationship of composition to press work, the length of time for production, proofreading practices, and printing conditions generally. The records of Cambridge University Press for its first decades, preserved entire, suggest that commonly held assumptions seriously misrepresent true conditions. Printing house conditions and practices were infinitely more complex than have been imagined.

E. SINGLE-WORK EDITIONS

The three most useful editions of *The Knight of the Burning Pestle* are by John Doebler, RRDS (1967), Andrew Gurr, Fountainwell Drama Series (1968), and Michael Hattaway, New Mermaid (1969). The play has also been edited by J. W. Lever (1962) and Benjamin W. Griffith, Jr. (1963), translated into Italian by Giuliano Pellegrini (1949) and French by M. T. Jones-Davies (1958), and issued in facsimile of the 1613 quarto by Da Capo Press, The English Experience, and Scolar Press. *Philaster* has been edited by Andrew Gurr for the Revels series

(1969), Brian Scobie for Fountainwell (1972), and Dora Jean Ashe for RRDS (1974); the 1620 quarto is in facsimile by Da Capo and English Experience, the 1622 quarto by Scolar. *The Maid's Tragedy* has been edited for RRDS by Howard B. Norland (1968), and for Fountainwell by Andrew Gurr (1969). There are facsimiles of the 1619 quarto by Da Capo and The English Experience. Pierre Messiaen included it in French translation in his *Théâtre anglais: moyen age et XVIe siècle* (1948) and Giuliano Pellegrini translated it as *La tragedia della fanciulla* (1948). The Regents, Fountainwell, and Mermaid editions provide general introductions (text, source, date, criticism, and so on).

Other plays in the canon exist in only one single-work edition. John H. Dorenkamp has edited *Beggar's Bush* (1967), J. D. Jump *Rollo, Duke of Normandy, or The Bloody Brother* (1948), W. W. Greg *Bonduca*, Malone Society (1951), Johan Gerritsen *The Honest Man's Fortune* (1952), Margaret McLaren Cook and F. P. Wilson *Demetrius and Enanthe*, Malone Society (1951), Robert K. Turner *A King and No King*, RRDS (1963), G. R. Proudfoot *The Two Noble Kinsmen*, RRDS (1970), and George B. Ferguson *The Woman's Prize* (1966). The *Spanish Curate* was translated and adapted by R. Ferdinand in *France Illustration Supplément*, No. 146 (Jan. 1954): 1-24.

Photofacsimile editions exist for *The Bloody Brother*, Da Capo (1969), *The Elder Brother*, Da Capo (1970), *A King and No King*, English Experience (1971) and Da Capo (1971), *The Scornful Lady*, English Experience and Da Capo (1972), *The Two Noble Kinsmen*, Tudor Facsimiles (1971), *Wit Without Money*, Da Capo (1970).

F. EDITIONS OF NONDRAMATIC WORKS

Beaumont's poems are in Alexander Chalmers, *The Works of the English Poets from Chaucer to Cowper*, vol. 6 (1810). Gwyn Jones edited *Salmacis and Hermaphroditus*, with engravings by John Buckland-Wright (1952); the poem is also in Elizabeth Story Donno, ed., *Elizabethan Minor Epics* (1963), and Alexander Nigel, ed., *Elizabethan Narrative Verse* (1967).

IV. SEE ALSO

A. GENERAL

Allen, Don Cameron. *The Star-Crossed Renaissance: The Quarrel about Astrology and Its Influence in England*. 1941.

Babb, Lawrence. *The Elizabethan Malady: A Study of Melancholia in English Literature from 1580 to 1642.* 1951.

Barber, C. L. *The Idea of Honour in the English Drama 1591-1600.* 1957.

Boas, Frederick S. "The Soldier in Elizabethan and Later Drama." *EDH* 19 (1942): 121-56. [Cites examples of "attractive pictures" of high-ranking soldiers in B&F]

Bowden, William R. *The English Dramatic Lyric, 1603-42: A Study in Stuart Dramatic Technique.* 1951.

Briggs, K. M. *Pale Hecate's Team: An Examination of the Beliefs on Witchcraft and Magic among Shakespeare's Contemporaries and His Immediate Successors.* 1962.

Cawley, Robert Ralston. *Unpathed Waters: Studies in the Influence of the Voyagers in Elizabethan Literature.* 1940.

Child, Harold H. "John Fletcher." In *Essays and Reflections,* ed. S. C. Roberts (1948), pp. 84-94. [Rpt. of 1925 *TLS* essay]

Clarkson, Paul S., and Warren, Clyde T., *The Law of Property in Shakespeare and the Elizabethan Drama.* 1942.

Cookman, A. V. "Shakespeare's Contemporaries on the Modern English Stage." *SU* 94 (1958): 29-41.

Dunn, T. A. *Philip Massinger: The Man and the Playwright.* 1957.

Ekeblad, Inga-Stina. "Anthony Trollope's Copy of the 1647 Beaumont and Fletcher Folio." *N&Q* 6 (1960): 153-55. [Trollope read 30-odd plays 1850-53.]

Evans, Ifor. *A Short History of English Drama.* 1948; rev. ed. 1965. [Five-page sketch]

Holzknecht, Karl J. *Outlines of Tudor and Stuart Plays 1497-1642.* 1947. [*Beggar's Bush, The Faithful Shepherdess, The Island Princess, The Knight of the Burning Pestle, The Maid's Tragedy, Philaster, Rule a Wife and Have a Wife, The Two Noble Kinsmen, The Wild Goose Chase*]

Kocourek, Rotislav. "Fletcherský dramatický kánon." *Časopis pro moderní filologii* 43 (1961): 26-33. [English summary p. 33; not seen]

Krzyzanowski, J. "Some Conjectural Remarks on Elizabethan Dramatists." *N&Q* 93 (1949): 233-34. [Suggests emendations in 6 plays]

Leech, Clifford. *Shakespeare's Tragedies and Other Studies in Seventeenth Century Drama.* 1950. [Scattered references]

M[cIlwraith], A. K. "John Fletcher (The Poet)." *N&Q* 92 (1947): 175. [Locates a Massinger mention of Fletcher]

Manifold, J. S. *The Music in English Drama from Shakespeare to Purcell.* 1956.

Masefield, John. "Beaumont and Fletcher." *Atlantic Monthly,* June 1957, pp. 71-74.

Meyers, Jay R. "Beaumont and Fletcher's Royalism: Once More." *Faculty Journal* (East Stroudsburg, Pa., State College) 1, i (1970): 29-35. [Not seen]

Ozu, Jiro. "Beaumont and Fletcher e no Kokoromi—Josho." *Eigo Seinen* (Tokyo) 119 (1974): 694-96. [Not seen]

Pellegrini, Giuliano. "Introduzione a Beaumont e Fletcher." *Rivista di letterature moderne* 2 (1947): 61-67.

———. "Motivi e procedimento barocchi i Beaumont and Fletcher." *Annali della Facoltá di Lettere e Filosofia della Universitá di Cagliari* 16 (1949): 5-78. [Not seen]

Reed, Robert Rentoul, Jr. *The Occult on the Tudor and Stuart Stage.* 1965.

Reul, Paul de. *Le triomphe du savoir-faire, joint aux dans poétiques: Beaumont and Fletcher.* Présentation du théâtre Jacobéen de Marston à Beaumont et Fletcher (1600-1625). Antwerp: n.d., pp. 189-302. [Not seen]

Schoenbaum, Samuel. "'Decadence' in Jacobean Drama." *History of Ideas Newsletter* 4 (1958): 50-55; 5 (1960): 3-11.

Silvestru, Valentin. "'Tragedia fecioarci.'" *România Literară*, 25 Jan. 1973, p. 22. [Not seen; a Romanian production]

Smet, Robert de [Romain Sanvic]. *Le théâtre élisabéthain.* 1955.

Smith, Irwin. *Shakespeare's Blackfriars Playhouse: Its History and Its Design.* 1964. [Lists B&F plays accepted at the Blackfriars]

Stroup, Thomas B. *Microcosmos: The Shape of the Elizabethan Play.* 1965.

Wertheim, Albert. "Fraternity and the Catches in Two Restoration Theater Productions." *Journal of the Catch Society of America* 1 (1969): 14-19.

Wilson, Edward M. "Did John Fletcher Read Spanish?" *PQ* 27 (1948): 187-90. [Yes.]

B. INDIVIDUAL PLAYS

Bloody Brother

Simpson, Percy. "Skiff." *TLS*, 2 Aug. 1947, p. 391. [In II.ii Fletcher attempted to transliterate *scyphus.*]

Elder Brother

Maxwell, J. C. "A Dramatic Echo of an Overburian Character." *N&Q* 192 (1948): 277. [In I.ii]

Fair Maid of the Inn

Sloman, Albert E. "The Spanish Source of *The Fair Maid of the Inn.*" In *Hispanic Studies in Honour of I. González Llubera*, ed. Francis William Pierce (1959), pp. 331-41. [Cervantes]

Faithful Shepherdess

Kempling, Wm. Bailey. "*The Faithful Shepherdess.*" *TLS*, 22 Jan. 1938, p. 60. [Inigo Jones adapted scenery for the production.]

Maid's Tragedy

Bejblík, Alois. "Poměr Zeyerova *Neklana* k Beaumontově a Fletcherově hře *The Maid's Tragedy.*" *Časopis pro moderni filologii* 32 (1949): 135-39. [Influence of *MT* on Zeyer; not seen]

Pellegrini, Giuliano. "Un in-quarto della *Maid's Tragedy.*" *Anglica* 1 (1946): 124-27. [Description of a copy in the National Library of Florence]

Nice Valor

Wasserman, Earl R. "The Source of Motherwell's 'Melancholye.'" *MLN* 55 (1940): 296. ["Hence, all you vain delights," from the play]

Philaster

Sekiya, Takeshi. "Shakespeare's Last Plays and Beaumont and Fletcher." *1967 Eibungaku Ronshu*, no. 1, pp. 69–91. [In Japanese; comparative study of *Philaster* and *Cymbeline*; not seen]

Prophetess

Bowers, Fredson. "A Bibliographical History of the Fletcher-Betterton Play, *The Prophetess*, 1690." *Library* 16 (1961): 169–75.

Thierry and Theodoret

Thorp, Willard. "A Shakespearian Echo in *Thierry and Theodoret*." *SAB* 9 (1934): 51–52. [Its final scene resembles *Lear* IV.vii.]

Valentinian

Wilson, J. Harold. "Satiric Elements in Rochester's *Valentinian*." *PQ* 16 (1937): 41–48.

Woman Hater

Weales, Gerald. "The Stage." *Commonweal* 92 (1970): 389–90. [Jestingly recommends it for production because of its relevance]

PHILIP MASSINGER

Terence P. Logan

William Gifford's *The Plays of Philip Massinger*, 4 vols. (1805; 2nd ed. 1813) is the standard collected edition of the fourteen non-collaborative plays it includes; the second edition is preferred. The third edition (1 vol., 1840) is available in several English and American reprints. Francis Cunningham's edition, *The Plays of Philip Massinger* (1871), prints Gifford's texts and adds his own of *Believe As You List*, omitted by Gifford. Three collaborative plays, *The Old Law*, *The Fatal Dowry*, and *The Virgin Martyr*, are included in the Gifford and Cunningham editions. Standard texts for the majority of Massinger's collaborative plays will appear in *The Dramatic Works in the Beaumont and Fletcher Canon*, gen. ed. Fredson Bowers (1966–), which is supplanting the earlier standard, *The Works of Francis Beaumont and John Fletcher*, ed. Arnold Glover and A. R. Waller, 10 vols. (1905-12). Bowers's edition of *The Dramatic Works of Thomas Dekker*, vol. 3 (1958), provides the standard text of *The Virgin Martyr*. T. A. Dunn's edition of *The Fatal Dowry* (1969) and the text of *The Old Law* included in A. H. Bullen's edition of *The Works of Thomas Middleton*, vol. 2 (1885), are standard for those titles. *The Poems of Philip Massinger, with Critical Notes*, ed. Donald S. Lawless (1968), is the definitive text for the nondramatic verse.

I. GENERAL

A. BIOGRAPHICAL

T. A. Dunn, *Philip Massinger: The Man and the Playwright* (1957), recounts most of the known facts and the myths of Massinger's biography. A brief life is also given in vol. 4 of G. E. Bentley's *The Jacobean and Caroline Stage* (1956). Bentley and Dunn agree that there is no solid evidence to support the speculation, first raised by Gifford in his editions, that Massinger was a Roman Catholic. Dunn, however, is inclined "to support Gifford's suggestion, at least in respect of Massinger's Roman Catholic sympathies," on the basis of his reading of the plays. Dunn also describes Massinger's working relations with Henslowe's and other companies, his literary associations, his patrons (perhaps including Philip Herbert), and his finances. A monograph by Donald Lawless, *Philip Massinger and His Associates* (1967), supplements the material in Dunn. Lawless relates the involvement of Massinger's mother's family in the Catholic cause and, on the basis of evidence other than that used by Dunn, is "inclined to believe that Massinger was a Roman Catholic." Lawless provides a more detailed account of Massinger's relations with other authors and his patrons, especially Philip Herbert. Much of the information in the monograph first appeared in a series of studies in *Notes and Queries*: "Massinger, Smith, Horner, and Selden," 4 (1957): 55-56; "Anne Massinger and Thomas Crompton," 4 (1957): 416-17; "Sir Robert Wiseman, Kt," 5 (1958): 185; "More About Anne Massinger (?) and Thomas Crompton," 5 (1958): 244; "A Further Note on Anne Massinger and Thomas Crompton," 5 (1958): 528; "Arthur Massinger of London," 7 (1960): 29-30; and "Sir Thomas Jay (Jeay)," 7 (1960): 30. Lawless's further biographical research is recorded in three *Notes and Queries* items published after his monograph: "The Parents of Philip Massinger," 15 (1968): 256-58, gives new information about Anne and Arthur Massinger, including Arthur's political connections with the Earl of Pembroke; "The Burial of Philip Massinger," 18 (1971): 29-30, describes the burial records and explains the funeral expenses; and "Massinger's Secretary," 19 (1972): 466-67, establishes that Joshua Poole's reference in *The English Parnassus* (1657) is not to a lost play by Philip but to a writers' guide written by Jean de la Serre and translated by John Massinger.

B. GENERAL STUDIES OF THE PLAYS

Dunn's 1957 book is the first full study since A. H. Cruickshank's *Philip Massinger* (1920) and Maurice Chelli's *Le drame de Massinger* (1923). The presentation is selective and limited. For example, "questions of collaboration and attribution" are excluded on the grounds that "the consideration of such problems here would have confused the reader and obscured the object of my study, Massinger himself." This decision rules out the largest part of the canon and Massinger's formative association with Fletcher. Dunn's organization is based on major aspects of the plays ("Plotting," "Stagecraft," "Characterization," "Criticism of Life," and "Style") and it precludes extended critical discussion of individual plays. Finally, the critical position developed in the book is as qualified and restricted as the organization and scope. Massinger is a "slave of habit" whose writing is "inelastic and mechanical. Massinger, in short, is not a poet. Only rarely is there any 'compelling emotion' behind his work." In a review, *RES* 10 (1959): 198-99, Philip Edwards found the book gravely flawed by Dunn's fondness for "casual and derogatory judgements which are not supported by critical argument." It is clearly, as other reviewers noted, a study written by a man who is not fond of his subject.

As the second half of its title indicates, Lawless's *Philip Massinger and His Associates* (1967) corrects Dunn's complete neglect of an important part of the canon. The "practice of collaboration must be held constantly in mind when we consider Massinger's dramatic career." Massinger learned in Henslowe's school and "had it not been for the system of collaboration then in vogue, he might possibly never have begun to write for the stage." Lawless's central critical position is significantly more favorable: "Massinger was the chief poet during the greater part of Charles I's reign, belonging to a school of playwrights that helped direct the course of English drama. Neither his position nor his virtues can be ignored."

T. S. Eliot, "Philip Massinger," in *The Sacred Wood* (1920), pp. 120-43 (rpt. in *Selected Essays* [1932], *Essays on Elizabethan Drama* [1934], and elsewhere), considers Massinger's frequent echoes of the greater Elizabethan dramatists and his inability to meet their standard. "Massinger's feeling for language had outstripped his feeling for things; . . . his eye and his vocabulary were not in cooperation." His stylistic complexity is not accompanied by depth of thought and feeling; his poetry "suffers from cerebral anæmia." Eliot excepts two plays from his general condemnation: *A New Way to Pay Old Debts* and *The City Madam* show that Massinger "might almost have been a great realist; he is killed by conventions which were suitable for the preceding literary generation, but not for his." A recent negative appraisal, Robert A. Fothergill, "The Dramatic Experiences of Massinger's *The City Madam* and *A New Way to Pay Old Debts*," *UTQ* 43 (1973): 68-86, reconsiders Eliot's two exceptions: "the dramatic experience of the plays is ultimately a confining one, a cramping of our possible range of responses into narrow and unenlivening satisfactions."

Another influential earlier essay, L. C. Knights, "The Significance of Massinger's Social Comedies—With a Note on 'Decadence,'" in *Drama and Society in the Age of Jonson* (1937), pp. 270-300 (rpt. in part under the title "Social Morality in *A New Way to Pay Old Debts*," in *Shakespeare's Contemporaries: Modern Studies in English Renaissance Drama*, ed. Max Bluestone and Norman Rabkin [1961], pp. 273-81; 2nd ed. [1970], pp. 378-86), presents a critical assessment distinctly more sympathetic than Eliot's. As a comic playwright, Massinger is "the last of the Elizabethans" and "each of his plays lives . . . . There is a fresh perception of a contemporary world." G. Wilson Knight, *The Golden Labyrinth: A Study of British Drama* (1962), is equally positive. Massinger "succeeds in making living drama from weightiest themes, striking a happy balance of statecraft and stagecraft. He is never unfair, always judicial."

Much of the criticism comments, at least in passing, on the moral values expressed in the plays. T. A. Dunn's view (I,A) that Massinger's "artistic conscience always succumbs to the conscience of the moralist" is challenged by Philip Edwards, "Massinger the Censor," in *Essays on Shakespeare and Elizabethan Drama in Honor of Hardin Craig*, ed. Richard Hosley (1962), pp. 341-50. The moral element is an integral part of the play's accomplishment, a strength, not a weakness. "To watch [Massinger] at work, bending an unlikely form of play to its moral mold, is perhaps to find a better artist and a more interesting moralist than has sometimes been recognized." Massinger's problems arise from his medium, Fletcherian tragicomedy, not his moral content. "The plays could not have been more successful if they had contained less morality, for without the moral scrutiny which is at their core they have no reason for existing." Similarly, A. L. Bennett, "The Moral Tone of Massinger's Dramas," *Papers on Language and Literature* 2 (1966): 207-16, finds that Massinger's surest writing is his political and social commentary; he is least adept when handling romantic elements.

In "Contemporary Politics in Massinger," *SEL* 6 (1966): 279-90, Alan G. Gross suggests that the criticism has made too much of possible topical political allusions in the plays. The plays reflect "an unflagging interest in general political theory," and it is even "possible to look upon Massinger as a topical writer partially frustrated in his aims"; however, the extant plays all avoid thrusts at specific persons and situations. An earlier monograph, more general in scope, Benjamin Townley Spencer's "Philip Massinger," in *Seventeenth Century Studies*, ed. Robert Shafer (1933), pp. 1-119, treats Massinger's social and political views at length. "Massinger in his social theory is essentially an aristocrat" and the plays reflect his bitter resentment of the rise of the bourgeoisie.

In *Massinger's Imagery*, Francis D. Evenhuis (1973) surveys and classifies the imagery along lines suggested by Henry W. Wells, *Poetic Imagery Illustrated from Elizabethan Literature* (1951) and Caroline F. E. Spurgeon, *Shakespeare's Imagery and What It Tells Us* (1935). Massinger's practice is compared with that of other dramatists, especially Marlowe and Shakespeare, and there is an overall assessment, heavily qualified, of the poetry of the plays. In an article with the same title as Evenhuis's book, *RenP*, 1955, pp. 47-54, John O. Lyons concludes that Massinger "can relate his imagery to the plot of his plays in a manner which is usually identified only with the best dramatic poetry."

A more precisely focused study of an aspect of Massinger's poetry, Cyrus Hoy's "Verbal Formulae in the Plays of Philip Massinger," *SP* 56 (1959): 600-618, finds it singularly inflexible: "the Massingerian method of meeting the dramatic occasion with a rhetorical formula . . . will not admit of nice adjustments to the demands of the particular moment. The formula is set; and once brought into play must unfold like a coiled spring." Because of Massinger's reliance on formulae, "emotional developments of stunning impact are rendered through what amount to little more than verbal posturings." In contrast, J. de Vos, "Philip Massinger and Dramatic Construction," *Studia Germanica Gandensia* 10 (1968): 67-77, praises Massinger's poetry "for its constant dignity and its rhetorical qualities." The fresh use of a poetic commonplace is noted by C. A. Gibson, "Massinger's 'Composite Mistresses,'" *AUMLA* 29 (1968): 44-51.

Massinger contributed a major share to the "Beaumont and Fletcher canon" and he is an important figure in much of the scholarship on those writers. That material is discussed in the essays on Beaumont and Fletcher in this volume. A few representative titles follow.

L. B. Wallis, *Fletcher, Beaumont, and Company: Entertainers to the Jacobean Gentry* (1947), gives critical appreciations, a history of the "Beaumont and Fletcher" critical reputation, and stage histories of the plays; Massinger's contribution was greater than Beaumont's and the omission of his name from the title page of the first folio was a real injustice. Detailed analyses of the styles of Beaumont, Fletcher, and Massinger, as well as some assignments of shares based on style, are given in Eugene M. Waith's *The Pattern of Tragicomedy in Beaumont and Fletcher* (1952).

Cyrus Hoy's attribution studies (III,A) have superseded most earlier material of this type. Three earlier books, however, remain useful for an understanding of the historical development of scholarship on Massinger's role in the collaboration: Maurice Chelli, *Étude sur la collaboration de Massinger avec Fletcher et son groupe* (1926); E. H. C. Oliphant, *The Plays of Beaumont and Fletcher: An Attempt to Determine Their Respective Shares and the Shares of Others* (1927); and Baldwin Maxwell, *Studies in Beaumont, Fletcher, and Massinger* (1939).

"Philip Massinger: The Spurious Legatee," a chapter in D. L. Frost's *The School of Shakespeare: The Influence of Shakespeare on English Drama. 1600–42* (1968), pp. 77–118, summarizes the current status of another large area of peripheral scholarship. Frost's main thrust is to reduce several hundred previously cited "borrowings" to the status of mere parallels: "Both writers spooned out of the same stock-pot."

Samuel A. Tannenbaum's *Philip Massinger (A Concise Bibliography)* was first published in 1938 and is reprinted in vol. 6 of *Elizabethan Bibliographies* (1967). This is updated (through 1965) in vol. 8 of *Elizabethan Bibliographies Supplements*, compiled by Charles A. Pennel and William P. Williams (1968). Selective lists of titles are given in Dunn (I,A); in Irving Ribner, *Tudor and Stuart Drama*, Goldentree Bibliographies (1966); and in *The New Cambridge Bibliography of English Literature*, ed. George Watson, vol. 1 (1974), and earlier *CBEL* editions.

II. CRITICISM OF INDIVIDUAL PLAYS AND STATE OF SCHOLARSHIP

A. INDIVIDUAL PLAYS

A New Way to Pay Old Debts

Robert Hamilton Ball's *The Amazing Career of Sir Giles Overreach* (1939) is a meticulously researched account of the play's background, its topical allusions to a contemporary political situation, and its stage history. *A New Way* was almost the only pre-Restoration play "acted almost continuously from Garrick to Hampden"; Ball establishes the public response to the play with generous citations from reviews and comments by figures like Thomas Jefferson. Its "extraordinary vitality" is a tribute to the "histrionic opportunities" found in the role of Sir Giles.

Class struggle is a recurring theme in Massinger's plays; three studies focus on that aspect of *A New Way*. Patricia Thomson, "The Old Way and the New Way in Dekker and Massinger," *MLR* 51 (1956): 168–78, finds that Massinger's main subject in *A New Way* is "the class struggle of his time, the struggle of the new gentry (Overreach) and the true gentry (Lovell)." Massinger treats the issue of interclass marriage far more seriously than Dekker. The Rose–Lord Lacy plot in *The Shoe-makers' Holiday* is a benevolent fairy tale; the Margaret Overreach–Lord Lovell plot, in contrast, is a vehicle for sustained social satire and argument. Unlike Dekker, Massinger is intensely aware of the deeper implications of class struggle; his "satire is amongst the greatest of his time not only because he can induce the requisite mood of indignation but also because he gets an intellectual grip on his situations." In partial disagreement, Alan Gerald Gross, "Social Change and Philip Massinger," *SEL* 7 (1967): 329-42, finds Massinger's treatment of social change in *A New Way* and *The City Madam* more emotional than intellectual. Massinger reveres the traditional hereditary class system and both fears and hates the rising trading class which threatens the stability of the older system. Alexander Leggatt, *Citizen Comedy in the Age of Shakespeare* (1973), considers the class conflict theme to be the play's most serious weakness. "Class awareness as a standard of judgment works well enough in the play's peripheral comic scenes . . . but, as a standard on which to base the central confrontation of good and evil, it breaks down." The play is a failure which "indicates the danger of imposing the wrong kind of seriousness on an intrigue comedy—or more precisely, perhaps, of embedding an intrigue comedy in a serious moral drama."

The play's topical allegory is stressed by Frederick M. Burelbach, Jr., "*A New Way to Pay Old Debts*: Jacobean Morality," *CLAJ* 12 (1969): 205-13. Massinger uses a thinly disguised attack on George Villiers to warn Charles not to follow James's example by encouraging upstarts. The play appeals "to the old aristocratic standard of gratitude" and supports "the conservative principles of the Pembrokes." R. H. Bowers, "A Note on Massinger's *New Way*," *MLR* 53 (1958): 214-15, suggests that a satirical ballad, now in the Folger Library, may provide additional information about Giles Mompesson whose career was the basis for Massinger's creation of Sir Giles Overreach.

Dunn (I,A) charts the play's six-strand plot and concludes that Massinger "has told a far-from-simple story surpassingly well." Muriel St. Claire Byrne's critical appraisal, in the introduction to her edition (1949), stresses the play's solid theatricality: "One calls it high class advisedly, because it is extremely well plotted and well written, in effective, easy blank verse: a highly finished, integrated piece of work, with everything handsomely symmetrical about it." A more qualified critical opinion is advanced by D. J. Enright, "Poetic Satire and Satire in Verse: A Consideration of Ben Jonson and Philip Massinger," *Scrutiny* 18 (1951): 211-23 (rpt. in his *The Apothecary's Shop: Essays in Literature* [1957], pp. 54-74), who contrasts Jonson's subtle and certain handling of Volpone with Massinger's inadequate treatment of Overreach, "the character whom his author could not control." Enright's title derives from his conclusion: "Jonson wrote poetic satire, Massinger wrote satire in verse—and there can be no doubt as to which of them was the greater dramatist." Robert A. Fothergill, "The Dramatic Experience of *The City Madam* and *A New Way to Pay Old Debts*," *UTQ* 43 (1973): 68-86, is even more negative. *A New Way* is superior to *The City Madam* but there is still "a needless ramming home of abundantly obvious satiric points"; Massinger's comedies "are seldom amusement of any kind."

The Roman Actor

In "The Theme and Structure of *The Roman Actor*," *AUMLA* 19 (1963): 39-51, Peter H. Davison defends the play from charges of structural weakness made by Eliot and others. While it touches on the conflict of lust and power in the profession of acting, the play's controlling theme is the nature of kingship. It derives artistic unity from "the relationship between the . . . theatre theme and the theme of power (especially divine right) in conflict with human weakness (cruelty and uxoriousness)." The equally positive reading given by Patricia Thomson, "World Stage and Stage in Massinger's *Roman Actor*," *Neophil* 54 (1970): 409-26, stresses the importance of the values represented by the principal characters. Domitian "deliberately confounds the life-like forms of drama with life itself." Paris's three major defenses of the stage, an important structural image in the play, are all correct in principle. The tyrannical political situation, however, corrupts the world of the theater and, while "Paris's ideals remain valid in principle, in practice their defeat makes *The Roman Actor* a tragedy not only of an actor, but of acting." The play is "brilliantly structured" according to A. P. Hogan, "Imagery of Acting in *The Roman Actor*," *MLR* 66 (1971): 273-81: "Domitian and his wife attempt to script and direct existence as their own pride dictates," and Paris's death is a "very ironic thing" because his final glory "derives from the tyrant's script, not from a triumphant career on stage."

Two recent articles treat Massinger's use of the device of plays within the play. Georges Borias, "Les personnages dans les pièces intérieurs à *L'Acteur Romain* de Massinger," *Revue d'Historie du Théâtre* 24 (1972): 289-99, closes his analysis of the play observing: "Il semble que le divorce soit complet entre le moraliste théorician qui ne réussit guère à nous convaincre, et le dramaturge, le practicien qui écrit *L'Acteur Romain* et construit ainse une pièce à la glorie du théâtre, glorie si differente de celle dont rêvait le moraliste que celui-ci ne l'aurait peut-être pas approuvée." In "The Play within a Play: An Elizabethan Dramatic Device," *E&S* 13 (1960): 36-48, Arthur Brown traces the use of the device from Kyd to Massinger. The interior plays in *The Roman Actor* are "the most consistent and fully integrated" of all; "so skilful a use of the play within a play is, I believe, unparalleled in Elizabethan tragedy."

Possible sources for the five-part outline of the classical oration which appears in many of the play's longer speeches are suggested by John H. Crabtree, Jr., "Philip Massinger's Use of Rhetoric in *The Roman Actor*," *FurmS* 7 (1960): 40-58. Other sources, including classical authors, Jonson's *Sejanus*, and Webster's *Duchess of Malfi*, are identified by C. A. Gibson, "Massinger's Use of His Sources for *The Roman Actor*," *AUMLA* 15 (1961): 60-72.

The Fatal Dowry

Fredson Bowers, *Elizabethan Revenge Tragedy, 1587-1642* (1940), holds that the play advances a "hard-headed bourgeois disapproval of revenge" which marks an important innovation in the revenge tradition: "For the first time in a play the romantic stage conventions of personal justice are outspokenly contrasted to the legal and moral code by which the vast majority of Elizabethans lived." Dunn (I,A) finds this collaboration with Field "unique among the plays of the Massinger canon in being both weak in plot and unusually strong in characterization." "The entire play is a working out of a situation" presented in a *controversia* by Seneca the Elder, according to Eugene M. Waith, "*Controversia* in the English Drama: Medwall and Massinger," *PMLA* 68(1953): 286-303.

An extended comparison of Massinger's play and Nicholas Rowe's adaptation, under the title *The Fair Penitent*, is given in Malcolm Goldstein's edition of the Rowe version (RRDS, 1969). Rowe cuts characters and action to create a more focused play than the original.

Donald B. Clark, "An Eighteenth-Century Adaptation of Massinger," *MLQ* 13 (1952): 239–52, finds that the structural changes "show the new preference for neoclassic simplicity" and that the adapted version reveals that Rowe lacks Massinger's ability "to perceive underlying moral principles." J. Frank Kermode briefly comments on the Rowe adaptation and one by Aaron Hill in "A Note on the History of Massinger's *The Fatal Dowry* in the Eighteenth Century," *N&Q* 192 (1947): 186–87.

The Virgin Martyr

Louise George Clubb, "*The Virgin Martyr* and the *Tragedia Sacra*," *RenD* 7 (1964): 103–26, classifies this collaborative work of Massinger and Dekker as a "saint's play"—a genre which developed under the influence of Counter-Reformation theology. *The Virgin Martyr* was "the only post-Reformation saint's play on the London stage before the theaters were closed in 1642." The play "fulfilled the aim of Counter-Reformation drama—to replace secular with sacred, specifically Catholic, themes." The original conception was probably Massinger's and he "must have realized" the obvious parallel between the situation of Catholics in England and "the position of Dorothea in Roman-governed Caesaria." Agreeing with M. T. Jones-Davies, *Un peintre de la vie londonienne, Thomas Dekker (circa 1572-1632)*, 2 vols. (1958), and G. E. Bentley, *The Jacobean and Caroline Stage*, vol. 3 (1956), Clubb finds that Sir George Buc's record of payment, 6 October 1620, "for new reforming the Virgin Martyr" refers to a fee for a second reading of a previously censored play, not to a Massinger revision of a play originally by Dekker. The Counter-Reformation attitudes in the play were earlier noted by Uve Christian Fischer, "Un dramma martirologico barocco: *The Virgin Martyr* di Philip Massinger," *Siculorum Gymnasium* 16 (1963): 1–19; Massinger perhaps intended the play "come un suo contributo personale contro un libro diffussimo e il più letto dopo la Bibbia, cioè quello di John Foxe, *Book of Martyrs*." In contrast to the Clubb and Fischer readings, Peter F. Mullany, "Religion in Massinger and Dekker's *The Virgin Martyr*," *Komos* 2 (1970): 89–97, finds the religious elements in the play superficial rather than serious. The religious story line is used "for exclusively theatrical purposes that preclude the play from having anything to say about what it means humanly to be willing to suffer martyrdom." The play is merely "another example of tragi-comedy designed to entertain, but not to illuminate the lives of its audiences."

Believe As You List

In the introduction to his Revels edition of Ford's *Perkin Warbeck* (1968) Peter Ure finds it "very probable" that *Believe As You List* and *Perkin* are closely related. Although the priority of performance cannot be established, "one can easily suppose that one of these two plays, proceeding from rival companies and rival theatres, was a deliberate attempt to match the other." Philip Edwards, "The Royal Pretenders in Massinger and Ford," *E&S* 27 (1974): 18–36, uses Ure's suggestion as the basis of a full comparative study. *Believe* is "a play on recent European history gone over with a paint-brush to make it look like ancient history." The Massinger and Ford plays are both "very pessimistic," reflect "a deep current of hostility to Charles," and have a common major theme in their explorations of "the meanings of the terms 'counterfeit' and 'natural' in the period of perturbed and perplexed relationships between monarch and people about the year 1620."

Machiavelli, whom Massinger "must have read" in a manuscript translation, is a source for many of the play's ideas, according to Roma Gill, "'Necessitie of State': Massinger's *Believe As You List*," *ES* 46 (1965): 407–16; "the evidence of this play . . . confirms the view that Massinger was a serious student of Machiavelli," and the play should be read as a "problem play," not a tragedy. Additional sources are discussed in the introduction to Charles J. Sisson's Malone Society edition (1928, for 1927).

The City Madam

Alan Gerald Gross, in an article in *SEL* (above, *A New Way to Pay Old Debts*), traces the theme of class conflict in *A New Way* and *The City Madam*. The characterization of Luke Frugal is central to the development of the theme in the latter play: "Luke is both a hypocrite and a personification of the financial ambitions of the trading class which uses hypocrisy as one of its weapons." *The City Madam* "entertains us with the spectacle of the loathsome persecuting the contemptible," according to Robert A. Fothergill (I,B). The play "is remarkable among satiric dramas for its economy of effort"; in the final analysis, however, it is little more than a social tract by a "grave conservative." The introduction to Cyrus Hoy's RRDS edition (1964) identifies the main themes as "vanity and hypocrisy," and finds that "the characterization of Luke is Massinger's crowning achievement in this play."

The Bondman

The sources, including a *controversia* by Seneca the Elder and items by Diodorus Siculus, Justin, and Herodotus, are discussed by Philip Edwards, "The Sources of Massinger's *The Bondman*," *RES* 15 (1964): 21-26. Edwards also stresses that the topical elements are not especially important: "the play explains itself as a moral entity, leaving very little to be accounted for in terms of political allegory." In "Massinger the Censor" (I,B) Edwards rates this "the finest of the more serious tragicomedies." *The Bondman*'s use as a major source is discussed by Warner G. Rice, "Sources of William Cartwright's *The Royal Slave*," *MLN* 45 (1930): 515-18.

The Duke of Milan

Leonora Leet Brodwin, *Elizabethan Love Tragedy 1587-1625* (1971), finds this Massinger's "greatest tragedy" and notes its use of worldly love rather than the more usual courtly love. The "exploration of the traditional Herod character is a consummate study of the bombastic quality in his nature." Massinger's treatment of the plot and characters of the Herod story is studied in a comparative context by Maurice Valency, *The Tragedies of Herod and Mariamne* (1940); over forty versions are included. Fredson Bowers, *Elizabethan Revenge Tragedy* (1940), considers the play in the context of another tradition; Massinger's "curious withholding of the comparatively just motives for Francisco's vengeance . . . a procedure which undoubtedly injures the chain of cause and effect so necessary for a satisfactory tragedy—may perhaps be laid to the influence of the growing disapproval of revenge."

The Emperor of the East

Both J. E. Gray, "The Source of *The Emperour of the East*," *RES* 1 (1950): 126-35, and Peter G. Phialas, The Sources of Massinger's *Emperour of the East*," *PMLA* 65 (1950): 473-82, identify the main source as *The Holy Court*, Sir Thomas Hawkins's translation (1626) of Nicholas Caussin's *La cour sainte*. Phialas discusses other influences, including a sketch in Burton's *Anatomy of Melancholy*, and ranks this as "the worst failure in the corpus of his plays." In "Massinger and the *Commedia dell'Arte*," *MLN* 65 (1950): 113-14, Phialas suggests that a scene in the play could be based on a *commedia* performed in London by Francis Nicoline and John Puncteus in 1630; "it is indeed possible that [Massinger] modeled his empiric on the ciarlatano of the *Commedia dell'Arte*."

The Maid of Honour

Peter F. Mullany, "Religion in Massinger's *The Maid of Honour*," *RenD* 2 (1969): 143-56, finds the play artificial and of little importance. "Massinger's dramatic intention, like that of Beaumont and Fletcher in *A King and No King*, is to create theatrical excitement in an improbable and escapist drama whose aim is not to explore human motives and action." Mullany again discusses *The Emperor* in an article listed below under *The Knight of Malta*. In "Marvel and Massinger: A Source of 'The Definition of Love,'" *RES* 23 (1947): 63-65, Pierre Legouis suggests that lines from the play are echoed in "the second-greatest of Marvell's love-poems." D. S. Bland, "Marvell and Massinger," *RES* 23 (1947): 267, glosses Massinger's meaning in the same passage.

The Unnatural Combat

T. A. Dunn's criticism (I,A) that "Massinger uses Belgarde and his affairs [in Act IV] merely in order to fill out the play to the required length" is disputed by Geraint Lloyd Evans, "*The Unnatural Combat*," *N&Q* 5 (1958): 96. Belgrade serves both to comment on the main action and to broaden the implications of Malefort's tragedy. In *Elizabethan Revenge Tragedy* (1940), Fredson Bowers finds that the play carries "to the logical conclusion of stage representation the religious ideas of the day about the intervention in human affairs of the personal retribution of Heaven." Malefort Senior, struck down by a thunderbolt, is a compelling example: "God Himself is shown as the avenger, and not merely the punisher of those who usurp His privilege."

The Knight of Malta

Peter F. Mullany, "The Knights of Malta in Renaissance Drama," *NM* 74 (1973): 297-310, compares Massinger's *Maid of Honour* and the Fletcher, Field, and Massinger collaboration, *The Knight of Malta*, with plays on similar subjects by Kyd, Marlowe, Webster, and others. The two plays in which Massinger had a hand show a more accurate sense of the history of the knights and use the order's rules and rubrics more correctly than other plays of the period. In both Massinger plays, however, the knights are merely "the vehicle with which they build their flawed and mechanical art." The plays "remain 'withered flowers' because they lack inner vitality and are devoid of any larger purpose that transcends simply the creation of intense theatrical moments." An error in source identification dating back to 1895 is corrected by Arthur Sherbo, "*The Knight of Malta* and Boccaccio's *Filocolo*," *ES* 33 (1957): 254-57; the *Filocolo* itself, not two stories in Painter's *Palace of Pleasure*, was the source.

A Very Woman

The principal source is identified by Roma Gill, "Collaboration and Revision in Massinger's *A Very Woman*," *RES* 18 (1967): 136-48, as *The Mirror of Knighthood* (1599), a translation of *Del espejo de principes y caballeros*. Massinger collaborated with Fletcher on the original version, which Gill partially reconstructs, and later revised the play alone. The revision adds the detailed treatment of Cardenes's melancholy, for which Burton's *Anatomy* was the main source. The final version is a gravely flawed play; it "tries to serve Massinger's God of giving an audience what it ought to want, and Fletcher's Mammon of pandering to easy tastes. Neither can be fully satisfied with the final product."

The Guardian

Glenn H. Blayney, "Massinger's Reference to the Claverly Story," *N&Q* 1 (1954): 17-18, compares Massinger's references to a crime committed by Walter Claverly in 1605 with the dramatic accounts of the same crime in *The Miseries of Enforced Marriage* (1606) and *A Yorkshire Tragedy* (1606). Massinger's version reveals a debt to *The Miseries* which he may have known in an acting version significantly different from the extant text. Philip Edwards, "Massinger the Censor" (I,B), praises the play and defends its explicit moralizing.

The Renegado

In "Massinger's *The Renegado*: Religion in Stuart Tragicomedy," *Genre* 5 (1972): 138-52, Peter F. Mullany compares this to other plays by Fletcher and by Massinger and to their collaborations. A common element of all their plays is that "religion is divorced from the real world and from human significance so as to become part of the artifice in plays that seek to move audiences rather than to inform them."

Love's Cure

Martin E. Erickson, "A Review of Scholarship Dealing with the Problem of a Spanish Source for *Love's Cure*," in *Studies in Comparative Literature*, ed. Waldo F. McNeir, Louisiana State University Studies, Humanistic Series No. 11 (1962), pp. 102-19, identifies "the principal source" as *La fuerza de la costumbre* by Guillén de Castro y Bellvis (1625); since this was never translated, "the dramatist who took the Spanish play for a model—probably Massinger—must have read it in Spanish."

The Picture

The main sources are an anonymous translation of André Favyn's *The Theater of Honour and Knighthood, or A Compendious Historie of the whole Christian World* (1623) and the twenty-eighth novel in the second volume of Painter's *Palace of Pleasure*, according to C. A. Gibson, "Massinger's Hungarian History," *Yearbook of English Studies* 2 (1972): 89-92.

B. OVER-ALL STATE OF CRITICISM

Massinger's claims to critical and scholarly attention are reasonably impressive. Dunn and Lawless (I,A) and the *Annals* credit him with whole or part authorship of more than fifty plays. Cyrus Hoy's attribution studies of the "Beaumont and Fletcher" canon (III,A) find Massinger's hand in nineteen of the fifty-four plays in that group, an involvement second only to Fletcher's. Massinger also collaborated with Dekker, Field, Middleton, and William Rowley. Robert Hamilton Ball's tracing of the stage history of *A New Way to Pay Old Debts* (II,B) indicates a performance record equalled by only the best Elizabethan and Jacobean plays. Dunn, whose book at times patronizes its subject, reminds us that Massinger was "the principal writer for the public theaters from 1625 to 1640."

Despite these solid accomplishments, relatively little has been written about Massinger's plays. Many of the better studies are peripheral: his role in collaborative plays, his value as a vane of prevailing winds of political and social thought, his sources, and his literary and historical allusions. The more obvious lacunae include total critical silence on a majority of the plays and only sparse comment on the few which have received attention in print.

Now that Hoy and others have made major progress toward more stable attributions and sound editions are available for some of the plays, Massinger may finally be the subject of more strictly literary study. A full critical reassessment, more sympathetic than Dunn's, is needed.

III. CANON

A. PLAYS IN CHRONOLOGICAL ORDER

This listing follows the preferred first performance dates given by Alfred Harbage, *Annals of English Drama, 975-1700* (1940; rev. S. Schoenbaum, 1964). This is the source of the dates of first performance (in italics), first editions (following the semicolons), types, and some information on lost plays. The early editions are described by W. W. Greg, *A Bibliography of the English Printed Drama to the Restoration*, 4 vols. (1939-59).

T. A. Dunn's *Philip Massinger* (I,A) discusses the canon in the text proper and his first two appendices list and date the definite, possible, and rejected collaborations. Much of Dunn's treatment, however, is not original; his lists are simply "compiled from evidence presented by Chelli," (*Étude sur la collaboration de Massinger avec Fletcher et son groupe* [1926]). Donald Lawless's monograph (I,A) provides a slightly different canon and chronology. G. E. Bentley, *The Jacobean and Caroline Stage*, vol. 4 (1956), and, less extensively, E. K. Chambers, *The Elizabethan Stage*, vol. 3 (1923), fully review the canon.

The canon sections of the essays in this series on Massinger's several collaborators supplement the material discussed here. The definitive treatment of Massinger's major collaborative effort appears in Cyrus Hoy's series "The Shares of Fletcher and His Collaborators in the Beaumont and Fletcher Canon," *SB* 8 (1956): 129-46; 9 (1957): 143-62; 11 (1958): 85-106; 12 (1959): 91-116; 13 (1960): 77-108; 14 (1961): 45-67; and 15 (1962): 71-90. While S. Schoenbaum, *Internal Evidence and Elizabethan Dramatic Authorship: An Essay in Literary History and Method* (1966), cautions that "Hoy's findings may one day be challenged in consequence of fuller understanding of the Beaumont and Fletcher texts," the series is the best available full study of an important part of Massinger's work. Virtually all discussions of the Beaumont and Fletcher canon devote considerable space to Massinger's role. Two representative titles are: Eugene M. Waith, *The Pattern of*

Tragicomedy in Beaumont and Fletcher (1952) and Clifford Leech, *The John Fletcher Plays* (1962).

Only plays which are listed as positively or possibly by Massinger in the *Annals* and in the *Supplements* by Schoenbaum (1966, 1970) are included below. Casual ascriptions, such as Dunn's contention, in a footnote, that "Massinger's hand can be demonstrated in *The Winter's Tale*," have been omitted.

The Jeweller of Amsterdam, or The Hague, with Fletcher and Field; tragedy (*1616-19;* lost)

Bentley, vol. 3 (1956), remarks that "the play is known only from the Stationers' Register entry" (8 April 1654). Andrew Clark, "An Annotated List of Lost Domestic Plays, 1578-1624," *RORD* 18 (1975): 29-44, agrees with Bentley that the play exploited an actual atrocity and concludes that "its actual date of writing was almost certainly soon after the crime, perhaps late 1616—early 1617."

Thierry and Theodoret, with Fletcher (and Beaumont?); tragedy (*1607-21;* 1621)

Hoy, *SB* 11 (1958): 85-106, assigns I.ii, II.i and iv, and IV.ii to Massinger and accepts Beaumont's participation.

The Knight of Malta, with Field and Fletcher; tragicomedy (*1618-19;* 1647)

Massinger wrote III.ii and iii and IV.i, iii, and iv according to Hoy, *SB* 12 (1959): 91-116.

The Old Law, or A New Way to Please You, with Middleton and William Rowley; comedy (ca. *1615-18;* 1656)

In "The Authorship and the Manuscript of *The Old Law,*" *HLQ* 16 (1953): 117-39, George R. Price assigns sixty percent of the play to Middleton and forty percent to Rowley. The original version was written in "1614 or 1615, at the beginning of the partnership between Middleton and Rowley." Massinger revised it, perhaps around 1626, for performance by the Queen's Men. "The prominence given to Massinger's name [on the title-page of the first edition] may be due to its having greater prestige at the time of publication."

The Fatal Dowry, with Field; tragedy (*1616-19;* 1632)

T. A. Dunn's edition (1969) assigns sixty percent of the play to Massinger. Nicholas Rowe's adaptation, under the title *The Fair Penitent,* has been edited by Malcolm Goldstein (RRDS, 1969).

The Little French Lawyer, with Fletcher; comedy (*1619-23;* 1647)

Hoy, *SB* 9 (1957): 143-62, gives Massinger I, III.iii, IV.v, part of vi, vii, and V. part of i and iii. Massinger is also responsible for "the final form of the extant text, with the result that the linguistic evidence is somewhat obscured."

Sir John van Olden Barnavelt, with Fletcher; tragedy (*Aug. 1619;* MS)

Hoy, *SB* 9 (1957), assigns shares; Massinger did I.i-ii, II.i, III.ii, v-vi, and part of V.i. An earlier influential division appears in the edition by Wilhelmina P. Frijlinck (1922).

The Virgin Martyr, with Dekker; tragedy (*licensed 6 Oct. 1620;* 1622)

Bowers provides an authorship analysis in vol. 3 of *The Dramatic Works of Thomas Dekker* (1958). See the discussion in the canon section of the Dekker essay in *The Popular School.*

The Custom of the Country, with Fletcher; comedy (*1619-23;* 1647)

Hoy's analysis is in *SB* 9 (1957). "The respective shares of their authorship are clear enough." Massinger did all of II, parts of III and IV, and all but a part of the fifth scene of V.

The Double Marriage, with Fletcher; tragedy (*1619-23;* 1647)

According to Hoy, *SB* 9 (1957), "it seems clear Massinger is responsible for the final form of the extant text." The play, however, "was originally a collaborated work."

The False One, with Fletcher; classical history (*1619-23;* 1647)

Hoy, *SB* 9 (1957), assigns I and V to Massinger. The manuscript of the first folio text preserves "the linguistic patterns which we know to distinguish the respective work of the two dramatists in a clear and immediately discernable manner."

Antonio and Vallia, comedy (ca. *1613–40;* lost)

Philenzo and Hypollita, tragicomedy (ca. *1613–40;* lost)

The Duke of Milan, tragedy (*1621–23;* 1623)

The Maid of Honour, tragicomedy (ca. *1621–23;* 1632)

A New Way to Pay Old Debts, comedy (*1621–25;* 1633)

In his book on the play (II,B), Robert Hamilton Ball suggests it was written in 1626.

The Woman's Plot, comedy (*5 Nov. 1621* [*acted*] *;* lost)

The Prophetess, with Fletcher; tragicomedy (*licensed 14 May 1622;* 1647)

Hoy, *SB* 9 (1957), assigns II, IV, and V.i–ii to Massinger. Betterton revised the play for performance as a dramatic opera in 1690.

The Sea Voyage, with Fletcher; comedy (*licensed 22 June 1622;* 1647)

Hoy, *SB* 9 (1957), gives Massinger II, III, and V; Fletcher was responsible for the play's final form, reversing the usual practice of the collaboration.

The Spanish Curate, with Fletcher; comedy (*licensed 24 Oct. 1622;* 1647)

Hoy, *SB* 9 (1957), finds this "one of the clearest examples of a Fletcher-Massinger collaboration in the canon." Massinger wrote I, III. iii, IV.i–ii, iv, and V.i, iii.

The Bondman (The Noble Bondman), tragicomedy (*licensed 3 Dec. 1623;* 1624)

The Renegado, or The Gentleman of Venice, tragicomedy (*licensed 17 April 1624;* 1630)

The Parliament of Love (with William Rowley?), comedy (*licensed 3 Nov, 1624;* MS [fragment])

Bentley discusses Rowley's possible involvement, vol. 4 (1956).

Love's Cure, or The Martial Maid (revising Beaumont and Fletcher?), comedy (*1625* [?]; 1647)

Hoy, *SB* 14 (1961): 45-67, finds "the one certainty about the authorship of this play is the presence of Massinger. In the only extant text, that of the 1647 folio, he is responsible for virtually all of Acts I, IV, and V." His role, however, was probably that of reviser, "not as one of the original authors." Earlier attribution studies, most of which credit Massinger with a major share of the play, are discussed in Martin E. Erickson's article on the sources (II,A).

The Painter, unknown (ca. *1613-40;* lost)

The Roman Actor, tragedy (*licensed 11 Oct. 1626;* 1629)

The Unnatural Combat, tragedy (*1621*-ca. *1626;* 1639)

The Great Duke of Florence (The Great Duke), tragicomedy (*licensed 5 July 1627;* 1636)

Bentley, vol. 4 (1956), has "serious misgivings" about the validity of a 1627 date of first production. Johanne M. Stochholm, in her edition (1933), dates composition between October 1623 and March 1625, on the basis of political allusions in the play.

The Judge, comedy (?) (*licensed 6 June 1627;* lost)

The Honour of Women, comedy (*licensed 6 May 1628;* lost)

The Tyrant, tragedy (ca. *1613-40;* lost)

Minerva's Sacrifice, tragedy (?) (*licensed 3 Nov. 1629;* lost)

The Picture, tragicomedy (*licensed 8 June 1629;* 1630)

Believe As You List, tragedy (*licensed 6 May 1631;* MS)

The Emperor of the East, tragicomedy (*licensed 11 March 1631;* 1632)

Revision "as a result of the unfavourable reception accorded to the original production" is suggested by A. K. McIlwraith, "Did Massinger Revise *The Emperour of the East?" RES* 5 (1929): 36-42. Bentley, vol.

4 (1956), finds "that the evidence for any sort of significant revision is not at all clear."

Fast and Welcome, comedy (ca. *1613–40;* lost)

The Unfortunate Piety, tragedy (?) (*licensed 13 June 1631;* lost)

For the confusion between this title and *The Italian Nightpiece* see Bentley, vol. 4 (1956). John Freehafer, "*The Italian Nightpiece* and Suckling's *Aglaura,*" *JEGP* 67 (1968): 249–65, suggests that Suckling's play reflects the influence of the lost play(s).

The City Madam, comedy (*licensed 25 May 1632;* 1658 or 1659)

"Allusions to the arrival of the French and Venetian ambassadors after a long absence from London establish that the comedy was written after 1629, while the references in the play to trade and exploration all closely fit English commercial activity between 1629 and 1632," according to C. A. Gibson, "Massinger's London Merchant and the Date of *The City Madam,*" *MLR* 65 (1970): 737–49. The play was anonymously adapted under the title *The Cure of Pride* in 1675.

The City Honest Man, unknown (ca. *1615–41;* lost)

The Forced Lady, tragedy (ca. *1615–41;* lost)

The *Annals* cross-references this title to *Minerva's Sacrifice* (1629).

The Guardian, comedy (*licensed 31 Oct. 1633;* 1655)

In 1680 the play was revised as a droll under the title *Love Lost in the Dark, or The Drunken Couple.*

Cleander (Lisander and Calista; revision of *The Wandering Lovers,* 1623), tragicomedy (*licensed 7 May 1634;* 1647)

Bentley, vol. 4 (1956), cites "external evidence that Fletcher wrote the original play and that Massinger gave it a thorough revision." Hoy, *SB* 9 (1957): 143–62, suggests shares and tends "to favor the theory that Massinger's role was that of reviser only and that originally the play stood as a product of Fletcher's sole authorship."

A Very Woman, or The Prince of Tarent (possibly a reworking of a Fletcher and Massinger play of ca. 1619-22), tragicomedy (*licensed 6 June 1634;* 1655)

According to Hoy, *SB* 9 (1957), "there is no doubt at all that it contains the work of both Fletcher and Massinger." Massinger probably revised it after Fletcher's death; Acts I, II, and V are most extensively reworked. An extended discussion of a possible revision and an attempted reconstruction of the original text are given by Roma Gill (II,A, *A Very Woman*).

The Orator, unknown (*licensed 10 Jan. 1635;* lost)

The *Annals* notes that this may or may not be the same play as *The Noble Choice,* included with this title in a 1653 entry in the Stationers' Register.

The Bashful Lover, tragicomedy (*licensed 9 May 1636;* 1655)

The King and the Subject, unknown (*licensed 5 June 1638;* lost)

Alexius, or The Chaste Lover (or *Gallant*), comedy (?) (*licensed 25 Sept. 1639;* lost)

The Fair Anchoress of Pausilippo, unknown (*licensed 26 Jan. 1640;* lost)

The Prisoner[s] , tragicomedy (ca. *1613-40* [?] *;* lost)

B. UNCERTAIN ASCRIPTIONS; APOCRYPHA

The Coxcomb, by Beaumont and Fletcher (revised by Massinger or William Rowley?), comedy (*1608-10;* 1647)

Chelli, *Étude sur la collaboration* (III,A), finds evidence of a possible revision by Massinger, perhaps ca. 1636. Hoy, *SB* 11 (1958): 85-106, sees "nothing in the play that points even remotely to Massinger and since his work elsewhere is so very distinctive it is hard to imagine he is present here."

The Honest Man's Fortune, by Fletcher (with Field? Massinger? Tourneur?), tragicomedy (*1613*; 1647 and MS)

Hoy, *SB* 12 (1959): 91–116, judges that this play "presents one of the most complex authorial problems in the canon." Massinger's role is debated, but he is "certainly present in Act III." Cruickshank (I,B) and Chelli (*Collaboration*, III,A) both see no evidence of Massinger's involvement. Chambers, vol. 3 (1923), summarizes earlier attribution studies. The most recent editor of the play, Johan Gerritsen (1952), is unable to assign a specific part to Massinger but is inclined to find that his hand, and that of Field, are present.

The Faithful Friends ("Francis Beaumont and John Fletcher" in the Stationers' Register; Daborne? Field? Massinger?), tragicomedy (*1613–*ca. *1621;* MS)

Chelli (*Collaboration*) rejects the Massinger attribution. Hoy, *SB* 15 (1962): 71–90, does not include the play in the Beaumont and Fletcher canon.

The Queen of Corinth, by Fletcher (and Massinger? Field?), tragicomedy (*1616*-ca. *1618;* 1647)

Chelli (*Collaboration*) considers Massinger's involvement certain. Hoy, *SB* 12 (1959): 91–116, assigns the first and last acts to Massinger, the second to Fletcher, and the third and fourth to Field.

The Bloody Brother (Rollo, Duke of Normandy), by Fletcher (with Massinger? Jonson? and another?) tragedy (*1616-24;* 1639)

In the introduction to his edition of the play (1948), J. D. Jump summarizes earlier attributions and offers fresh evidence for the certain involvement of Fletcher and Massinger and the likely participation of Chapman and Jonson. Jump assigns a relatively small share to Massinger: I.i and V.i, lines 1–89. Hoy, *SB* 14 (1961): 45–67, is also certain that Massinger's role was more than merely that of a reviser. All of I and most of V.i were originally written by Massinger; he shared the remainder of V.i and part of V.ii with Fletcher.

Beggars' Bush, by Fletcher (with Massinger?), comedy (ca. *1615-22;* 1647 and MS)

Hoy, *SB* 11 (1958): 85–106, divides the play almost equally between Beaumont, Fletcher, and Massinger. Attribution scholarship and the nature and history of the printed texts are discussed at length in the introduction to John H. Dorenkamp's edition (1967). Dorenkamp's assignment of specific shares differs slightly from Hoy's. The introduction also compares the original with adaptations by Thomas Hull (*The Royal Merchant*, 1768) and by Douglas Kinnaird (*The Merchant of Bruges, or Beggars' Bush*, 1815).

The Wandering Lovers (The Lovers' Progress. Cleander), by Fletcher (and Massinger?), tragicomedy (*licensed 6 Dec. 1623; revised, 1634,* by Massinger; 1647)

Massinger's "work is present in the play beyond any doubt," according to Hoy, *SB* 9 (1957): 143-62; while "the evidence is far from conclusive," Massinger's role probably "was that of reviser only."

The Elder Brother, by Fletcher (revised by Massinger?), comedy (*1625* [?]; 1637 and MS)

Hoy, *SB* 9, considers this "a Fletcherian original, the first and last acts of which have been virtually rewritten by Massinger."

The Fair Maid of the Inn, by Fletcher (with Massinger? William Rowley? and Ford?), comedy (*licensed 22 Jan. 1626;* 1647)

Hoy, *SB* 13 (1960): 77-108, believes that the play is by Fletcher, Ford, Massinger, and Webster. He assigns all of I and part of V.iii to Massinger.

C. CRITIQUE OF THE STANDARD EDITION

Gifford's second edition is "standard" by virtue of being the only edition to include all of Massinger's non-collaborative plays, except *Believe As You List*. The Massinger canon is textually complex and the need for a more reliable edition has been recognized for almost fifty years. In 1931 A. K. McIlwraith began work on a new complete edition for the Oxford University Press; Philip Edwards and C. A. Gibson are continuing that project. In the meantime, recent editions of single titles, when available, provide texts superior to those of Gifford and Cunningham.

Fredson Bowers's edition of *The Virgin Martyr* in vol. 3 of *The Dramatic Works of Thomas Dekker* (1958) and those, by Bowers and others, of Massinger's collaborations which have and will appear in *The Dramatic Works in the Beaumont and Fletcher Canon,* gen. ed., Fredson

Bowers (1966-), are of exceptional quality. When the *Beaumont and Fletcher* is completed, almost all of Massinger's collaborative plays will be available in definitive editions.

The editorial work and related studies, like Hoy's, recently done on the collaborative plays have made the inadequacies in these same areas of the non-collaborative plays more obvious. A textually accurate and annotated edition of the entire corpus is needed both for its own sake and as an aid to further critical study.

D. TEXTUAL STUDIES

Cyrus Hoy's series of articles in *SB* (III,A) is an impressive study of a large portion of the Massinger canon. Hoy's ascriptions are consistently and convincingly argued; their cumulative effect is to bring order to an area previously regarded as gray, hopelessly confused, or plain impossible (Dunn, I,A). Hoy also makes substantial contributions to our knowledge of Massinger's writing habits, his language practices, and the nature and history of the collaborative texts. Hiroshi Yamashita, "The Printing of Philip Massinger's Plays," *Shakespeare Studies* (Tokyo) 10 (1971-72): 16-38, reviews much of the earlier textual scholarship, treats the texts of *The Duke of Milan* and *The Maid of Honour* at length, and establishes the nature of the copy behind several texts. *The City Madam* "is the only one of Massinger's plays which was definitely printed from a prompt-book." *The Duke of Milan* and *The Maid of Honour* were set from "authorial fair copies." Two textual studies by Johann Gerritsen treat specific points: "The Printing of the Beaumont and Fletcher Folio of 1647," *Library* 3 (1949): 233-64, analyzes the division of press work between William Wilson and Suzan Islip; several of Massinger's collaborations are discussed in "The Dramatic Piracies of 1661," *SB* 11 (1958): 117-31.

E. SINGLE-WORK EDITIONS

There are few recent editions of single titles by Massinger. *A New Way to Pay Old Debts* had been edited for the New Mermaids series by T. W. Craik (1964); the brief introduction concentrates on Massinger's style. The extensive introduction and notes to an earlier edition by Muriel St. Clare Byrne (1949) cover most of the play's background and provide a sensitive response to the text. There are also two facsimile editions of *A New Way* (1969 and 1970).

Cyrus Hoy's RRDS edition of *The City Madam* is the only other text of a Massinger non-collaborative play published since 1935. Hoy's text is based on a collation of six copies of the 1685 quarto and his introduction includes extensive bibliographical and critical comment. The introduction to an earlier edition by Rudolph Kirk (1934) supplements Hoy by giving the provenance of some copies of the first quarto, a history of adaptations and influence, and other details.

The following editions post-date Gifford, generally offer texts superior to his, and often have complete introductions and apparatus: *Believe As You List*, ed. Charles J. Sisson (Malone Society, 1928, for 1927); *The Bondman*, ed. Benjamin Townley Spencer (1932); *The Great Duke of Florence*, ed. Johanne M. Stochholm (1933); *The Maid of Honour*, ed. Eva A. W. Bryne (1927); *The Parliament of Love*, ed. Kathleen M. Lea (1928); *The Roman Actor*, ed. William Lee Sandidge (1929); and *The Unnatural Combat*, ed. Robert S. Telfer (1932).

Except for titles included in the Bowers editions of Dekker and of Beaumont and Fletcher and in other editions of the "Beaumont and Fletcher" plays (see the discussions of editions in the Beaumont and Fletcher essay in this volume), T. A. Dunn's edition of *The Fatal Dowry* (1969) is the only collaborative title published in a new edition during the time limits of this survey. Dunn determines that the copy text for the 1632 quarto was probably a holograph in the hands of Massinger and Field, with stage directions in another hand, and he provides an analysis of authorship shares and a critical commentary.

Three uncertain ascriptions have been edited since 1948. The edition of *Rollo, Duke of Normandy (The Bloody Brother)* by J. D. Jump (1948) is notable for its impressive analysis of authorship division; the introduction is the best available general study of the play. Johan Gerritsen's *A Critical Edition of MS Dyce 9 (1625): "The Honest Man's Fortune"* (1952) makes available an important alternate to the text printed in the 1647 Beaumont and Fletcher folio. A full introduction, textual notes, and a detailed commentary make this an unusually helpful edition. *Beggars' Bush* has been edited by John H. Dorenkamp (1967): this has generous apparatus, including textual variants from all earlier editions.

IV. SEE ALSO

A. GENERAL

Anderson, Donald K. "The Banquet of Love in English Drama (1595-1642)." *JEGP* 63 (1964): 422-32.

Appleton, William W. *Beaumont and Fletcher, A Critical Study*. 1956.

Babb, Lawrence. *The Elizabethan Malady: A Study of Melancholia in English Literature from 1580 to 1642.* 1951.

Barber, C. L. *The Idea of Honour in the English Drama 1591-1700.* 1957.

Bentley, Gerald Eades. *The Profession of Dramatist in Shakespeare's Time 1590-1642.* 1971.

Boas, F. S. *An Introduction to Stuart Drama.* 1946.

Bowden, William R. *The English Dramatic Lyric, 1603-42.* 1951.

Bradbrook, M. C. *Themes and Conventions of Elizabethan Tragedy.* 1935.

———.*The Growth and Structure of Elizabethan Comedy.* 1955.

Brown, Arthur. "Citizen Comedy and Domestic Drama." In *Jacobean Theatre,* SuAS 1 (1960), pp. 62-83.

Cazamian, Louis. *The Development of English Humor.* 1952.

Clarkson, Paul S., and Warren, Clyde T. *The Law of Property in Shakespeare and Elizabethan Drama.* 1942.

Coleridge, Samuel Taylor. *Coleridge on the Seventeenth Century,* ed. Roberta Florence Brinkley. 1955.

Cunningham, John E. *Elizabethan and Early Stuart Drama.* 1965.

Davies, H. Neville. "Dryden's *All for Love* and Thomas May's *The Tragedie of Cleopatra Queen of AEgypt.*" *N&Q* 12 (1965): 139-44.

Dent, Alan. *Preludes and Studies.* 1942.

Doran, Madeleine. *Endeavors of Art: A Study of Form in Elizabethan Drama.* 1954.

Edwards, Philip. "The Danger Not the Death: The Art of John Fletcher." In *Jacobean Theatre,* SuAS 1 (1960), pp. 159-77.

Ekelblad, Inga-Stina. "Anthony Trollope's Copy of the 1647 Beaumont and Fletcher Folio." *N&Q* 6 (1959): 153-55.

Ellis-Fermor, Una M. *The Jacobean Drama.* 1939; 5th ed. 1965.

Enright, D. J. "Elizabethan and Jacobean Comedy." In *The Age of Shakespeare* (1955; vol. 2 of *The Pelican Guide to English Literature,* ed. Boris Ford), pp. 416-28.

Gentilli, Vanna. *Le figure della pazzia nel teatro elisabettiano.* N. d.

Harbage, Alfred. *Cavalier Drama: An Historical Supplement to the Study of the Elizabethan and Restoration Stage.* 1936.

Herrick, Marvin T. *Tragicomedy: Its Origin and Development in Italy, France, and England.* 1955.

Histrio. "John Fletcher (The Poet)." *N&Q* 192 (1947): 38. [A Massinger reference to Fletcher]

Ingram, R. W. "Patterns of Music and Action in Fletcherian Drama." In *Music in English Renaissance Drama,* ed. John H. Long (1968), pp. 75-95.

Jones, Eldred. *Othello's Countrymen: The African in English Renaissance Drama.* 1965.

Klein, David. *The Elizabethan Dramatists as Critics.* 1963.

Leech, Clifford. "The Caroline Audience." *MLR* 36 (1941): 304-19.

———.*Shakespeare's Tragedies and Other Studies in Seventeenth Century Drama.* 1950.

M[cIlwraith], A. K. "John Fletcher (The Poet)." *N&Q* 192 (1947): 175.

McKeithan, Daniel Morley. *The Debt to Shakespeare in the Beaumont and Fletcher Plays.* 1938.

McManaway, James G. "Massinger and the Restoration Drama." *ELH* 1 (1934): 276-304 (rpt. in *Studies in Shakespeare, Bibliography, and Theater*, ed. Richard Hosley, et al. [1969], pp. 3-30).

Manifold, J. S. *The Music in Elizabethan Drama from Shakespeare to Purcell.* 1956.

Mills, Laurens J. *One Soul in Bodies Twain: Friendship in Tudor Literature and Stuart Drama.* 1937.

Muir, Kenneth. *Shakespeare as Collaborator.* 1960.

Oras, Ants. *Pause Patterns in Elizabethan and Jacobean Drama: An Experiment in Prosody.* UFMH, no. 3 (1960).

Parrott, Thomas Marc, and Ball, Robert Hamilton. *A Short View of Elizabethan Drama.* 1943; rev. ed. 1958.

Pellegrini, Giuliano. "La cultura italiana di Philip Massinger." *Giornale Italiano di Filologia* 3 (1950): 22-43 (rpt. in his *Barocco inglese* [1953], pp. 157-94).

"Philip Massinger (1583-1640). A Master of Plot and Tragi-Comedy." *TLS*, 16 March 1940, pp. 134, 140.

Quennell, Peter. "Philip Massinger." In *The Singular Preference: Portraits and Essays* (1952), pp. 37-43.

Reed, Robert Rentoul, Jr. *Bedlam on the Jacobean Stage.* 1952.

———.*The Occult on the Tudor and Stuart Stage.* 1965.

Rulfs, Donald J. "Beaumont and Fletcher on the London Stage, 1776-1833." *PMLA* 63 (1948): 1245-64.

Salingar, L. G. "The Decline of Tragedy." In *The Age of Shakespeare* (1955; vol. 2 of *The Pelican Guide to English Literature*, ed. Boris Ford), pp. 429-40.

Smet, Robert de [Romain Sanvic]. *Le théâtre élisabéthain.* 1955.

Spencer, Theodore. *Death and Elizabethan Tragedy: A Study of Convention and Opinion in the Elizabethan Drama.* 1936.

Staub, Hans V. *Massingers Versuch eines Idiendramas.* 1950.

Stroup, Thomas B. *Microcosmos: The Shape of the Elizabethan Play.* 1965.

Swinburne, Algernon Charles. *Contemporaries of Shakespeare*, ed. Edmund Gosse and Thomas J. Wise. 1919.

Symons, Arthur. "Philip Massinger." In *Studies in the Elizabethan Drama* (1920), pp. 161-94.

Wells, Henry W. *Elizabethan and Jacobean Playwrights.* 1939.

Wilson, F. P. *Elizabethan and Jacobean.* 1945.

B. INDIVIDUAL PLAYS

Adams, John Cranford. *The Globe Playhouse: Its Design and Equipment.* 1942. [*The Double Marriage*]

Armstrong, William A. "'Canopy' in Elizabethan Theatrical Terminology." *N&Q* 4 (1957): 64-65. [*The Maid of Honour*]

Freehafer, John. "A Textual Crux in *The Two Noble Kinsmen.*" *ELN* 7 (1970): 254-57. [*The Double Marriage*]

Gibson, C. A. "'Behind the Arras' in Massinger's *The Renegado.*" *N&Q* 16 (1969): 296-97.

———."The Date of *The Broken Heart.*" *N&Q* 18 (1971): 458. [*The Picture*]

Holzknecht, Karl J. *Outlines of Tudor and Stuart Plays 1497-1642.* 1947. [*Beggars' Bush, The Fatal Dowry, The Maid of Honour, A New Way to Pay Old Debts*]

Hunter, G. K. "Notes on Webster's Tragedies." *N&Q* 4 (1957): 53-55. [*The Double Marriage*]

McCullen, Joseph T., Jr. "Madness and the Isolation of Characters in Elizabethan and Early Stuart Drama." *SP* 48 (1951): 206-18. [*A New Way to Pay Old Debts*]

———."The Use of Parlor and Tavern Games in Elizabethan and Early Stuart Drama." *MLQ* 14 (1953): 7-14. [*The Spanish Curate*]

McManaway, James G. "Smooth Tongued Shakespeare, 1650." *SQ* 14 (1963): 92. [*The Picture*]

Martin, L. C. "Marvell, Massinger, and Sidney." *RES* 2 (1951): 374-75. [*The Maid of Honour*]

Mathews, Ernst G. "Cockain's *The Obstinate Lady* and the *Araucana*." *MLN* 57 (1942): 57-58. [*A Very Woman* as a source]

Maxwell, Baldwin. *Studies in Beaumont, Fletcher, and Massinger.* 1939 [*The Famous History of the Life of King Henry VIII, The Mad Lover, The Spanish Curate, A Very Woman*, etc.]

———."The Source of the Principal Plot of *The Fair Maid of the Inn*." *MLN* 59 (1944): 122-27.

Maxwell, J. C. "A Dramatic Echo of an Overburian Character." *N&Q* 192 (1947): 277. [*The Elder Brother*]

Pellegrini, Giuliano. "Un matiro di S. Dorotea nel teatro barocco inglese." In *Barocco inglese* (1953), pp. 195-219. [*The Virign Martyr*]

Quennell, Peter. "Massinger's Play *A New Way to Pay Old Debts* from which the Greatest of English Actors Evoked the Most Terrific Exhibition of Human Passion." *New Statesman and Nation* 39 (1950): 40-42.

Rashbrook, R. F. "Keats and Massinger." *N&Q* 194 (1949): 424-25. [*The Duke of Milan*]

Rattray, R. F. "Skiff." *TLS* 9 Aug. 1947, p. 403. [*The Bloody Brother*]

Simpson, Percy. "Skiff." *TLS*, 2 Aug. 1947, p. 391. [*The Bloody Brother*]

———."Skiff." *TLS*, 16 Aug. 1947, p. 415.

Sloman, Albert E. "The Spanish Source of *The Fair Maid of the Inn*." In *Hispanic Studies in Honour of I. González Llubera*, ed. Frank Pierce (1959), pp. 331-41.

Waith, Eugene M. "The Sources of *The Double Marriage* by Fletcher and Massinger." *MLN* 64 (1949): 505-10.

———."John Fletcher and the Art of Declamation." *PMLA* 66 (1951): 226-34. [*The Double Marriage, The Queen of Corinth*]

Worthington, F. L. "Tudor Plays on the Way to Production." In *Ashland Studies for Shakespeare*, ed. Margery Bailey (1959), pp. 1-24. [*Believe As You List*]

C. CANON AND TEXTUAL STUDIES

Baillie, W. M. "Authorship Attribution in Jacobean Dramatic Texts." In *Computers in the Humanities*, ed. J. L. Mitchell (1973), pp. 73-81. [Not seen]

Bald, R. C. *Bibliographical Studies in the Beaumont and Fletcher Folio of 1647.* 1938.

Barker, Richard H. "The Authorship of *The Second Maiden's Tragedy* and *The Revenger's Tragedy*." *ShAB* 20 (1945): 51-62. [Rejects Massinger as a possible author of *The Second Maiden's Tragedy*]

Battle, Guy A. "The Case of the Altered 'C'—A Bibliographical Problem in the Beaumont and Fletcher First Folio." *PBSA* 42 (1948): 66-70.

Bennett, A. L. "The Early Editions of Philip Massinger's Plays." *Papers on Language and Literature* 1 (1965): 177-81.

Bowers, Fredson. "A Bibliographical History of the Fletcher-Betterton Play, *The Prophetess*, 1690." *Library* 16 (1961): 169-75.

Crundell, H. W. "Actors' Parts and Elizabethan Play-Texts." *N&Q* 180 (1941): 350-51.

Gray, J. E. "Still More Massinger Corrections." *Library* 5 (1950): 132-39.

Hook. F. S. "Marlowe, Massinger, and Webster Quartos." *N&Q* 4 (1957): 64-65. [*A New Way to Pay Old Debts*]

Jump, J. D. "*Rollo, Duke of Normandy:* Some Bibliographical Notes on the Seventeenth-Century Editions." *Library* 18 (1937): 279-86.

Kocourek, Rotislav. "Fletcherský dramatický kánon." *Časopis pro Moderni Filologii* 43 (1961): 26-33.

McIlwraith, A. K. "Marginalia on Press Corrections in Books of the Early Seventeenth Century." *Library* 4 (1950): 238-48. [*The Bondman*]

———."The Manuscript Corrections in Massinger's Plays." *Library* 6 (1951):213-16.

Muir, Kenneth. *Shakespeare as Collaborator.* 1960. [Rejects Massinger as a possible author of *The Two Noble Kinsmen*]

Oliphant, E. H. C. *The Plays of Beaumont and Fletcher: An Attempt to Determine Their Respective Shares and the Shares of Others.* 1927. [*The Famous History of the Life of King Henry VIII, The Two Noble Kinsmen,* etc.]

Povey, K. "Variant Formes in Elizabethan Printing." *Library* 10 (1955): 41-48. [*The Bondman*]

Turner, Robert K., Jr. "Notes on the Text of *Thierry and Theodoret* Q1." *SB* 14 (1961): 218-31.

D. EDITIONS

Chapman, Robin, and Grant, Allan, eds. *The City and the Court: Five Seventeenth-Century Comedies of London Life.* 1968. [*The City Madam*]

Ferdinand, Roger, trans. and adapter. "*Le curé espagnol (The Spanish Curate).*" *France Illustration Supplément*, no. 146 (Jan. 1954), pp. 1-24.

Garrod, H. W., ed. *Londons Lametable Estate, in any great Visitation.* In *Genius Loci and Other Essays* (1950), pp. 87-131. [Poem by Massinger]

Lockert, Charles Lacy, Jr., ed. *The Fatal Dowry.* 1918.

McIlwraith, A. K., ed. *Five Stuart Tragedies.* 1953. [*The Roman Actor*]

Messiaen, Pierre, ed. *Théâtre anglais, moyen-age et XVIe siècle: Anonymes, Marlowe, Dekker, Heywood, Ben Jonson, Webster, Tourneur,* etc. *Nouvelle traduction française avec remarques et notes.* 1948. [Not seen]

Strachey, J. St. Loe, ed. *Beaumont and Fletcher.* 2 vols. 1887; rpt. 1949, 1950. [*Thierry and Theodoret, The Spanish Curate*]

JOHN FORD

Donald K. Anderson, Jr.

The standard edition is that by William Gifford and Alexander Dyce, *The Works of John Ford*, 3 vols. (1869; reissued 1895, 1965). Another collected edition consists of two complementary volumes published separately: W. Bang's *John Fordes Dramatische Werke*, Materialien zur Kunde des älteren englischen Dramas, no. 23 (1908), and H. de Vocht's *John Ford's Dramatic Works*, Materials for the Study of the Old English Drama, n.s. no. 1 (1927).

I. GENERAL

A. BIOGRAPHICAL

M. Joan Sargeaunt's *John Ford* (1935), although mainly a critical study (I,B), contains most of the very scanty biographical information available on Ford. Especially noteworthy is her discussion of his career at the Middle Temple, where, she concludes, he probably "pursued some kind of legal profession, though not that of a barrister." R. G. Howarth, "John Ford," *N&Q* 4 (1957): 241, contends that Ford probably was still living in 1640 since two works printed at that time— Thomas Bancroft's *First Booke of Epigrammes* (1639) and the miscellany *Witts Recreations* (1640)—allude to him by name and "seem to imply that Ford was then alive." A useful compilation of biographical data appears in the section on Ford in Gerald Eades Bentley's *The Jacobean and Caroline Stage*, vol. 3 (1956).

B. GENERAL STUDIES OF THE PLAYS

Significant criticism of Ford began in 1808 with Charles Lamb, who in *Specimens of English Dramatic Poets* admired Calantha's death in *The Broken Heart* and "the grandeur of the soul" in *'Tis Pity She's a Whore*. William Hazlitt responded adversely in *Lectures Chiefly on the*

Dramatic Literature of the Age of Elizabeth (1820), charging the playwright with "wire-drawn sentiment" and "playing with edged tools." For the following one hundred years, commentators tended to accept these battle lines. Among those who shared Lamb's view of Ford as sympathetic portrayer of suffering were Algernon Swinburne, *Essays and Studies* (1875); Hippolyte A. Taine, *Historie de la littérature anglaise* (1866); and Havelock Ellis, ed., *John Ford*, Mermaid Series (1888). Among those who, siding with Hazlitt, saw Fordian drama as decadent were George Saintsbury, *A History of Elizabethan Literature* (1887); James R. Lowell, *Conversations on Some of the Old Poets* (1893); Felix E. Schelling, *Elizabethan Drama* (1908); Ashley H. Thorndike, *Tragedy* (1908); and Stuart P. Sherman, "Forde's Contribution to the Decadence of the Drama" (pp. vii–xix), in the edition by Bang cited in the initial paragraph above.

This preoccupation with morality was broken in the 1930s, unfavorably by T. S. Eliot, favorably by Sargeaunt and Una Ellis-Fermor. Eliot, *Selected Essays* (1932), shifts the focus of Fordian criticism by attacking the dramatist on esthetic rather than ethical grounds. Ford's work, asserts Eliot, is "of the surface," lacks "inner significance" and "symbolic value," and is "the result of the stock of expressions of feeling accumulated by the greater men." Eliot's views have not prevailed. Sargeaunt (I,A) concludes the first book-length study of Ford by denying his decadence and extolling his poetry and perceptivity: "It may indeed be that in this age we are in outlook nearer to Ford than the generations of the intervening centuries. . . . Ford's ribaldry offends us not so much by reason of its indecencies as because of its lack of humour. . . . But . . . there yet remains a body of poetry direct in expression and of grave and passionate import penetrated by a knowledge of the motives that sway the actions of mankind." Ellis-Fermor, *The Jacobean Drama: An Interpretation* (1936; 4th ed. 1958), sees Ford primarily concerned not with the violent and sensational but with "the study of characters whose strongest quality was a reticent dignity in endurance"; though his work, because of its narrow scope, may, according to Ellis-Fermor, mark "a conclusion" to Elizabethan drama, it "brings us back, serenely, economically, untheatrically, to the dominant which last sounded clearly in Greene and Peele and in the early work of Marlowe."

Although, as the next paragraph will illustrate, the majority of recent critics have admired Ford's plays, some have not. The most frequent charges are decadence, sensationalism, and excessive imitation of earlier dramatists. Mary E. Cochnower, in her section "John Ford," in

Seventeenth Century Studies, ed. Robert Shafer (1933), pp. 123-278, concludes that Ford was a "decadent" as evidenced by his "morbid or perverted themes" and by his "use of old dramatic material." Muriel C. Bradbrook, *Themes and Conventions of Elizabethan Tragedy* (1935), condemns Ford, in a chapter entitled "The Decadence," for "limited intensity," "abstractness," and "a split between dramatic and poetic method"; Ford, she continues, "took over conventions passively and therefore they were largely useless to him." Even more outspoken is Wallace A. Bacon, "The Literary Reputation of John Ford," *HLQ* 11 (1948): 181-99: Ford's characters, though "invested with traces of the lyrical, . . . are at the same time drenched in sensationalism." T. B. Tomlinson, *A Study of Elizabethan and Jacobean Tragedy* (1964), states in his chapter "Decadence: The Hollowness of Chapman and Ford" that Ford's plays "lack the substance which comes from . . . the business of living and common experience." George C. Herndl, *The High Design: English Renaissance Tragedy and the Natural Law* (1970), accuses him of sacrificing "almost anything . . . for theatrical effect or the heightening and vivifying of code extravagances which must fill the vacuum in tragedy." And Arthur C. Kirsch, *Jacobean Dramatic Perspectives* (1972), reiterates Eliot's indictment of "poetry of the surface" and claims that "the characteristic dramatic situations and effects in the plays of Beaumont and Fletcher and of Ford are similar, if not often identical."

Yet, in retrospect, the strong affirmations of Fordian drama by Sargeaunt and Ellis-Fermor forty years ago seem to have had an enduring effect, if most subsequent studies of Tudor and Stuart drama in general and of Ford's plays in particular are a reliable indication. For the former group, a brief look at several studies must suffice. Thomas M. Parrott and Robert H. Ball, *A Short View of Elizabethan Drama* (1943; rev. ed. 1958), find Ford's plays distinguished by "lovely poetry, subtle psychology, and a profound pity for the unhappy lot of man." Frederick S. Boas, *An Introduction to Stuart Drama* (1946), takes a similar position: Ford displays "a finely sensitive poetic gift" and, in his tragedies, bestows upon his audience "the delight which springs from seeing human sufferings transmuted into high artistic form." C. V. Wedgwood, *Seventeenth-Century English Literature* (1950), calls him "the only outstanding dramatist of the Caroline epoch" and "remarkable for . . . a gloomy fatalism which sees men and women as victims of fate. His poetry frequently achieves a soft descriptive sweetness, a melodiousness oddly at variance with the subjects he chose to handle."

Even higher praise is accorded Ford by Robert Ornstein, *The Moral Vision of Jacobean Tragedy* (1960): "he wrote with a deeper sense of the communion between the individual and society than did Chapman or Webster. And unlike Middleton he had a clear view of the ideal in man's thought and conduct." Speaking in much the same vein is G. Wilson Knight, *The Golden Labyrinth: A Study of British Drama* (1962): "Faith in human excellence runs as an elixir through his dramas. . . . This trust beats as a heart within his dark and militant tragedies." Irving Ribner, *Jacobean Tragedy: The Quest for Moral Order* (1962), stresses Ford's use of paradox based upon "Caroline skepticism": his greatest contribution, says Ribner, is "the tragedy of man's inability to find certainty, to understand reality or to grasp his own position in the universe."

Since Sargeaunt's work in 1935 (I,A), a good number of other books on Ford have appeared. These include, in chronological order, S. Blaine Ewing, *Burtonian Melancholy in the Plays of John Ford* (1940); George F. Sensabaugh, *The Tragic Muse of John Ford* (1944); Robert Davril, *Le drame de John Ford* (1954); Harold J. Oliver, *The Problem of John Ford* (1955); Clifford Leech, *John Ford and the Drama of His Time* (1957); Mark Stavig, *John Ford and the Traditional Moral Order* (1968); Donald K. Anderson, Jr., *John Ford*, TEAS (1972); and Tucker Orbison, *The Tragic Vision of John Ford*, Salzburg Studies in English Literature: Jacobean Drama Studies, no. 21 (1974). All of these books have contributed significantly to Fordian scholarship. In some ways, Davril's work may be the most helpful: it is by far the longest and contains informative chapters on Ford's sources, characterization, themes, "L'émotion dramatique," technique, and language. In his concluding chapter, Davril rebuts the customary charge of decadence by asserting that Ford gives love supremacy and uses sensationalism with discretion. If *'Tis Pity She's a Whore* and *Love's Sacrifice* do have a flaw, says Davril, it is an intellectualization that has lost touch with reality and common sense.

The books by Ewing, Sensabaugh, and Stavig differ from the others in their greater emphasis upon thesis. Ewing argues for the playwright's indebtedness in all of his dramas to Burton's *The Anatomy of Melancholy* (1621): "The range of Ford's interest in melancholy is the whole of Burton's treatise and more. As we advance through his plays, we view a gallery of melancholy types representing almost every major type in *The Anatomy*." Unlike Ewing's views, which have been generally accepted, those of Sensabaugh and Stavig have generated considerable debate. Sensabaugh contends that Ford stresses "scientific determinism" and "unbridled individualism" and hence is "modern": "By thus making what ordinarily passes for sin seem innocent and pure, Ford . . . raises poignant dilemmas"; in *'Tis Pity*, "tragedy springs not from Giovanni's breaking the world's moral order but from a misunderstanding of the nature of his celestial love." Whereas Sensabaugh sees Ford challenging society, Stavig finds him defending the traditional moral order: "Ford is . . . a serious dramatist who . . . in his own exaggerated, often satiric style . . . writes plays that will delight his sophisticated audience by their very outrageousness and at the same time reassure them that the values of their Anglican, Christian-humanist society still have validity." Most commentators agree neither with Stavig's view of Ford as a conservative moralist nor with Sensabaugh's view of him as an amoral defender of the religion of love; rather, critics usually put Ford somewhere between these two extremes.

The studies by Oliver, Leech, Anderson, and Orbison have a broader approach than the three just discussed, yet differ from one another appreciably. Oliver sees Ford as "a constant experimenter with dramatic form," a writer "concerned to portray not the sequence of emotions but the single, static feeling." Ford's skill, says Oliver, "lay in dissecting the emotion of a character under stress"; Ford's "women, particularly, are probably second only to Shakespeare's." Leech contends that *'Tis Pity She's a Whore* is not so typical of Ford as are *Perkin Warbeck*, *The Broken Heart*, and *Love's Sacrifice*, which present "exalted human beings whose actions never come within the scope of censure. Suffering, not action, is the dominant strain in their world." This "aristocratic code" in Ford, says Leech, is "a product of the 'private' theatres of his time." Anderson examines Ford's "knowledgeable dramaturgy" and concludes that he is "usually successful, and always interested, in arranging his material." As unifying principles in the plays, Anderson cites "the threatened marriage" and the esthetic subordination of vengeance to love; he also offers new interpretations (II,A) of *The Lover's Melancholy* and *Love's Sacrifice*. Orbison, in his study of Ford's tragedies, concludes that as Ford turns from *'Tis Pity She's a Whore* to *Love's Sacrifice*, *Perkin Warbeck*, and *The Broken Heart*, he moves "further away from the tensions and unresolvable situations of the tragic vision."

In addition to the books surveying Tudor and Stuart drama or dealing exclusively with Ford's plays, there are, of course, many relevant books on other topics as well as a good number of articles on Ford. At least some of the more noteworthy of these should be mentioned. R. J. Kaufmann, "Ford's Tragic Perspective," *TSLL* 1 (1960): 522-37, describes Ford as "a student of the arbitrary"; his characters are "self-defining and nonpolitical. They do not so much defy society as deny its relevance to their lives." Also dealing with Ford's conception of tragedy is Alan Brissenden, "Impediments to Love: A Theme in John Ford," *RenD* 7 (1964): 95-102, who claims that "the most recurrent of Ford's themes" is "the hindering of love's fulfillment." Concerning Ford's characterization, Robert Rentoul Reed, Jr., *Bedlam on the Jacobean Stage* (1952), praises him for "the refinement of bedlam" and states that his personae are "invariably more important than the theatrical spectacle which, when presented, is the natural result of the carefully analyzed motives." Jeanne A. Roberts, "John Ford's Passionate Abstractions," *Southern Humanities Review* 7 (1973): 322-32, asserts that Fordian drama might be "puzzling to an audience committed to seeing characters as multi-dimensional people, but to the receptive interpreter of allegorical abstractions the moral involvement becomes intense and unforgettable." The structure of Ford's dramas is discussed by Juliet McMaster in "Love, Lust, and Sham: Structural Pattern in the Plays of John Ford," *RenD* 2 (1969): 157-66: "Nearly all his plays have a triple plot. The main one is always seriously if not tragically conducted; the secondary one may be wholly serious or partly comic . . . ; the tertiary plot . . . is always comic." Richard Levin, *The Multiple Plot in English Renaissance Drama* (1971), shares McMaster's viewpoint, particularly concerning *'Tis Pity* and *Love's Sacrifice*. Moody E. Prior describes Ford's language in *The Language of Tragedy* (1947) and notes its "effect of inaction" and "the masque-like character of his plays." Songs in Ford's plays are discussed by William R. Bowden, *The English Dramatic Lyric, 1603-42: A Study in Stuart Dramatic Technique* (1951); a very informative appendix describes most of the dramatic lyrics of the period.

C. THE WORKS AT LARGE

The books on Ford by Sargeaunt, Davril, Oliver, and Anderson (I,B) devote chapters to his five nondramatic works: the poems *Fame's Memorial* (1606) and *Christ's Bloody Sweat* (1613) and the prose pamphlets *Honour Triumphant* (1606), *The Golden Mean* (1613), and *A Line of Life* (1620). Concerning these early works Oliver says, "But of the dramatic genius there is practically no sign; and this fact alone may suggest—if a paradox may be permitted—how purely dramatic Ford's genius was." Anderson concludes that "continuity in both theme and language marks Ford's entire output. Love, beauty, fame, antihedonism, repentance, Stoicism, and able kingship appear both in his nondramatic and in his dramatic works." Frederick M. Burelbach, Jr., "John Ford's Style: The Apprentice Years," *McNR* 17 (1966): 58-73, discusses the poems, the pamphlets, and those dramas written in collaboration: "he gradually learned to overcome his excessive dependence on strict rhetorical rules, his addiction to Ciceronian artifice, and his predilection for high-sounding clichés."

An influential article has been M. Joan Sargeaunt's "Writings Ascribed to John Ford by Joseph Hunter in *Chorus Vatum*," *RES* 10 (1934): 165-76. Following Hunter's suggestion that *Christ's Bloody Sweat* and *The Golden Mean* are by Ford, Sargeaunt effectively documents these attributions. The two works are now generally accepted as part of the Ford canon. G. D. Monsarrat, "John Ford's Authorship of *Christes Bloodie Sweat*," *ELN* 9 (1971): 20-25, offers additional evidence of Ford's authorship by citing parallel passages and word clusters in both the poem and his other works. George F. Reinecke, "John Ford's 'Missing' Ralegh Passage," *ELN* 6 (1969): 252-54, states that Ford's reference to Sir Walter in at least one manuscript of *A Line of Life* and in at least one copy of the 1620 edition may mean that "Ford wrote precisely at the time of Ralegh's execution on October 29, 1618." Cyril Falls, "Penelope Rich and the Poets: Philip Sidney to John Ford," EDH 28 (1956): 123-37, mentions Ford's praise of Penelope and the Earl of Devonshire in *Fame's Memorial* and surmises: "To the eyes of John Ford the great days were gone and the survivors of the Elizabethan age were living amongst the chaff." Robert Davril, "John Ford et les *caractères overburiens*," *EA* 6 (1953): 122-26, suggests Ford's authorship of the characters of "The Wise Man" and "The Noble Spirit," which were added to the 1614 edition of Sir Thomas Overbury's *The Wife*; Leech (I,B) is not convinced.

Samuel A. Tannenbaum's *John Ford (A Concise Bibliography)* was published in 1941, reprinted in *Elizabethan Bibliographies* by Samuel A. and Dorothy R. Tannenbaum, vol. 2 (1967), and continued by Charles A. Pennel and William P. Williams in *Elizabethan Bibliographies Supplements*, vol. 8 (1968). Selected lists appear in Irving Ribner's *Tudor and Stuart Drama*, Goldentree Bibliographies (1966), and in Anderson's book (I,B).

II. CRITICISM OF INDIVIDUAL PLAYS AND STATE OF SCHOLARSHIP

A. INDIVIDUAL PLAYS

'Tis Pity She's a Whore

Many salvos have been fired at this most controversial of Ford's plays; mention of three must suffice. In 1831, the drama and its title were omitted from the two-volume *The Dramatic Works of John Ford*, Harper's Stereotype Edition, published in New York; the Introduction substitutes the title *Annabella and Giovanni* for "a much coarser one"; and the anonymous editor states that, in the play, Ford's language "flings a soft and soothing light over what, in its natural state [,] would glare with salutary and repulsive horror." In 1908, Sherman (I,B) condemns the playwright's handling of Giovanni and Annabella: "He crowns their adulterous and incestuous loves with roses, and attempts to irradiate their crime with celestial light. This play stands for the ultimate corruption of the romantic ideal. When the last ugliness of unnatural lust and crime is clothed in a veil of divine illusion, decadence can go no farther." Tomlinson, writing as recently as 1964 (I,B), declares: "Plays must inevitably refer to a moral framework, and though they don't of course have to adopt uncritically the moral standards they find in respectable society, there is no sense in deliberately and wantonly controverting these." But the barrage against "decadence" has diminished greatly since Sherman's era, and even Eliot's sniping from another quarter in 1932 (I,B) that the play lacks "general significance and emotional depth" and that the love between Giovanni and Annabella "hardly rises above the purely carnal infatuation" has drawn little support.

During the past four decades, most critics have found not weakness but strength in *'Tis Pity She's a Whore*. Perhaps the most provocative commentary on the play is that by Antonin Artaud in *Le théâtre et son double* (1938). Artaud, in an essay overlooked by most Ford scholars, likens tragic drama to the plague because both of them exteriorize latent evil. He uses *'Tis Pity* as his paradigm: both Annabella and Giovanni exemplify absolute freedom in revolt as they proceed from excess to excess and vindication to vindication. Influenced by Artaud yet disagreeing with him in some important respects, Carol C. Rosen, "The Language of Cruelty in Ford's *'Tis Pity She's a Whore*," *CompD*

8 (1974): 356-68, contends that Artaud has underestimated "the torrential language of *'Tis Pity* [that] engulfs the drama . . . in the twisted redundancies of ruthless words." Among the various recent approaches to Ford, those of Sensabaugh (I,B) and Stavig (I,B) are at opposite ends of the spectrum. According to Sensabaugh, Giovanni and Annabella "stand exempt from the toils of accepted ethical law." This view is supported by S. Gorley Putt, "The Modernity of John Ford," *English* 18 (1969): 47-52, who finds the dramatist "not so much a debased Elizabethan" as a modern existentialist. Stavig, on the other hand, sees Giovanni satirized by Ford as "a combination of the passionate sinner and the rationalizing fool." Of a similar persuasion is Kenneth A. Requa, "Music in the Ear: Giovanni as Tragic Hero in Ford's *'Tis Pity She's a Whore*," *Papers on Language and Literature* 7 (1971): 13-25: "Giovanni from the first is self-blinded, seeking but never finding an adequate excuse for his action."

The great majority of contemporary commentators agree with neither Sensabaugh nor Stavig; instead, they tend to find in the play an ambivalence that both censures and sympathizes with Giovanni. Ornstein and Ribner, in their books on Jacobean and Caroline tragedy (I,B), are typical. Ornstein, having claimed that neither Giovanni nor the Friar is Ford's spokesman, asserts that "Ford dares to find beauty, tenderness, and devotion in a forbidden love." Ribner maintains that in *'Tis Pity* "the impossibility of good makes all the more striking the reality of evil"; Ford is "not a champion of moral anarchy" but does arouse "pity for the incestuous lovers." Since the mid-1950s, most books on Ford have taken the same middle ground, though their emphases understandably vary. Davril (I,B), in a section entitled "Le sensationnel," states that Ford inherits this colorful aspect of his dramaturgy from the Elizabethan playwrights but utilizes it selectively to enhance action and characterization. Oliver (I,B) believes that the play presents "incestuous love as the tragic flaw in otherwise admirable characters"; he also argues for the work's "complete validity of characterization" and for the excellence of its construction, including the Bergetto subplot. Leech (I,B) finds in *'Tis Pity* "the horrible and the shocking," which, unlike Artaud, he regards as a "blemish": Ford, says Leech, "shows something of a mere desire to make our flesh creep." N. W. Bawcutt, in his edition (III,E), reaffirms Davril's thesis of discreet sensationalism: "Throughout Ford portrays events which, barely narrated, could easily be regarded as crudely sensationalist, but in his hands they take on difficult and disturbing meanings that are not easily defined." Anderson (I,B) cites Ford's audacious virtuosity: "To have an incestuous adulterer seek vengeance upon the cuckolded husband surely is a remarkable variation on a familiar theme, but the playwright makes it credible." Orbison (I,B) reiterates the theme of ambivalence: "Though the validity of moral law is asserted in the fall of the sinner, easy formulas are tested and facile answers rejected."

The similarity of *'Tis Pity* to *Romeo and Juliet* has often been noted. Kirsch (I,B), for example, says that Ford "does not merely recollect *Romeo and Juliet*, but attempts to rework it, to translate it, into terms . . . viable . . . for . . . his Caroline audience." Sidney R. Homan, Jr., "Shakespeare and Dekker as Keys to Ford's *'Tis Pity She's a Whore*," *SEL* 7 (1967): 269-76, thinks that both Shakespeare's tragedy and *The Witch of Edmonton*, on which Ford collaborated with Dekker and Rowley, are formative; Homan finds the character of Frank Thorney in the latter play "very much the ancestor of Giovanni." Cyrus Hoy, however, in "'Ignorance in Knowledge': Marlowe's Faustus and Ford's Giovanni," *MP* 57 (1960): 145-54, sees *'Tis Pity* more indebted to *Doctor Faustus* than to *Romeo and Juliet*, for both Giovanni and Faustus are guilty of intellectual pride and misuse reason with tragic consequences.

Other aspects of the play have been discussed in other studies. T. J. King, "Staging of Plays at the Phoenix in Drury Lane, 1617-42," *Theatre Notebook* 19 (1965): 146-66, concludes that because both *'Tis Pity She's a Whore* and *Love's Sacrifice*, which were produced at the Phoenix, seem to require "a discovery space and an acting area above," these staging devices probably were used at that theater, perhaps by means of a curtained booth. Larry S. Champion, "Ford's *'Tis Pity She's a Whore* and the Jacobean Tragic Perspective," *PMLA* 90 (1975): 78-87, sees in the play an indictment both of the individual and of society, the latter "not as a microcosmic unit of God's larger order but as a cluster of degree-vizarding individuals. . . . The path from Faustus to Giovanni is . . . the journey of Jacobean tragedy." Donald K. Anderson, Jr., "The Heart and the Banquet: Imagery in Ford's *'Tis Pity* and *The Broken Heart*," *SEL* 2 (1962): 209-17, believes that in both plays the imagery "not only is sustained but also progresses from the figurative to the literal and underlines the theme of each drama."

The Broken Heart

The play has long vied with *'Tis Pity She's a Whore* as Ford's greatest work. "*The Broken Heart* is, to most of Ford's readers, the supreme reach of his genius," says Ellis-Fermor (I,B); she praises the drama for its effect of "rapidity of inner realization and stillness of outward demeanour simultaneously indicated." Leech (I,B) finds *The Broken Heart* more characteristic of Ford than is *'Tis Pity*: "his most impressive characters have an aristocratic code of endurance, remembering always in their anguish that they are courtiers and princes." Oliver (I,B) thinks it "quieter, more restrained, more poetic" than *'Tis Pity* but also "less credible and in both subject and treatment essentially less dramatic."

The treatment of love and of marriage in the play has received considerable attention. Ewing (I,B) believes that Ford is indebted to Burton for the symptoms of Bassanes's jealousy and for the melancholy of both Penthea and Orgilus. Sensabaugh (I,B) contends that the play's idealization of love is influenced by the Platonic coterie of Queen Henrietta; Davril (I,B) disagrees, but does point out some similarities to George Wilkins's *The Miseries of Enforced Marriage* (1607). Peter Ure, "Marriage and the Domestic Drama in Heywood and Ford," *ES* 32 (1951): 200-16, asserts that the marriage of Penthea and Bassanes is "a denial of the rights of precontract"; in the portrayal of Penthea, continues Ure, "Ford cleverly combines the theme of the false wife stricken by conscience . . . and the theme of the enforced marriage." A similar argument is made by Glenn H. Blayney in "Convention, Plot, and Structure in *The Broken Heart*," *MP* 56 (1958): 1-9: the drama is "written in protest against the practice of enforced marriage in seventeenth-century society. . . . The form of the entire play is governed by Ford's use of this theme."

More recently, other views of *The Broken Heart* have been expressed. Charles O. McDonald, "The Design of John Ford's *The Broken Heart*: A Study in the Development of Caroline Sensibility," *SP* 59 (1962): 141-61, calls the play "fragile, more uneven, and more pathetic than tragic in its effects. . . . But pathos is equally clearly that which Ford considered his special province." Roger T. Burbridge, "The Moral Vision of Ford's *The Broken Heart*," *SEL* 10 (1970): 397-407, sees Ford stressing futility: "The world of *The Broken Heart*, then, is a world of shifting values, in which finally there is no reference for belief, no recourse but to endure, no resolution except in death." A more positive view is attributed to the dramatist by Michael J. Kelly in "The Values of Action and Chronicle in *The Broken Heart*," *Papers on Language and Literature* 7 (1971): 150-58: "A man may achieve dignity . . . by acting so as to deserve a 'chronicle' which will reorder the experience of a disjointed world into an intelligible and meaningful pattern for posterity." Ford's attitude towards seventeenth-century drama is discussed by David Malouf in "The Dramatist as Critic: John Ford and *The Broken Heart*," *Southern Review: An Australian Journal of Literary Studies* 5 (1972): 197-206; Malouf sees Ford as an anti-Jacobean rejecting the conventional speech and actions of the earlier drama and cites the portrayal of Bassanes as the best example. Anderson, in his chapter on the play (I,B), believes that Ford utilizes the motifs of fate and revenge "to pace his story and to achieve a denouement nicely poised between expectation and surprise"; Anderson also claims that the playwright carefully sets up in Act I a central situation which he then discards in Act II.

More attention has been paid to the language of *The Broken Heart* than to that of any of Ford's other plays. Besides Anderson's article in 1962 on the iterative imagery of the heart and the banquet in both *The Broken Heart* and *'Tis Pity* (above, *'Tis Pity*), three studies have appeared. Brian Morris, in his 1966 edition of *The Broken Heart* (III,E), claims that Ford's language is "remarkable for its lack of figures." Instead, says Morris, the style is "periphrastic," with "the core of meaning ... overlaid with a complicated yet loosely articulated syntax which gives . . . an aureate grandeur of utterance." R. J. Kaufmann, "Ford's 'Waste Land': *The Broken Heart*," *RenD* 3 (1970): 167-87, contends that "The atmosphere of the play is controlled by images of truncation, frustration, and desiccation which reach their culmination in the powerfully realized death scenes in the last acts." Kaufmann also sees *The Broken Heart* as a "tragedy of manners." Thelma N. Greenfield, "The Language of Process in Ford's *The Broken Heart*," *PMLA* 87 (1972): 397-405, agrees with and adds to Morris's comments: "Significant names, pinpointing of cause and effect, heavy use of verbs that produce metaphors showing cause and operation, a style detached and observational although alternately complex-vague and simple-direct . . .—these are qualities of language that Ford puts to work in this play."

There is no literary source for the main story of *The Broken Heart*. Early in this century, Stuart P. Sherman, in "Stella and *The Broken Heart*," *PMLA* 24 (1909): 274-85, suggested as a source for the Orgilus-Penthea tragedy the relationship between Sir Philip Sidney and Penelope Devereux. The possible influence of the *Arcadia* also has been noted; for example, Morris (III,E) finds a similarity between the story of Argalus and Parthenia and that of Orgilus and Penthea. Earlier English dramatists may have influenced *The Broken Heart*. Robert Davril, "Shakespeare and Ford," *SJ* 94 (1958): 121-31, believes that

Penthea's madness resembles that of Ophelia. Félix Carrère, "*La tragédie espagnole* de Thomas Kyd et *Le coeur brisé* de John Ford," *EA* 8 (1955): 1-10, argues, on the basis of many parallels, Ford's indebtedness to Kyd. G. Fitzgibbon, "An Echo of *Volpone* in *The Broken Heart*," *N&Q* 22 (1975): 248-49, finds a "close verbal correspondence" between lines spoken by Bassanes and Corvino and infers Ford's "identifying Bassanes with Jonson's earlier jealous husband." Possible origins have been suggested for two of the play's more spectacular scenes. Robert Davril, "John Ford and La Cerda's *Inés de Castro*," *MLN* 66 (1951): 464-66, discerns in the Spanish tragedy a source for the marriage-in-death of Calantha and Ithocles in the final scene. R. Jordon, "Calantha's Dance in *The Broken Heart*," *N&Q* 16 (1969): 294-95, points out that Calantha's insistence upon continuing to dance despite the three announcements of death may be based upon Plutarch's account of the Spartans' refusal to stop festive dance upon receiving news of military disaster.

The possible reference of the phrase "a truth" in the Prologue to a particular historical incident has been the topic of three articles. Giovanni M. Carsaniga, "'The Truth' in John Ford's *The Broken Heart*," *CL* 10 (1958): 344-48, not only mentions the possible model (noted by Sherman) of Sidney and Stella but also cites, as a source for Ithocles's murder, a Bandello novella based on a murder in Antwerp in 1551 involving the same kind of chair in which Orgilus traps Ithocles. Frederick M. Burelbach, Jr., "'The Truth' in John Ford's *The Broken Heart* Revisited," *N&Q* 14 (1967): 211-12, suggests that the phrase refers to an allegedly true story in Castiglione's *Courtier* of a lady who, forbidden to marry the man she loved, preserved an unbroken continence until her death. Michael Neill, "New Light on 'The Truth' in *The Broken Heart*," *N&Q* 22 (1975): 249-50, discovers, in a letter written by Philip Gawdy in 1600, historical analogues for the deaths of both Penthea and Calantha: Margaret Ratcliffe, one of Elizabeth's maids of honor, grief-stricken at the death of her brother, starved herself to death; an autopsy found her body "well and sounde, saving certaine stringes striped all over her harte"—a possible explanation for "the rather embarrassing literalness ('cracke, cracke') with which 'silent griefs . . . cut the hart-strings' of the play's other heroine, Princess Calantha."

Finally, a little known commendation of *The Broken Heart* made almost eighty years ago by an eminent scholar must not be forgotten. Robert Speaight, *William Poel and the Elizabethan Revival* (1954), quotes at length from a program note written by Edmund Gosse for a

London performance of the play in 1898. Gosse, having likened *The Broken Heart* to seventeenth-century French tragedy, concludes: "Racine might have envied the skill with which, from the very first, the fate of Ithocles and Calantha, apparently so secure and so fortunate, flutters in the closed hand of Orgilus. His revenge has a quiet resolution which is absolutely demoniac."

Perkin Warbeck

Eliot (I,B) has praised the drama as "unquestionably Ford's highest achievement, and . . . one of the very best historical plays outside of the works of Shakespeare in the whole of Elizabethan and Jacobean drama." Most commentators disagree with the first part of Eliot's statement, for they find either *The Broken Heart* or *'Tis Pity* to be Ford's best; but there has been little argument about the stature of *Perkin Warbeck* as a history play. Irving Ribner, *The English History Play in the Age of Shakespeare* (1957; rev. ed. 1965), ranks it with the English historical plays of Marlowe and Shakespeare; *Perkin Warbeck*, says Ribner, achieves "a faithful representation of the past (truth) and an exposition of significant political doctrine (state)."

Criticism of the play in the past four or five decades has centered upon the psychological, the political, and the paradoxical. The psychological approach usually concerns the sanity of Warbeck. Lawrence Babb, "Abnormal Psychology in John Ford's *Perkin Warbeck*," *MLN* 51 (1936): 234-37, sees Warbeck depicted as a Burtonian melancholic with delusions of grandeur. Ewing (I,B) states: "The real Warbeck may have been only a consummate imposter; Ford's is not. . . . Fully deluded, he is worthy of pity as well as of death." Davril (II,B), disagreeing with Babb and Ewing, asserts that Warbeck is neither ill nor possessed and, indeed, is the least abnormal of Ford's tragic heroes. Leech (I,B) calls Warbeck "a Fordian aristocrat, dignified by his own steadfastness in delusion," and points out that "Ford never exposes him to the pity which we may give to the sick."

Assessments of the play's political content have varied considerably. Sargeaunt (I,A) believes that, in *Perkin Warbeck*, "Ford is not really concerned at all with the fortunes of England, with its traditions, its politics and its countryside." Most critics view the drama otherwise, but in turn differ as to the nature of its political emphasis. Mildred C. Struble, in her 1926 edition of the play (III,E), asserts that Ford, in the characters of Henry VII and Warbeck respectively, is contrasting responsible Tudor sovereignty and irresponsible Stuart autocracy. Ribner, sharing Struble's view, sees Ford presenting a tragedy in political terms, idealizing Henry VII and offering "some subtle questioning of the doctrine of the divine right of kings." Donald K. Anderson, Jr., "Kingship in Ford's *Perkin Warbeck*," *ELH* 27 (1960): 177-93, finds not only a contrast between the astute statecraft of Henry and the inept leadership of Warbeck but also a James IV of Scotland shifting his political philosophy, in the course of the play, towards the pragmatism of the English monarch. At variance with these views is Jonas A. Barish, "*Perkin Warbeck* as Anti-History," *Essays in Criticism* 20 (1970): 151-71; Barish argues that the play favors Warbeck and undercuts Henry: "If it is Henry who wins the political struggle, it is Perkin who continues to marshal our imaginative allegiance." Philip Edwards, "The Royal Pretenders in Massinger and Ford," *E&S* 27 (1974): 18-36, supports Barish: "the play's contrast between the ruler and the claimant is, in personal terms, entirely on the side of the claimant."

The relative merits of Warbeck and Henry have led some critics to cite paradox as informing the play. Ribner (I,B) asserts that "the audience is left in a state of doubt and ambivalence"; Peter Ure, in his edition (III,E), states that Ford, in handling the drama's "complex relations, . . . blends some of them together, softly cradled in an antithesis"; and Anderson, in his chapter on the play (I,B), concludes: "the two antagonists complement rather than neutralize one another. Both men triumph: the statesman over his less far-sighted and 'provident' adversary; the Stoic, over death."

The principal source for the drama is Sir Francis Bacon's *History of the Reign of King Henry VII* (1622). To this Mildred C. Struble has added, in "The Indebtedness of Ford's *Perkin Warbeck* to Gainsford," *Anglia* 49 (1925): 80-91, Thomas Gainsford's *True and Wonderful History of Perkin Warbeck* (1618). Michael Neill notes Ford's use of the same source for his comic portrayal of John a Water, one of Warbeck's advisors, in "Ford and Gainsford: An Unnoticed Borrowing," *N&Q* 15 (1968): 253-55. Donald K. Anderson, Jr., "*Richard II* and *Perkin Warbeck*," *SQ* 13 (1962): 260-63, points out a parallel between Richard's (III.ii) and Warbeck's (IV.v) landings in England, especially their reliance upon the divine right of kings. John J. O'Connor, "William Warner and Ford's *Perkin Warbeck*," *N&Q* 2 (1955): 233-35, states that Ford's characterizations of Katherine and Daliell may have been suggested by Warner's *Albion's England* (ca. 1586).

John J. O'Connor, "A Lost Play of Perkin Warbeck," *MLN* 70 (1955): 566-68, cites a reference to an earlier Warbeck play in Gainsford's *True History of the Earl of Tyrone* (1619). Donald K. Anderson, Jr., "The Date and Handwriting of a Manuscript Copy of Ford's *Perkin Warbeck*," *N&Q* 10 (1963): 340-41, dates a manuscript of the drama as of 1745, since a name of the actor Furnival, who played Henry VII in a performance at Goodman's Fields in that year, appears in the dramatis personae. Margaret Crum accepts this date and suggests that the manuscript resembles the 1714 reprint more than it does the 1634 quarto, in "A Manuscript of Ford's *Perkin Warbeck*: An Additional Note," *N&Q* 12 (1965): 104-5. Both Harbage (III,A) and Homan (III,A) state that Ford may have had a collaborator, Thomas Dekker.

Love's Sacrifice

Many critics have found this play—especially Act V—the most puzzling of Ford's works. Ewing (I,B) attributes the final catastrophe of three deaths to the duke's melancholy: "Like Bassanes he goes through the jealous man's changeableness: successive feelings of outrage and pitying sorrow." Peter Ure, "Cult and Initiates in Ford's *Love's Sacrifice*," *MLQ* 11 (1950): 298-306, contends that Bianca is chiefly responsible for the tragic outcome because her "feeble attempt at the Platonic relationship breaks down at an early stage." Kaufmann (above, *'Tis Pity*) protests that "the Duke has thoroughly botched everything . . . . We find his final act [suicide] gratuitous, his joining the dead lovers (whose relationship possesses at least a shred of validity) an intrusion." A. L. and M. K. Kistner, "The Dramatic Functions of Love in the Tragedies of John Ford," *SP* 70 (1973): 62-76, hold Bianca responsible: "An audience . . . presented with a choice between a generous-minded, blameless husband and a cruelly jeering wife, innocent in deed but certainly not in intent, is likely to decide that the scope of infidelity is broader than a bed."

A differing view of the play is offered by Cyrus Hoy, McMaster, and Anderson. Hoy, "Renaissance and Restoration Dramatic Plotting," *RenD* 9 (1966): 247-64, argues for the work's "Platonic love ethic" and maintains that Bianca belongs among those heroines who, because they "seek to suppress their passion at any cost when fulfillment implies a violation of honor, are therefore to be accounted virtuous." McMaster, in her 1969 article (I,B) on the triple-plot structure of Ford's dramas, states that the "central love of Fernando and Bianca" should be seen as "a deep and admirable kind of love." Anderson, in his chapter on the play (I,B), claims that "The key word in *Love's Sacrifice* is *lust*" meaning "illicit sexual intercourse, which is the unforgivable sin in Ford's Pavia." According to Anderson, the duke, goaded by D'Avolos, mistakenly regards the actions of Bianca and Fernando as "lust," and so kills his wife.

The Lover's Melancholy

This play is gradually being seen as something more than an imitation of *The Anatomy* or of Elizabethan drama. George F. Sensabaugh, "Burton's Influence on Ford's *The Lover's Melancholy*," *SP* 33 (1936): 545–71, finds the drama structured upon "the Burtonian formula of the causes, symptoms, and cures of melancholy" and "little more than a pseudo-scientific study of diseased people." Marvin T. Herrick, *Tragicomedy: Its Origin and Development in Italy, France, and England* (1955), describes the work as "utilizing most of the familiar tragicomic devices found in Fletcher and others, but seasoned with Ford's own peculiar kind of abnormal emotionalism." Oliver (I,B) states that "Ford's first unaided drama . . . shows clearly some of his limitations. The typical Elizabethan story of the girl in disguise is, as it were, put to the test of Burtonian psychology and not found wanting." Leech (I,B) sees Ford combining, in *The Lover's Melancholy*, "a dependence on Burton with a frequent asseveration that Providence watches and guides all." Anderson (I,B), besides noting Ford's use of an art-versus-nature motif, sees him "presenting in his main plot—six scenes in which the melancholy of Prince Palador and Lord Meleander is diagnosed and cured—psychotherapy as spectacle." These recoveries, continues Anderson, "owe much more to Ford's imagination and artistry than to Burton's psychology."

The Witch of Edmonton

Written by Ford in collaboration with Dekker and Rowley, the play is praised by Leonora Leet Brodwin in "The Domestic Tragedy of Frank Thorney in *The Witch of Edmonton*," *SEL* 7 (1967): 311–28; Brodwin calls the Frank Thorney plot "probably the most sophisticated treatment of domestic tragedy in the whole of the Elizabethan-Jacobean drama." Sargeaunt (I,A) states that Winifred "must have been Ford's creation" and that "her courage, combined with a certain tenderness and strength of feeling, . . . [is] found in all his women." Oliver (I,B) praises the opening scene, which he believes to be Ford's; Leech (I,B) notes, in the scene between Thorney and Katherine in Act IV, a compelling fusion of "naturalistic detail and supernatural intervention";

and Anderson (I,B) asserts that both the Thorney plot and the Mother Sawyer plot "have the theme of damnation and are overtly linked by the devil dog."

The Fancies Chaste and Noble

Juliet Sutton, "Platonic Love in Ford's *The Fancies, Chaste and Noble*," *SEL* 7 (1967): 299-309, believes that many critics have been unduly harsh towards the play. Sutton states, "Ford expected us to realize . . . that Octavio's Bower of Fancies, besides being an academy for his nieces, is an establishment for the practice of Platonic love." She also contends that Octavio's advances to Castamela are both genuine and Platonic. Anderson (I,B) finds in the play's title an ironic commentary by Ford on the mistaken notions not only of his characters but of his audience: "We must confess to ourselves that whereas Octavio's three wards are eminently chaste and noble, our own fancies—not to mention those of Livio, Romanello, Castamela, Camillo, Vespucci, Secco, and Spadone—certainly have not been."

The Lady's Trial

Oliver (I,B), reflecting on the peaceful resolution of the story's potential tragedy, states: "Ford never was interested in the tragedy of blood. . . . But to make a play only from what people think and feel is to strain drama to its utmost limits." James Howe, "Ford's *The Lady's Trial*: A Play of Metaphysical Wit," *Genre* 7 (1974): 342-61, asserts that the vocabulary of law dominates the main plot and that incidents parallel the progressive stages of legal proceedings. Howe also claims that the play gives priority to thematic rather than psychological considerations.

The Sun's Darling

This collaboration with Dekker is discussed by H. K. Russell, "Tudor and Stuart Dramatizations of the Doctrines of Natural and Moral Philosophy," *SP* 31 (1934): 1-27. According to Russell, Dekker and Ford "have combined . . . the two dramatic forms in which natural and moral philosophy has hitherto been presented. The form of the morality has been used to stage the conflict in man's soul. . . . The form of the masque has been used to present the properties of the four elements and the affections." Oliver (I,B) states that "of Ford the play tells us little except that he was willing apparently to collaborate sometimes in work that was far removed from his usual interests."

B. STATE OF SCHOLARSHIP

The standard edition of Ford still is that by Gifford and Dyce and is not adequate (III,C). Twentieth-century single-work editions, most of them quite satisfactory, unfortunately are limited—if dissertations are excluded—to three plays: *'Tis Pity She's a Whore, The Broken Heart*, and *Perkin Warbeck* (III,E). At present, agreement on the canon is almost unanimous; of the uncertain ascriptions (III,B), *The Queen* is now generally accepted as Ford's, and the others are generally not. Fordian criticism is in somewhat better state than the editing: beginning with Sargeaunt's work in 1935, a good number of books have been written on the playwright (I,B), and they complement one another effectively. When all modern criticism of Ford—articles as well as books—is considered, however, preoccupation with the same three plays reappears; *The Fancies* and *The Lady's Trial* may deserve this neglect, but *The Lover's Melancholy* and *Love's Sacrifice* do not. Concerning Ford's three major plays, twentieth-century criticism has handled *The Broken Heart* the best: commentary on this drama is both informative and varied as it turns from analogues to language to theme (II,A). Recent criticism of *Perkin Warbeck* also has contributed much of value (II,A), one instance being the current debate about the relative merits of Warbeck and Henry VII. But criticism of *'Tis Pity She's a Whore* has been disappointingly repetitious, probably because of its almost exclusive concentration upon theme (II,A).

III. CANON

A. PLAYS IN CHRONOLOGICAL ORDER

The chronology, dates, and type of play are those of Alfred Harbage, *Annals of English Drama, 975-1700* (1940; rev. S. Schoenbaum, 1964); *A Second Supplement to the Revised Edition* by S. Schoenbaum appeared in 1970. Following the title of each entry, the dates in parentheses refer to the first performance (in italics) and the first edition. The Ford canon is discussed in Bentley's *The Jacobean and Caroline Stage*, vol. 3 (1956). Descriptions of the editions published before 1660 are given in W. W. Greg's *A Bibliography of the English Printed Drama to the Restoration*, 4 vols. (1939-59).

The Witch of Edmonton, with Dekker and W. Rowley; tragicomedy (*1621;* 1658)

H. Dugdale Sykes, "The Authorship of *The Witch of Edmonton,*" *N&Q* 151 (1926): 435-38 and 453-57, attributes three of the twelve scenes to Ford, one to Dekker, and four to Ford and Dekker; he sees Ford's hand in three of the remaining four. Oliver (I,B) thinks Sykes has exaggerated Ford's share, but does call the dramatist's contributions, "from a man writing possibly his first play, astounding." Bentley, vol. 3, is skeptical about "attempts to assign to the three dramatists their respective shares." Brodwin, in her article on the Frank Thorney plot (II,A), thinks Dekker primarily responsible for its conception and Ford for its execution.

The Bristow Merchant, with Dekker; comedy? (*licensed 22 Oct. 1624;* lost)

E. K. Chambers, *The Elizabethan Stage* (1923), vol. 3, has suggested that this was the same play as *The London Merchant* (below), but Bentley, vol. 3, calls this suggestion "pure conjecture."

The Fairy Knight, with Dekker; mask? (*licensed 11 June 1624;* lost)

The Late Murder in White Chapel, or Keep the Widow Waking (The Late Murder of the Son upon the Mother), with Dekker, W. Rowley, and Webster; comedy and tragedy (*licensed Sept. 1624;* lost)

C. J. Sisson, *Lost Plays of Shakespeare's Age* (1936), a book based in part upon his article "*Keep the Widow Waking*: A Lost Play by Dekker," *Library* 8 (1927): 39-57, 233-59, documents the authorship of the work as well as the circumstances of its composition. The main plot is based upon a murder trial in 1624; the secondary plot, upon the notorious victimizing of a widow in the same year.

The London Merchant, with Dekker?; comedy (*1624?;* lost)

Chambers, vol. 3, thought this was perhaps the same play as *The Bristow Merchant* (above). Bentley, vol. 3, states: "The play is known only from the entry in the Stationers' Register [1660], for Warburton's record of it may well be only a copy of the register entry and no evidence that he had ever seen the manuscript."

The Sun's Darling, with Dekker; moral mask *(licensed 3 March 1624 and revised 1638–39;* 1656)

The mask was once thought to be a revision by Ford of Dekker's lost *Phaethon,* written for Henslowe in 1598; but William L. Halstead, "Dekker's *Phaethon,*" *N&Q* 175 (1938): 380-85, sees little similarity between *The Sun's Darling* and the Phaethon myth. Bentley, vol. 3, agrees. Attempts to assign parts of the play to Ford and to Dekker have been made by Frederick E. Pierce, "The Collaboration of Dekker and Ford: The Authorship of *The Sun's Darling,*" *Anglia* 36 (1912): 141-68; by H. Dugdale Sykes, *Sidelights on Elizabethan Drama* (1924); and by Sargeaunt (I,A). But Oliver (I,B) does "not see any hope of making a satisfactory division." The mask very likely was revised after 1624; W. J. Lawrence, "The Problem of Lyly's Songs," *TLS,* 20 Dec. 1923, p. 894, suggests 1638 or 1639, since the first part of Act V relates to the political situation in those years. A song in Act II seems based upon the cuckoo song in Lyly's *Alexander and Campaspe;* this song, however, did not appear in Lyly's drama until the 1632 edition, and John Robert Moore, "The Songs in Lyly's Plays," *PMLA* 42 (1927): 623-40, contends that the song in *The Sun's Darling* is not extraneous and hence probably not taken from Lyly.

The Lover's Melancholy, tragicomedy *(licensed 24 Nov. 1628;* 1629)

Bentley, vol. 3, points out that the acting of the play by the King's company is indicated "not only by Herbert's licence and the title-page of the 1629 quarto, but by the list, which was printed in the quarto, of the seventeen actors of the King's company who took part in the original performance."

The Broken Heart, tragedy (ca. *1625–33;* 1633)

W. J. Lawrence, *TLS,* 12 July 1923, p. 472, dates the play no earlier than 1631, maintaining that Ford's phrase "The garland of good-will" refers to Thomas Deloney's *The Garland of Good Will,* which was published in that year. Ewing (I,B) dates *The Broken Heart* in 1632 for three reasons: an apparent reference to the drama in William Hemming's *Elegy on Randolph's Finger* (ca. 1632); the omission of the

Globe theater from the play's title page; and Crashaw's line, in *Delights of the Muses* (1646), "What is *Loves Sacrifice*, but *The broken Heart*." Bentley, vol. 3, challenges the conclusions of both Lawrence and Ewing. C. A. Gibson, "The Date of *The Broken Heart*," *N&Q* 18 (1971): 458, argues, because of a possible borrowing from Massinger's *The Picture*, which was licensed for performance in 1629 and published in 1630, that the work may have been written ca. 1630-31.

Beauty in a Trance, genre unknown (*acted 28 Nov. 1630;* lost)

Love's Sacrifice, tragedy (*1632?;* 1633)

Frederick Gard Fleay, *A Biographical Chronicle of the English Drama, 1559-1642* (1891), vol. 1, contends that the phrase "women anticks" in Act III alludes to French actresses performing in London in 1629; he thus dates *Love's Sacrifice* around 1630. Bentley, vol. 3, believes that the phrase more likely refers to the proposed court performance of Queen Henrietta and her ladies in 1632.

'Tis Pity She's a Whore, tragedy (*1629?-33;* 1633)

Ford's reference to the play, in his dedication to the Earl of Peterborough, as "These *First Fruites* of my leasure" has led some commentators to regard *'Tis Pity* as the earliest of his unassisted dramas; but Bentley, vol. 3, argues that the play simply "was the product of some newly acquired leisure—conceivably a leisure connected with the 'particular Ingagement' Ford owed to Peterborough." Oliver (I,B) agrees with Bentley, and also rejects the notion, advanced by Sargeaunt (I,A) and Davril (I,B), that similarities in versification between *'Tis Pity* and *Love's Sacrifice* put them close together chronologically, and before the other plays.

Perkin Warbeck, with Dekker?; history (ca. *1629-34;* 1634 & MS)

Schoenbaum, in his 1970 supplement to the *Annals*, changes the terminus a quo date for the play from 1629 to 1625. Bentley, vol. 3, finds odd the phrase "Acted (some-times)" on the title page, and suggests that it may signify either that the play "was not often or not recently acted, and therefore that 1633 was too late for a composition date" or that performances had been suppressed. Alfred Harbage, "The Mystery of *Perkin Warbeck*," *Studies in the English Renaissance Drama in Memory of Karl Julius Holzknecht*, ed. J. W. Bennett, Oscar Cargill, and Vernon Hall, Jr. (1959), pp. 125-41, noting that some commentators have found *Perkin Warbeck* not typical of Ford and that Ford and Dekker collaborated on other plays, concludes that perhaps Dekker "wrote part of *Perkin Warbeck* and shaped the play as a whole." Of the same opinion is Sidney R. Homan, Jr., "Dekker as Collaborator in Ford's *Perkin Warbeck*," *ELN* 3 (1965): 104-6; Homan contends that parallel situations as well as a name in common ("Warbeck") in both *Perkin Warbeck* and *The Witch of Edmonton* indicate Dekker's participation in the former drama. Homan also suggests an earlier date of composition (ca. 1621-24) for the play. Peter Ure, in his 1968 edition (III,E), discusses at length the collaboration theory, but rejects it. In "A Pointer to the Date of Ford's *Perkin Warbeck*," *N&Q* 17 (1970): 215-17, Ure suggests that the play may have been written in late 1632 or 1633 because of the probable relationship between "Ford's precise and careful allusion to the remote ancestry of the Stuart kings" in Act I and allegedly treasonable activities of the Earl of Menteith in the early 1630s.

The Fancies Chaste and Noble, comedy (*1635-36;* 1638)

Fleay (above, *Love's Sacrifice*), vol. 1, asserts that the play must have been performed before May of 1636, when Queen Henrietta's men stopped using the Phoenix, the theater mentioned on the title page. Fleay also argues that the "old man of one hundred and twelve" mentioned by Ford in Act V alludes to Old Parr and thus probably dates the play around 1635, when the old man came to London and was a topic of conversation. Paul Reyher, *Les masques anglais* (1909), argues for 1636 on the basis of the possible influence on the play's concluding mask of Davenant's *Triumphs of the Prince D'Amour*, licensed and performed early in 1636. Ewing (I,B), however, suggests 1631, stating that *The Fancies* was ridiculed in Shirley's *Changes*, which was licensed in January of 1632. Harbage, *Annals*, lists Ford's play as possibly a revision of a 1631 version.

The Lady's Trial, comedy (*licensed 3 May 1638;* 1639)

Bentley, vol. 3, notes, at the end of the prologue in some copies of the play, a "Mr. Bird," and believes this appears as a signature to indicate the authorship of the prologue by Theophilus Bird, whose name is also attached to *The Witch of Edmonton* and *The Sun's Darling*.

The Royal Combat, comedy (ca. *1621-42;* lost)

B. UNCERTAIN ASCRIPTIONS; APOCRYPHA

A Bad Beginning Makes a Good Ending, comedy (*acted 1612-13;* lost)

According to Harbage, this is probably the same play as *An Ill Beginning Has a Good End,* assigned to Ford in the Stationers' Register, 1660. Thomas M. Parrott, "A Note on John Ford," *MLN* 58 (1943): 247-53, argues that Ford could not have written the play.

The Laws of Candy by Fletcher; tragicomedy (*1619-23;* 1647)

Though the play has been and still is generally assigned to Fletcher, E. H. C. Oliphant, *The Plays of Beaumont and Fletcher; An Attempt to Determine Their Respective Shares and the Shares of Others* (1927), cites verbal parallels to show that *The Laws of Candy* is "wholly Ford's, save for one little bit of Fletcher." Leech (I,B) believes Oliphant has made "a reasonable case," but Bentley, vol. 3, and Davril (I,B) are skeptical. Cyrus Hoy, "The Shares of Fletcher and His Collaborators in the Beaumont and Fletcher Canon (V)," *SB* 13 (1960): 77-108, claims, on the basis of linguistic patterns—e.g., the incidence of *ye*—in *The Laws of Candy* and in Ford's unaided plays, that "it seems best to regard *The Laws of Candy* as wholly his." Hoy also attributes part of *The Fair Maid of the Inn* (below) to Ford in the same manner. S. Schoenbaum, *Internal Evidence and Elizabethan Dramatic Authorship* (1966), finds these attributions of Hoy "inconclusive."

The Queen, or The Excellency of Her Sex, tragicomedy (ca. *1621-42;* 1653)

Published anonymously by Alexander Gough in 1653, the play was first attributed to Ford in 1906 by W. Bang in his edition of it in Materialien zur Kunde des älteren englischen Dramas, no. 13. Bang's claim, based entirely on internal, stylistic evidence, has been supported and strengthened by Stuart P. Sherman, "A New Play by John Ford," *MLN* 23 (1908): 245-49; by Sykes (III,A); by Sargeaunt (I,A); and by Anderson (I,B). Although *The Queen* is now generally accepted as part of the Ford canon, its dates of composition and initial performance are highly conjectural. Because Gough, its publisher, had acted with the King's men, Oliver (I,B) is inclined to regard *The Queen* as one of Ford's earlier plays, and calls it "certainly closest to *The Lovers Melan-*

choly in its use of Burton." Tucker Orbison, "The Date of *The Queen*," *N&Q* 15 (1968): 255-56, argues for a dating of 1624-33 because of the work's incidence of rhymes and double and triple endings relative to that of Ford's other plays.

The Spanish Gypsy by Middleton and W. Rowley; tragicomedy (*licensed 9 July 1623;* 1653)

Although the title page lists only Middleton and Rowley as authors, H. Dugdale Sykes, "John Ford the Author of *The Spanish Gipsy*," *MLR* 19 (1924): 11-24, reprinted in *Sidelights* (III,A), claims the entire play for Ford because of its style. Sargeaunt (I,A) agrees with Sykes, except for the gypsy scenes. But Bentley, vol. 4, regards the work as "an ordinary collaboration between Middleton and Rowley"; so does Schoenbaum (above, *The Laws of Candy*), who questions at length Sykes's general methods of attribution. Ronald M. Huebert, "On Detecting John Ford's Hand: A Fallacy," *Library* 26 (1971): 256-59, strongly argues against one criterion—the incidence of *d'ee* and *t'ee*—used by Sykes in attributing *The Spanish Gypsy* to Ford. Examining all of the unassisted plays of both Ford and Shirley, Huebert discovers a higher average incidence of *d'ee* in Shirley; he therefore concludes that this criterion, "made by Sykes and supported by Sargeaunt, Harbage, Lloyd, Davril, and Hoy," is "suspect, if not invalid."

The Welsh Ambassador, or A Comedy in Disguises by Dekker; pseudo-history (ca. *1623?;* MS)

The anonymous play, extant in a manuscript in the Cardiff Public Library, has generally been considered Dekker's since Abraham Hill's attribution of it to him ca. 1678. Bertram Lloyd, "The Authorship of *The Welsh Embassador*," *RES* 21 (1945): 192-201, agrees except for parts of Act III and of Act V, which he believes Ford wrote. Oliver (I,B) supports Lloyd, and wonders if the drama may be a revision, by Ford alone or by Ford and Dekker, of "an earlier play of which Dekker had written at least part."

The Fair Maid of the Inn by Fletcher, with Massinger?, W. Rowley?, and Ford?; comedy (*licensed 22 Jan. 1626;* 1647)

Although the drama was licensed as Fletcher's, Sykes, in *Sidelights* (III,A), believes it to be "a Webster-Massinger play" save for the first scene of Act IV, which he assigns to Ford. F. L. Lucas, *The Complete Works of John Webster* (1927), vol. 4, sees Ford's hand in three scenes; but Oliver (I,B) believes one scene probably is Ford's. Bentley, vol. 3, finds the arguments for authorship other than Fletcher's unconvincing. Hoy (above, *The Laws of Candy*) asserts that Ford wrote all of Act III and, with Fletcher, the first scene of Act IV; Schoenbaum (above, *The Laws of Candy*) is dubious.

The Spanish Duke of Lerma by Henry Shirley; foreign history (*before 1627;* lost)

Alfred Harbage, "Elizabethan-Restoration Palimpsest," *MLR* 35 (1940): 287–319, claims that this lost play was written not by Henry Shirley but by Ford and that much of the drama is extant in Sir Robert Howard's *The Great Favourite, or The Duke of Lerma* (1668). The latter work, according to Harbage, "bears the stamp of Ford in its plot materials, its characters, and its style." Agreeing with Harbage are George F. Sensabaugh, "Another Play by John Ford," *MLQ* 3 (1942): 595–601, and Leech (I,B); some others—Bentley, Davril (I,B), and Oliver (I,B)—have expressed varying degrees of doubt.

C. CRITIQUE OF THE STANDARD TEXT

The Works of John Ford, edited by William Gifford and Alexander Dyce (1869; reissued 1895, 1965), 3 vols., remains the standard edition but needs to be replaced. Its emendations are sometimes questionable, its quarto collations—usually between only two copies—very few, and its explanatory notes inadequate. Two complementary single-volume editions (already cited in the initial paragraph of this study) containing all of Ford's plays are those by W. Bang in 1908 and H. de Vocht in 1927; the two volumes closely follow particular copies of the quartos but list no variants and have no editorial apparatus. More recently, helpful single-work editions of *'Tis Pity She's a Whore*, *The Broken Heart*, and *Perkin Warbeck* have been published (III,E); Ford's other plays sorely need similar attention.

D. TEXTUAL STUDIES

Studies of Ford's texts have, for the most part, sought either to determine his sole or partial authorship or to ascertain the dates of various plays (III,A and B) and nondramatic works (I,C). Descriptions of some of Ford's texts appear in the single-work editions (III,E) of Anderson, Bawcutt, Morris, and Ure.

E. SINGLE-WORK EDITIONS

With the exception of Bang's 1906 edition of *The Queen* (III,B), single-work editions have been confined to and almost equally divided among Ford's three major plays. This neglect of his four other unaided dramas is most regrettable. *'Tis Pity She's a Whore* has been edited by N. W. Bawcutt for the RRDS (1966), by Mark Stavig for Crofts Classics (1966), and by Brian Morris for the New Mermaids (1969); a facsimile of the 1633 quarto was published by the Scolar Press in 1969. *The Broken Heart* has been edited by Morris for the New Mermaids (1966) and by Donald K. Anderson, Jr., for the RRDS (1968). *Perkin Warbeck* has been edited by Mildred C. Struble for the University of Washington Publications in Language and Literature, no. 3 (1926); by Anderson for the RRDS (1965); and by Peter Ure for the Revels Plays (1968). All of these editions provide helpful introductions and notes, and most of them contain useful appendices.

A single volume consisting of *'Tis Pity She's a Whore* and *The Broken Heart* was edited by Stuart P. Sherman for the Belles-Lettres Series (ca. 1915); a single volume containing the same two plays and *Perkin Warbeck* was edited by Keith Sturgess for the Penguin English Library (1970); and a single volume containing those three plays plus *The Lover's Melancholy* and *Love's Sacrifice* was edited by Havelock Ellis for the Mermaid Series (1888) and reissued in 1957.

Mention should also be made of the informative bibliographical descriptions in Arthur H. Nethercot's introductions to Ford, to *The Witch of Edmonton*, to *The Broken Heart*, and to *Perkin Warbeck* in *Stuart Plays* (1971), the second volume of his two-volume revision of the anthology *Elizabethan and Stuart Plays*, ed. A. H. Nethercot, C. R. Baskervill, and V. B. Heltzel (1934).

F. EDITIONS OF NONDRAMATIC WORKS

There have been no twentieth-century editions of the five nondramatic works now generally attributed to Ford: *Fame's Memorial* (1606), *Honour Triumphant* (1606), *Christ's Bloody Sweat* (1613), *The Golden Mean* (1613), and *A Line of Life* (1620). *Fame's Memorial*, *Honour Triumphant*, and *A Line of Life* appear in the standard edition of Ford by Gifford and Dyce, vol. 3. *Fame's Memorial* was edited separately by Joseph Haslewood in 1819, and a single volume consisting of editions of *Honour Triumphant* and *A Line of Life* was published by The Shakespeare Society in 1843. For both *Christ's Bloody Sweat* and *The Golden Mean*, only seventeenth-century editions are available.

IV. SEE ALSO

A. GENERAL

Adams, Henry Hitch. *English Domestic or, Homiletic Tragedy, 1575 to 1642.*1943.

Ali, Florence. *Opposing Absolutes: Conviction and Convention in John Ford's Plays.* Salzburg Studies in English Literature: Jacobean Drama Studies, no. 44 (1974).

Anderson, Donald K., Jr. "The Banquet of Love in English Drama (1595-1642)." *JEGP* 63 (1964): 422-32.

Anderson, Ruth L. "Kingship in Renaissance Drama." *SP* 41 (1944): 136-55.

Armstrong, William A. *The Elizabethan Private Theatres: Facts and Problems.* The Society for Theatre Research Pamphlet Series, no. 6 (1958).

Babb, Lawrence. *The Elizabethan Malady: A Study of Melancholia in English Literature from 1580 to 1642.* 1951.

Barber, C. L. *The Idea of Honour in the English Drama, 1591-1700.* 1957.

Baskervill, Charles Read. *The Elizabethan Jig and Related Song Drama.* 1929.

Bentley, Gerald Eades. *The Profession of Dramatist in Shakespeare's Time, 1590-1642.* 1971.

Bergeron, David M. *English Civic Pageantry, 1558-1642.* 1971.

Bevington, David M. *From "Mankind" to Marlowe: Growth of Structure in the Popular Drama of Tudor England.* 1962.

——. *Tudor Drama and Politics: A Critical Approach to Topical Meaning.* 1968.

Blayney, Glenn H. "Enforcement of Marriage in English Drama (1600-1650)." *PQ* 38 (1959): 459-72.

Boas, F. S. "Charles Lamb and the Elizabethan Dramatists." *E&S 1943* 29 (1944): 62-81.

Bose, Tirthankar. "Ford's Understanding of Honour." *LCrit* 8 (1969): 19-26.

——. "John Ford on Poetry." *The Visvabharati Quarterly* 37 (1971-72): 52-58.

Bowers, Fredson Thayer. *Elizabethan Revenge Tragedy, 1587-1642.* 1940.

——. *On Editing Shakespeare and the Elizabethan Dramatists.* 1955.

——. *Textual and Literary Criticism.* 1959.

Bradbrook, M. C. *The Rise of the Common Player: A Study of Actor and Society in Shakespeare's England.* 1962.

——. *English Dramatic Form: A History of Its Development.* 1965.

Bridges-Adams, W. *The Irresistible Theatre.* 1957.

Briggs, K. M. *Pale Hecate's Team: An Examination of the Beliefs on Witchcraft and Magic among Shakespeare's Contemporaries and His Immediate Successors.*1962.

Brodwin, Leonora Leet. *Elizabethan Love Tragedy, 1587-1625.* 1971.

Brown, Arthur. "Studies in Elizabethan and Jacobean Drama since 1900." *ShS* 14 (1961): 1-14.

Campbell, Lily B. "Theories of Revenge in Renaissance England." *MP* 28 (1931): 281–96.

Cazamian, Louis. *The Development of English Humor.* 1952.

Cecil, Lord David. *The Fine Art of Reading, and Other Literary Studies.* 1957.

Clarkson, Paul S., and Warren, Clyde T. *The Law of Property in Shakespeare and the Elizabethan Drama.* 1942.

Cookman, A. V. "Shakespeare's Contemporaries on the Modern English Stage." *SJ* 94 (1958): 29–41.

Crane, Milton. *Shakespeare's Prose.* 1951.

Davison, Peter. "La dramaturgie en Angleterre à la veille de la Guerre Civile: John Ford et la comédie." In *Dramaturgie et société: Rapports entre l'oeuvre théâtrale, son interprétation et son public aux XVIᵉ et XVIIᵉ siècles,* ed. Jean Jacquot (1968), vol. 2, pp. 805–14.

Davril, Robert. "Swinburne et Ford." *Letterature Moderne* 44 (1950): 114–15.

Dessen, Alan C. *Jonson's Moral Comedy.* 1971.

Doran, Madeleine. *Endeavors of Art: A Study of Form in Elizabethan Drama.* 1954.

Downer, Alan S. *The British Drama: A Handbook and Brief Chronicle.* 1950.

Farnham, Willard. *The Medieval Heritage of Elizabethan Tragedy.* 1936.

Fraser, Russell. "Elizabethan Drama and the Art of Abstraction." *CompD* 2 (1968): 73–82.

Freehafer, John. "Leonard Digges, Ben Jonson, and the Beginning of Shakespeare Idolatry." *SQ* 21 (1970): 63–75.

Frost, David L. *The School of Shakespeare: The Influence of Shakespeare on English Drama, 1600–42.* 1968.

Green, A. Wigfall. *The Inns of Court and Early English Drama.* 1931.

Greg, W. W. *Some Aspects and Problems of London Publishing between 1550 and 1650.* 1956.

Gurr, Andrew. *The Shakespearean Stage, 1574–1642.* 1970.

Harbage, Alfred. *Cavalier Drama: An Historical and Critical Supplement to the Study of the Elizabethan and Restoration Stage.* 1936.

——. *Shakespeare and the Rival Traditions.* 1952.

Hawkins, Harriett. "What Kind of Pre-contract Had Angelo? A Note on Some Non-problems in Elizabethan Drama." *CE* 36 (1974): 173–79.

Haydn, Hiram. *The Counter-Renaissance.* 1950.

Hodges, C. Walter. *The Globe Restored: A Study of the Elizabethan Theatre.* 1953; 2nd ed. 1968.

——. *Shakespeare's Second Globe: The Missing Monument.* 1973.

Holzknecht, Karl J. *Outlines of Tudor and Stuart Plays, 1497–1642.* 1947. ['Tis Pity; Broken Heart; Perkin Warbeck; Witch of Edmonton]

Hoskins, Frank L. "Misalliance: A Significant Theme in Tudor and Stuart Drama." *RenP,* 1956, pp. 72–81.

Hunter, G. K. "The Marking of Sententiae." *Library* 6 (1951): 171–88.

Hyde, Mary Crapo. *Playwriting for Elizabethans, 1600–1605.* 1949.

Lauren, Barbara. "John Ford: A Caroline Alternative to Beaumont and Fletcher." *Modern Language Studies* 5 (1975): 53–66.

Lawrence, W. J. *Those Nut-Cracking Elizabethans: Studies of the Early Theatre and Drama.* 1935.

Leech, Clifford. *John Ford*. WTW, no. 170 (1964).

Lever, J. W. *The Tragedy of State*. 1971.

Lievsay, John L. *The Elizabethan Image of Italy*. 1964.

Linthicum, M. Channing. *Costume in the Drama of Shakespeare and His Contemporaries*. 1936.

McCullen, Joseph T., Jr. "Madness and the Isolation of Characters in Elizabethan and Early Stuart Drama." *SP* 48 (1951): 206–18.

McDonald, Charles Osborne. *The Rhetoric of Tragedy: Form in Stuart Drama*. 1966.

Manifold, J. S. *The Music in English Drama from Shakespeare to Purcell*. 1956.

Mehl, Dieter. *The Elizabethan Dumb Show: The History of a Dramatic Convention*. 1965; German ed. 1964.

Nicoll, Allardyce. *The Elizabethans*. 1957.

Oras, Ants. *Pause Patterns in Elizabethan and Jacobean Drama: An Experiment in Prosody*. 1960.

Orsini, Napoleone. "'Policy': Or the Language of Elizabethan Machiavellianism." *JWCI* 9 (1946): 122–34.

Partridge, A. C. *Orthography in Shakespeare and Elizabethan Drama: A Study of Colloquial Contractions, Elision, Prosody, and Punctuation*. 1964.

Praz, Mario. *Il dramma elisabettiano: Webster-Ford*. 1946.

Quennell, Peter. *The Singular Preference: Portraits and Essays*. 1952.

Ramsey, Jarold W. "The Provenance of *Troilus and Cressida*." *SQ* 21 (1970): 223–40.

Reed, Robert Rentoul, Jr. *The Occult on the Tudor and Stuart Stage*. 1965.

Rocco-Bergera, Niny. *John Ford*. 1962.

Saagpakk, Paul F. "A Survey of Psychopathology in British Literature from Shakespeare to Hardy." *L&P* 18 (1968): 135–65.

Salingar, L. G. "The Decline of Tragedy." In *The Age of Shakespeare* (1955; vol. 2 of *A Guide to English Literature*, ed. Boris Ford), pp. 429–40.

Sasayama, Takashi. "A Note on 'Decadence' in John Ford's Tragedies." *SELit*, English Number (1966): 1–14.

Sensabaugh, G. F. "John Ford and Platonic Love in the Court." *SP* 36 (1939): 206–26.

———. "John Ford and Elizabethan Tragedy." *PQ* 20 (1941): 442–53.

———. "John Ford Revisited." *SEL* 4 (1964): 195–216.

Silvette, Herbert. *The Doctor on the Stage: Medicine and Medical Men in Seventeenth-Century England*. 1967.

Smet, Robert de [Romain Sanvic]. *Le théâtre élisabéthain*. 1955.

Spencer, Theodore. *Death and Elizabethan Tragedy: A Study of Convention and Opinion in the Elizabethan Drama*. 1936.

Spencer, T. J. B. "Shakespeare v. the Rest: The Old Controversy." *ShS* 14 (1961): 76–89.

Stroup, Thomas B. *Microcosmos: The Shape of the Elizabethan Play*. 1965.

Sugden, Edward H. *A Topographical Dictionary to the Works of Shakespeare and His Fellow Dramatists*. 1925.

Sypher, Wylie. *Four Stages of Renaissance Style: Transformations in Art and Literature, 1400–1700*. 1955.

Tayler, Edward William. *Nature and Art in Renaissance Literature*. 1964.

Taylor, Michael. "The Conflict in *Hamlet*." *SQ* 22 (1971): 147–61.

Tilley, Morris Palmer. *A Dictionary of the Proverbs in England in the Sixteenth and Seventeenth Centuries: A Collection of the Proverbs Found in English Literature and the Dictionaries of the Period*. 1950.

Venezky, Alice S. *Pageantry on the Shakespearean Stage*. 1951.

Waith, Eugene M. *The Herculean Hero in Marlowe, Chapman, Shakespeare, and Dryden*. 1962.

Wickham, Glynne. *Early English Stages, 1300–1660*. 2 vols. 1959–72.

Wilcox, John. "On Reading John Ford." *SAB* 21 (1946): 66–75.

Wilson, F. P. *Elizabethan and Jacobean*. 1945.

Young, Steven C. *The Frame Structure in Tudor and Stuart Drama*. Salzburg Studies in English Literature: Jacobean Drama Studies, no. 6 (1974).

Zanco, Aurelio. *Il teatro di John Ford*. 1950.

———. "Modernità di John Ford." *Ulisse* 10 (1956): 1097–1105.

B. INDIVIDUAL PLAYS

'Tis Pity She's a Whore

Andrieu, Lucette. *Dommage qu'elle soit une p . . .* (*'Tis Pity She's a Whore*) de John Ford: Vitalité et devenir scénique de la tragédie." *Cahiers Elisabéthains* 3(1973): 16–40.

Bawcutt, N. W. "Seneca and Ford's *'Tis Pity She's a Whore*." *N&Q* 14 (1967): 215.

Felperin, Howard. "Shakespeare's Miracle Play." *SQ* 18 (1967): 363–74.

Hobbs, Mary. "Robert and Thomas Ellice, Friends of Ford and Davenant." *N&Q* 21 (1974): 292–93.

Jacquot, Jean. "International Notes." *ShS* 15 (1962): 132–33.

Johnson, Jeffrey L. "The Spoils of Love and Vengeance: A Study of the Jacobean Revenge Tragedy Motivated by Lust." *Xavier University Studies* 7 (1968): 31–43.

Kroll, Jack. "The Final Explosion." *Newsweek*, 30 Oct. 1967, p. 92.

Levin, Richard. "'The Ass in Compound': A Lost Pun in Middleton, Ford, and Jonson." *ELN* 4 (1966): 12–15.

MacCarthy, Desmond. "The Tragedy of Evil." *New Statesman and Nation*, 18 May 1940, pp. 641–42.

Ravignani, Donatella. "Ford e Burton: Riesame di un rapporto." *EM* 17 (1966): 211–47.

Ribner, Irving. "By Nature's Light: The Morality of *'Tis Pity She's a Whore*." *TSE* 10 (1960): 39–50.

Rubenstein, Roberta. "Virginia Woolf and Anna Karenina." *Descant* 16 (1972): 37–41.

Woolf, Virginia. *The Common Reader*. 1925.

The Broken Heart

Feldman, A. Bronson. "The Yellow Malady: Short Studies of Five Tragedies of Jealousy." *L&P* 6 (1956): 38–52.

Hartnoll, Phyllis. "Library Drama Comes to Life." *Theatre Arts*, Dec. 1959, pp. 79–81 and 83.

Novarr, David. "'Gray Dissimulation': Ford and Milton." *PQ* 41 (1962): 500–504.

Pellizzi, Giovanna. "The Speech of Ithocles on Ambition in Ford's *The Broken Heart*." *EM* 20 (1969): 93–99.

Presson, Robert K. "Two Types of Dreams in the Elizabethan Drama, and Their Heritage: Somnium Animale and the Prick-of-Conscience." *SEL* 7 (1967): 239–56.

Perkin Warbeck

Kistner, A. L. and M. K. "The Fine Balance of Imposture in John Ford's *Perkin Warbeck*." *ES* 52 (1971): 419–23.

Maxwell, J. C. "A Neglected Emendation in Ford's *Perkin Warbeck*." *N&Q* 17 (1970): 215.

Sanna, Vittoria. "Problemi e aspetti del *Perkin Warbeck*." *AION-SG* 8 (1965): 117–73.

Ure, Peter. "'Addition' (*Troilus and Cressida*, IV.v.141)." *N&Q* 13 (1966): 135.

Weathers, Winston. "*Perkin Warbeck*: A Seventeenth-Century Psychological Play." *SEL* 4 (1964): 217–26.

Love's Sacrifice

Johnson, S. F. "'A Table of Green Fields' Once More." *SQ* 10 (1959): 450–51.

Sensabaugh, G. F. "Ford's Tragedy of Love-Melancholy." *Englische Studien* 73 (1939): 212–19.

The Lover's Melancholy

Findlay, Robert R. "Macklin's 1748 Adaptation of Ford's *The Lover's Melancholy*." *Restoration and 18th Century Theatre Research* 8 (1969): 13–22.

Leech, Clifford. "A Projected Restoration Performance of Ford's *The Lover's Melancholy*?" *MLR* 56 (1961): 378–81.

Sutton, Juliet. "Ford's Use of Burton's Imagery." *N&Q* 10 (1963): 415.

The Witch of Edmonton

West, Edward Sackville. "The Significance of *The Witch of Edmonton*." *Criterion* 17 (1937): 23–32.

The Lady's Trial

Cutts, John P. "British Museum Additional Ms. 31432: William Lawes' Writing for the Theatre and the Court." *Library* 7 (1952): 225–34.

The Late Murder of the Son upon the Mother

Forker, C. R. "*Wit without Money*: A Fletcherian Antecedent to *Keep the Widow Waking*." *CompD* 8 (1974): 172–83.

The Spanish Gypsy

Burelbach, Frederick M., Jr. "Theme and Structure in *The Spanish Gypsy*." *HAB* 19 (1968): 37–41.

JAMES SHIRLEY

Albert Wertheim

The standard edition of the plays, masks, and poems is William Gifford and Alexander Dyce's *The Dramatic Works and Poems of James Shirley*, 6 vols. (1833; rpt. 1966). A selection of plays for the Mermaid series (1888) was edited by Edmund Gosse; *The Poems of James Shirley* (1941) was edited by Ray Livingstone Armstrong. An old-spelling edition, with textual and expository notes, of all the plays, masks, and poems, edited by Richard E. Morton for the Clarendon Press's Oxford English Dramatists series, is currently in progress.

I. GENERAL

A. BIOGRAPHICAL

Arthur Huntington Nason's *James Shirley Dramatist* (1915; rpt. 1967) continues to offer the most complete biography of Shirley. Biography, however, comprises only one of the three parts of Nason's book and concerns itself mostly with recorded data on the life of Shirley, and on the presentation and publication of the plays; Nason has little to say about Shirley's associates, the Caroline theatre, or the times in which Shirley lived. The second section of Nason's study is a plot summary of the dramatic works, and the third is a bibliographic list.

J. Schipper's *James Shirley: sein Leben und seine Werke* (1911) is also divided into three sections. The first is devoted to biography but is not as complete as Nason's. The second section offers plot summaries of Shirley's plays; and the third is a translation into German of *The Royal Master*.

Providing useful biographical information on Shirley's years in Ireland are four articles by Allan H. Stevenson: "James Shirley and the Actors of the First Irish Theatre," *MP* 40 (1942): 147-60; "Shirley's Years in Ireland," *RES* 20 (1944): 19-28; "Shirley's Publishers: The

Partnership of Crooke and Cooke," *Library* 25 (1945): 140-61; and "Shirley's Dedications and the Date of his Return to England," *MLN* 61 (1946): 140-61.

A chronological list of biographical data is provided by F. G. Fleay, "Annals of the Careers of James and Henry Shirley," *Anglia* 8 (1885): 405-14.

B. GENERAL STUDIES OF THE PLAYS

A thorough critical study of Shirley's plays has not yet been written. Nason and Schipper (I,A) provide only plot outlines of the dramatic works. Robert Stanley Forsythe, *The Relations of Shirley's Plays to the Elizabethan Drama* (1914) attempts to demonstrate that Shirley's plays are "the aggregate, the sum total, of the similar plays, incidents, or characters, of earlier and contemporary playwrights." Forsythe first provides plot outlines for all of Shirley's plays and follows this with an outline of analogues, taken from 520 Elizabethan plays, for every major incident and scene. The amount of information in this study is staggering, but the book is more worthwhile as a catalogue of stock scenes in Elizabethan drama than as a discussion of Shirley's plays. More recently, Anna Maria Crinò has provided a short general survey of the works in *James Shirley: Drammaturgo di corte* (1968) as has Richard Gerber in *James Shirley Dramatiker der Dekadenz* (1952).

The best discussions of Shirley's plays are those limited to an examination of a particular group of plays or to a particular aspect of Shirley's drama. Karl Roeloffs, *James Shirleys Beitrag zur Entwicklung der "Comedy of Manners"* (1959) is a good example of such a study. It traces Shirley's comedies back to the humours comedies of Jonson and shows as well that especially *The Witty Fair One*, *Hyde Park*, and *The Lady of Pleasure* look ahead to the comedies of Wycherley, Etherege, and Congreve. This point is made in the second chapter of Kathleen Lynch, *The Social Mode of Restoration Comedy* (1926), and the last chapters of Dale Underwood, *Etherege and the Seventeenth-Century Comedy of Manners* (1957).

Richard Morton discusses the failure of communication between different social levels in Shirley's plays in "Deception and Dislocation: An Aspect of James Shirley's Drama," *RenD* 9 (1966): 227-45; and Shirley's plays are used as an index of the playwright's attitude toward the Caroline court and toward his own preferment there in Marvin Morillo, "Shirley's 'Preferment' and the Court of Charles I," *SEL* 1 (1961): 101-17. Juliet McGrath, "Shirley's Use of Language," *SEL* 6 (1966):

323-39, argues that Shirley uses noticeably colorless language in his plays and that his "distrust of language handicaps him in his presentation of character, and the consistent separation he maintains between thought and the verbal expression of that thought precludes well-developed conceptual or philosophical emphases in the plays."

The later reputation of Shirley and the stage history of his plays is the subject of Gebhard Josef Scherrer, *James Shirleys Nachruhm* (1951); and the particular effect of Shirley's drama upon sentimental comedies of the early eighteenth century is discussed by Robert R. Reed, "James Shirley and the Sentimental Comedy," *Anglia* 73 (1955): 149-70. A section on Shirley's tragicomedies appears in Marvin T. Herrick, *Tragicomedy: Its Origin and Development in Italy, France, and England* (1955), but Herrick merely provides plot outlines for the tragicomedies he surveys.

Valuable information has come to light on the reaction to some of Shirley's plays by one of his contemporaries, Abraham Wright (1611-90), whose commonplace book, "Excerpta Quaedam per A. W. Adolescentem" is part of Add. MS. 22068 of the British Museum. That manuscript and its importance is made clear in James G. McManaway, "Excerpta Quaedam per A. W. Adolscentem," in *Studies in Honor of De-Witt T. Starnes*, ed. Thomas P. Harrison et al. (1967), pp. 117-29. McManaway describes the manuscript, dates it no earlier than 1639, and explains that it contains quotations from works of the period, primarily plays. Of the twenty-eight plays Wright mentions, quotes from, and comments upon, eleven are by Shirley, who seems to have been Wright's favorite playwright. The Shirley works in Wright's commonplace book are: *The Traitor, Hyde Park, The Contention for Honour and Riches, Changes, Bird in a Cage, Young Admiral, Lady of Pleasure, Royal Master, Wedding, School of Compliment*, and *Gentleman of Venice*. Arthur C. Kirsch, "A Caroline Commentary on the Drama," *MP* 66 (1969): 256-61 reproduces Wright's remarks on each of the plays. Kirsch concludes that what Wright admired most was the tradition of tragicomedy established by Beaumont and Fletcher and maintained by Shirley. Wright is especially enthusiastic about *The Young Admiral*; his reaction to it is illuminating not only for Shirley's dramaturgy but for the whole tragicomic tradition from Fletcher to Dryden.

C. THE WORKS AT LARGE

A brief assessment of Shirley as a poet is given in the general introduction to Ray Livingstone Armstrong's edition of *The Poems of James Shirley* (1941). G. E. Bentley prints eight previously unpublished poems and uses them to show Shirley's affiliation with Thomas Stanley during the early Commonwealth period in "James Shirley and a Group of Unnoted Poems on the Wedding of Thomas Stanley," *HLQ* 2 (1938-39): 219-31. *Narcissus, or The Self-Lover* is reprinted in Elizabeth Story Donno's anthology of Ovidian epics, *Elizabethan Minor Epics* (1963); the introduction to this anthology mentions that Shirley's poem was modeled on Shakespeare's *Venus and Adonis*. *Narcissus* is also briefly noted in Douglas Bush's *Mythology and Renaissance Tradition* (1932; rev. ed. 1963). John P. Cutts, "British Museum Additional MS. 31432, William Lawes' Writing for the Theatre and the Court," *Library* 7 (1952): 225-34, has found some musical settings for two poems.

Vivian Salmon, "James Shirley and Some Problems of Seventeenth-Century Grammar," *Archiv* 197 (1961): 287-96, explores some specialized problems, using the school texts Shirley wrote during his years as a schoolmaster after the closing of the theaters.

II. CRITICISM OF INDIVIDUAL PLAYS AND STATE OF SCHOLARSHIP

A. INDIVIDUAL PLAYS

The Lady of Pleasure

The comic structure of *The Lady of Pleasure* is treated in Richard Levin, *The Multiple Plot in English Renaissance Drama* (1971), and a short but perceptive treatment of its particular relation to the Restoration comedy of manners is given by Dale Underwood, *Etherege and the Seventeenth-Century Comedy of Manners* (1957). George Sensabaugh, "Platonic Love in Shirley's *The Lady of Pleasure*" in *A Tribute to George Coffin Taylor*, ed. Arnold Williams (1952), pp. 168-77, explores the possibility that the play is a commentary on the Platonic love cult that flourished in the Caroline court under Queen Henrietta Maria. In C. S. Lewis's essay "Variation in Shakespeare and Others" that appeared in his collection *Rehabilitations and Other Essays* (1939), *The Lady of Pleasure* is singled out for scorn. Looking at speeches which list London vices, Lewis concludes that in *The Lady of Pleasure* Shirley as a dramatist has, on the whole, extremely little to say and that he stretches out that little through variation, repeating the same idea again and again.

Hyde Park

Richard Levin, "The Triple Plot of *Hyde Park*," *MLR* 62 (1967): 17–27, describes the three disparate plots of *Hyde Park* and argues for their thematic unity through analogous action. Each plot, argues Levin, is "constructed about a love-triangle involving a woman and two male rivals," and each plot turns on a surprising change in the woman's position within the triangle. The setting of the play within London's Hyde Park provides a backdrop for all three plots, which Levin describes as high comedy appealing to the intellect, sentimental comedy appealing to ethical sensibilities, and simple situation comedy. He then demonstrates that "the separate comic levels are brought into a functional relationship by the analogical scheme of comparisons and contrasts, so that our response to each of them is qualified by our response to the others." Levin reiterates his argument more briefly in *The Multiple Plot in English Renaissance Drama* (1971).

The most extensive discussion of *Hyde Park* is Albert Wertheim's "Games and Courtship in James Shirley's *Hyde Park*," *Anglia* 90 (1972): 71–91. Like Levin, Wertheim concentrates on the analogous action of the comedy's three plots. During the course of *Hyde Park*, horse and foot races are being carried on and in them a "dark horse" contender triumphs. Wertheim sees these races and their outcomes as an appropriate background for the play's three plots, in each of which a surprising "dark horse" suitor wins the hand of a lady. Each of the comedy's plots is, further, shot through with the language and imagery of sports and games; and each of the plot structures is based upon games, tricks, and trials.

The comic dialogue and the relationship of *Hyde Park* to the later comedies of language in the Restoration is the subject of Richard Gerber, "Shirleys Komodiendialog und der Welt am Hyde Park," *SJH* 95 (1959): 98–111. The use of Hyde Park as the physical location for the comedy is treated in Theodore Miles, "Place-Realism in a Group of Caroline Plays," *RES* 18 (1942): 428–40.

The Cardinal

Fredson Bowers, in *Elizabethan Revenge Tragedy 1587–1642*(1940), discusses *The Cardinal* as a "coherent Kydian revenge tragedy, polished and simplified in his best manner." Bowers's comments are reprinted in Max Bluestone and Norman Rabkin, ed., *Shakespeare's Contemporaries* (1961, pp. 295–300; 2nd ed., 1970, pp. 406–11). The most detailed treatment of the play, however, is provided by Charles R. Forker in the introduction to his edition (1964). He discusses the specific problems facing an editor of *The Cardinal*, comments on the possible topical references and dramatic sources, and shows how Shirley both adheres to and departs from conventional revenge tragedy traditions. In "Shirley's *The Cardinal*: Some Problems and Cruces," *N&Q* 6 (1959): 232-33, Forker clears up some problems about which characters are actually present on stage during the play's fatal mask in Act III; and in "The Death of Hernando in Shirley's *Cardinal*," *N&Q* 12 (1965): 342-43, Frank Manley provides a convincing argument that Hernando's death may not be suicide, as the Gifford and Dyce stage directions would have us believe, but the result of wounds inflicted by Antonelli and the Cardinal's servants. That Archbishop Laud may be the model for Shirley's eponymous villain, a suggestion later reiterated in his edition, is the subject of Charles Forker's "Bishop Laud and Shirley's *The Cardinal*," *Transactions of the Wisconsin Academy of Sciences Arts and Letters* 47 (1958): 241-51.

The Triumph of Peace

By far the most thorough and illuminating research on *The Triumph of Peace* has been done by the musicologist Murray Lefkowitz. In his chapter on the masks in his *William Lawes* (1960), he provides the general political background for the occasion of *The Triumph of Peace*. Then, drawing upon the material in *Memorials of the English Affairs* (1682) by Bulstrode Whitelocke, who was a musician, a parlimentarian, the representative from one of the Inns of Court producing the music, and the person in charge of the musical arrangments for the mask, Lefkowitz provides a vivid description of what the mask must have been like in performance. He gives as well some analysis of William Lawes's music for the mask. In "The Longleat Papers of Bulstrode Whitelocke: New Light on Shirley's *Triumph of Peace*," *Journal of the American Musicological Society* 18 (1965): 42-60, Lefkowitz recounts his discovery at Longleat of Whitelocke's unpublished papers. These provide a treasure trove for students of the Caroline mask in general and of *The Triumph of Peace* in particular, for Whitelocke's papers contain a cast list, the names and voice parts of all singers, the names and instruments of all the musicians, diagrams with musicians' names for soloists and chorus positions during the mask, a cue sheet for the serious part of the mask, names of musicians who played at the Blackfriars and Cockpit, as well as other data relating to the music and musicians. Lefkowitz's article is accompanied by several photographic reproductions from the papers, some of which show the staging for musicians complete with an indication of which particular musicians stood where. In *Trois masques a la cour de Charles Ier D'Angleterre* (1970), Lefkowitz gives his fullest treatment of *The Triumph of Peace*, with a discussion of the mask and a descriptive reconstruction of its performance. He provides as well the complete text and Lawes's music for the songs. The music for two of those songs appears as well in Andrew J. Sabol's *Songs and Dances for the Stuart Masque* (1959).

The Triumph of Peace and Shirley's reliance upon Jonson's techniques are discussed in Enid Welsford, *The Court Masque* (1927), but the fullest discussion of the mask's complexity, allegory, and political statement is made in Stephen Orgel and Roy Strong, *Inigo Jones*, 2 vols. (1973). Orgel also provides a short historical background on *The Triumph of Peace* in *The Illusion of Power: Political Theater in the English Renaissance* (1975). Similar background material as well as the surviving Inigo Jones designs for the mask are given in John Harris, Stephen Orgel, and Roy Strong, *The King's Arcadia: Inigo Jones and the Stuart Court* (1973). A sound reconstruction of the mask can be found in Allardyce Nicoll, *Stuart Masques and the Renaissance Stage* (1938). There is also much useful information in *Designs by Inigo Jones for Masques and Plays at Court*, ed. Percy Simpson and C. F. Bell (1924), though this volume has been largely superseded by Orgel and Strong. The mask and its music are described in Edward J. Dent, *Foundations of English Opera* (1928), and notes for a 1974 production may be found in Robert K. Sarlos, "From Historical to Modern Production: A Stuart Masque," in *Regie in Dokumentation, Forschung und Lehre*, ed. Margaret Dietrich (1975).

The Traitor

As a preface for discussing Richard Lalor Sheil's *Evadne* (1819), an adaptation of *The Traitor*, Joseph W. Donohue, *Dramatic Character in the English Romantic Age* (1970), provides a discussion of the dramatic strategies of Shirley's play. Donohue argues that the strength of *The Traitor* lies "in a highly theatrical presentation of shocking and pathetic events and equally unprepared reversals of character" and that the situations of the play provide dramatic tests for the goodness or villainy of the characters and provide as well a basis for character reversals.

The place of *The Traitor* in Elizabethan revenge tradition is discussed by Fredson Bowers, *Elizabethan Revenge Tragedy 1587-1642* (1940). Bowers sees Lorenzo as a typical Machiavellian villain and feels that in the figure of Sciarrha, Shirley is indebted to Foreste in Davenant's *Cruel Brother*. A. P. Riemer, "A Source for Shirley's *The Traitor*," *RES* 14 (1963): 380-83, shows that the secondary plot of *The Traitor* is based upon Shirley's reading of the murder of Buondelmonte in Thomas Bedingfield's translation (1595) of Machiavelli's *Le istorie fiorentine*.

St. Patrick for Ireland

In the context of their histories of the Irish theater, *St. Patrick for Ireland* is discussed by William Smith Clark, *The Early Irish Stage* (1955), and La Tourette Stockwell, *Dublin Theatres and Theatre Customs* (1938). A brief sketch of the play is also provided by John Eglinton (pseud. for William Kirkpatrick Magee), *Anglo-Irish Essays* (1917). Hugh MacMullan, "The Sources of Shirley's *St. Patrick for Ireland*," *PMLA* 48 (1933): 806-14, shows that Jocelyn's account of St. Patrick's life was obviously Shirley's source for the play.

The fullest discussion of *St. Patrick* is that by Albert Wertheim, "The Presentation of James Shirley's *St. Patrick for Ireland* at the First Irish Playhouse," *N&Q* 14 (1967): 212-15. Wertheim concentrates particularly upon the range of theatrical tricks and stage devices used by Shirley ostensibly to win the favor of the audience at the St. Werburgh Street Theatre, Dublin, for whom this play was written. In a reply to Wertheim's article, Elizabeth M. McConnell, *N&Q* 15 (1968): 268-69, asserts that the emphasis of the play is less upon spectacular stage effects than upon Christian miracles.

The Ball

Hanson T. Parlin's *A Study in Shirley's Comedies of London Life* (1914) is primarily a discussion of *The Ball*; Parlin examines Chapman's practice as a comic playwright in order to dismiss the claim that Chapman may have had a share in the writing of the play. Parlin provides as well a good deal of general and historical background for the play. The presentation of *The Ball* on the Restoration stage and its appropriateness for a Restoration audience is the subject of Dana G. McKinnen, "A Description of a Restoration Promptbook of Shirley's *The Ball*," *Restoration and Eighteenth-Century Theatre Research* 19 (1971): 25-28.

The Constant Maid

A. P. Riemer convincingly argues that *The Constant Maid* was written early in the 1630s rather than in 1636-40 in "Shirley's Revisions and the Date of *The Constant Maid*," *RES* 17 (1966): 141-48.

The Contention of Ajax and Ulysses

Edwin F. Ochester, "A Source for Shirley's *The Contention of Ajax and Ulysses*," *N&Q* 17 (1970): 217, points to Book xiii of Ovid's *Metamorphoses* as a probable source.

Cupid and Death

Edward J. Dent has reproduced the Gifford and Dyce text together with the complete musical score by Matthew Locke and Christopher Gibbons in an edition of *Cupid and Death* appearing in *Musica Brittanica*, vol. 2 (1951). In his preface to the text, Dent provides an outline of the mask with emphasis on its music as well as its stage history. In general, Dent feels that *Cupid and Death* "is much more like a Court Masque than any of Shirley's other school Masques."

The Duke's Mistress

Using the subplot of *The Duke's Mistress* as his example, Peter Ure provides a useful footnote on the relationship between the deformed mistress theme and its relevance to Platonic preciosité in "The 'Deformed Mistress' Theme and the Platonic Convention," *N&Q* 193 (1948): 269-70.

The Gamester

Shirley's use of the bed trick in *The Gamester* is the subject of Richard Levin, "'Measure beyond Measure' and *The Gamester*," *RN* 18 (1965): 1-3.

Love Tricks or The School of Compliment

According to C. R. Baskervill, "The Source of the Main Plot of Shirley's *Love Tricks*," *MLN* 24 (1909): 100-101, Shirley drew his material for this play from "Of Phylotus and Emilia," the eighth history in Barnabe Riche's *Farewell to Militarie Profession*.

The Sisters

A Restoration promptbook of *The Sisters* first mentioned in Gifford and Dyce is discussed by Montague Summers in "A Restoration Prompt Book," *TLS*, 24 June 1920, p. 400. It is examined in some detail by Edward A. Langhans, "The Restoration Promptbook of Shirley's *The Sisters*," *Theatre Annual* 14 (1956): 51-65.

The Triumph of Beauty

The Triumph of Beauty has received the barest notice from mask scholars. The composer for its music, however, has been discovered in recent years to have been William Lawes, who also provided the music for *The Triumph of Peace*: see Murray Lefkowitz, "New Facts Concerning William Lawes and the Caroline Masque," *Music and Letters* 40 (1959): 324-33.

The Wedding

Alfred Harbage, "Shirley's *The Wedding* and the Marriage of Sir Kenelm Digby," *PQ* 16 (1937): 35-40, asserts that "no member of the fashionable world of London . . . could have read this play . . . without thinking of the affair of Sir Kenelm Digby and Venetia Stanley."

B. STATE OF SCHOLARSHIP

It is astonishing how very little of substance has been wirtten about James Shirley; in fact, it is astonishing how very little of anything has been written about Shirley. Richard Morton's article (I,B), which treats a limited topic, is one of the few pieces in recent decades that attempts an overview of the plays. Yet of the authors writing for the Caroline stage, Shirley was clearly the most popular; the admiration expressed by Andrew Wright (I,B) is probably typical of the sentiments of audiences in the private playhouses that supported Shirley's many plays, rivalled in number only by those of Shakespeare and by the combined efforts of Beaumont and Fletcher and their collaborators. Shirley wrote more plays in more different genres than any other single playwright of his time. The large number of plays means that there is an excellent opportunity for studying Shirley in considerable detail—and not only Shirley, but also the nature of the Caroline stage and the tastes of its audiences. As yet none of these possibilities has been explored.

III. CANON

A. PLAYS AND MASKS IN CHRONOLOGICAL ORDER

The source for the type of play, the acting date (in italics preceding semicolon), and the original date of publication, as well as information on lost plays, is Alfred Harbage, *Annals of English Drama, 975–1700*, rev. S. Schoenbaum (1964), and the *Supplements* by Schoenbaum (1966, 1970). Readers are also directed to G. E. Bentley, *The Jacobean and Caroline Stage*, vol. 5 (1956).

St. Albans, tragedy (ca. *1625–40;* lost)

The only record of this play is in the Stationers' Register for 14 February 1639/40, entered to William Cooke.

The School of Compliment (Love Tricks), comedy (*licensed 11 Feb. 1625;* 1631)

The Brothers, unknown (*licensed 4 Nov. 1626;* lost)

There is much uncertainty about this play. A play entitled *The Brothers* was licensed by Sir Henry Herbert in 1626; but a play entitled *The Brothers* was published in Shirley's *Six New Playes* (1653) and bears a separate title page giving the date 1652. It seems likely that *The Brothers* of 1626 is lost and that *The Brothers* of 1641 is identical with a play called *The Politique Father*, licensed in 1641 but never printed under that title. It has also been suggested that the 1626 play was revised as *The Politique Father*. In his article on *The Wedding*, Alfred Harbage (II,A) suggests that *The Brothers* may be an alternate title for *The Wedding*.

The Maid's Revenge, tragedy (*licensed 9 Feb. 1626;* 1639)

The Wedding, comedy (*1626–29;* 1629)

Since there is no license date for this comedy, Harbage (II,A) speculates that it may be identical with *The Brothers* licensed in 1626 but for which there is no performance record.

The Witty Fair One, comedy (*licensed 3 Oct. 1628;* 1633)

The Grateful Servant (The Faithful Servant), tragicomedy (*licensed 3 Nov. 1629;* 1630)

Bentley suggests that this play was licensed under the title *The Faithful Servant.*

The Contention for Honour and Riches, moral (ca. *1625–32;* 1633)

The Humorous Courtier (The Duke), comedy (*licensed 17 May 1631;* 1640)

Love's Cruelty, tragedy (*licensed 14 Nov. 1631;* 1640)

The Traitor, tragedy (*licensed 4 May 1631;* 1635)

The Ball, comedy (*licensed 16 Nov. 1632;* 1639)

Some confusion about the authorship of this play has occurred because the 1639 title page ascribes it to George Chapman and James Shirley. Hanson T. Parlin (II,A) does not altogether discount Chapman as a possible author for this play, but the view of both Thomas Marc Parrott, in his edition of *The Plays of George Chapman: The Comedies,* 2 vols. (1913), and of Allan H. Stevenson, in "Shirley's Publishers" (I,A), is that the joint ascription is a publisher's error.

The Changes, or Love in a Maze, comedy (*licensed 10 Jan. 1632;* 1632)

Hyde Park, comedy (*licensed 20 April 1632;* 1637)

The Bird in a Cage (The Beauties), comedy (*licensed 21 Jan. 1633;* 1633)

This play was probably licensed under the title *The Beauties,* as Bentley (III,A) suggests.

The Gamester, comedy (*licensed 11 Nov. 1633;* 1637)

The Young Admiral, tragicomedy (*licensed 3 July 1633;* 1637)

The Example, comedy (*licensed 24 June 1634;* 1637)

The Opportunity, comedy (*licensed 29 Nov. 1634;* 1640)

The Triumph of Peace, mask (*licensed 3 Feb. 1634;* 1634)

The Coronation, comedy (*licensed 6 Feb. 1635;* 1640)

The 1653 edition of Shirley's *Six New Plays* bears a statement that *The Coronation* had been falsely ascribed to John Fletcher, and *The Coronation* was later published in the 1679 Beaumont and Fletcher second folio. There is almost no question, however, that *The Coronation* is Shirley's play: see Bentley (III,A).

The Lady of Pleasure, comedy (*licensed 15 Oct. 1635;* 1637)

The Duke's Mistress, tragicomedy (*licensed 18 Jan. 1636;* 1638)

The Royal Master, comedy (*1637;* 1638)

Allan H. Stevenson, "James Shirley and the Actors at the First Irish Theatre" (I,A) claims that *The Royal Master* was the first play at the new St. Werburgh Street playhouse in Dublin in 1637. It was licensed a year later for its London performance. See Bentley (III,A).

The Constant Maid (Love Will Find out the Way), comedy (ca. *1630–40;* 1640)

No license exists for this comedy and it may have been first produced, therefore, at the St. Werburgh Street playhouse in Dublin. The limits for this play are given as 1636?–40 in *The Annals,* but S. Schoenbaum revises the limits to ca. 1630–40 in the second *Supplement* (1970) to the *Annals* in accord with A. P. Riemer's article (II,A) which gives evidence that *The Constant Maid* was written early in the 1630s.

The Doubtful Heir (Rosania, or Love's Victory), tragicomedy (ca. *1638;* 1653)

This play was originally presented at the St. Werburgh Street playhouse in Dublin and Shirley provides a prologue for it under the name *Rosania, or Love's Victory.* The title was licensed in London by Sir Henry Herbert in 1640 also under the title *Rosania;* it was, however, changed to *The Doubtful Heir* after the licensing and before the protecting of the repertory of the King's company in 1641. The play is published as *The Doubtful Heir* in Shirley's *Six New Plays* (1653). See Bentley (III,A).

The Gentleman of Venice, tragicomedy (*licensed 30 Oct. 1639;* 1655)

Although this tragicomedy was licensed for the Queen's company in 1639, it may have been first performed earlier in Dublin: see Allan H. Stevenson, "Shirley's Dedications" (I,A) and Bentley (III,A).

The Politician, tragedy (ca. *1639?;* 1655)

There is no licensing date for this play. Because it was published by Humphrey Moseley at the same time and in the same way as *The Gentleman of Venice,* it has been believed to have been licensed at the same time and, like that play, possibly to have been performed earlier in Dublin: see Bentley (III,A).

I St. Patrick for Ireland, neo-miracle (ca. *1637-40;* 1640)

This play was written for the Dublin stage during Shirley's residence in Ireland, 1636-40. There is no license for a London performance. In the prologue and epilogue to the play, Shirley says that he will write a sequel, but there is no record of one.

The Imposture (The Impostor), tragicomedy (*licensed 10 Nov. 1640;* 1653)

This play was licensed as *The Imposter.*

The Brothers (The Politic Father), comedy (*licensed 26 May 1641;* 1653)

This is likely the play licensed under the title *The Politique Father* and published as *The Brothers;* it may or may not be identical with, or a revised version of, the play licensed in 1626 as *The Brothers* (q.v.).

The Cardinal, tragedy (*licensed 25 May 1641;* 1653)

The Court Secret, tragicomedy (*unacted;* 1653)

The theaters were closed before *The Court Secret* could be produced, though it seems to have been produced during the Restoration.

The Sisters, comedy (*licensed 26 Apr. 1642;* 1653)

The Triumph of Beauty, mask (*unknown;* 1646)

The title page says that this mask "was personated by some young Gentlemen, for whom it was intended, at a private Recreation." As Bentley (III,A) suggests, it may be a school mask but the date is too early to allow one to say this with certainty. Bentley further says that "the masque could have been written almost any time during Shirley's career, though it seems more characteristic of his activities after the closing of the theatres."

Cupid and Death, mask (*26 March 1653;* 1653)

The Contention of Ajax and Ulysses for the Armour of Achilles, entertainment (ca. *1645-58;* 1658)

The title page says that this entertainment was "nobly represented by young Gentlemen of quality, at a private Entertainment of some persons of Honour" though no specific performance date is known. It may be that *The Contention of Ajax and Ulysses* was written for the schoolboys Shirley taught after the closing of the theaters.

Honoria and Mammon, moral (*unacted?;* 1658)

Honoria and Mammon is a five-act allegory that is an expansion of *The Contention for Honour and Riches* (above) and may have been revised by Shirley for presentation by his students during his career as a schoolmaster.

B. UNCERTAIN ASCRIPTIONS; APOCRYPHA

The Night Walker, or The Little Thief, by John Fletcher, rev. Shirley; comedy (ca. *1611?;* 1640)

John Fletcher's *The Night Walker* was probably first acted ca. 1611 and was revised in 1633 by Shirley for a production by the Queen's Men. An identification of Shirley's revisions is given by Cyrus Hoy in "The Shares of Fletcher and his Collaborators in the Beaumont and Fletcher Canon (IV)," *SB* 12 (1959): 108-11.

Chabot, Admiral of France, by George Chapman, rev. Shirley; tragedy (*1611-1622?;* 1639)

This is almost certainly George Chapman's play revised for the stage in 1635 by Shirley. In the preface to his edition of the play (1906),

Ezra Lehman concludes that it is principally the work of Chapman. This is reaffirmed with some pertinent factual material by Thomas Marc Parrott, the editor of *The Plays of George Chapman: The Tragedies*, 2 vols. (1910). The shares of Shirley and Chapman have been determined with some precision by Derek Crawley in "The Effect of Shirley's Hand on Chapman's *The Tragedy of Chabot Admiral of France*," SP 63 (1966): 677-96.

The Country Captain (Captain Underwit), by William Cavendish; comedy (ca. *1639*-ca. *1640;* 1649)

William Cavendish, Duke of Newcastle, is almost certainly the author of this comedy. When A. H. Bullen reprinted the play in *A Collection of Old English Plays* (1833), he proposed Shirley as a possible author. This suggestion is accepted by Robert S. Forsythe (I,B) and Henry Ten Eyck Perry, *The First Duchess of Newcastle and Her Husband as Figures in Literary History* (1918), and also by the *Annals*. There are no facts that would warrant attribution of the play to Shirley.

The Arcadia, pastoral tragicomedy (*1640;* 1640)

There is no license for this play, but the title page of the 1640 edition announces that it was acted by "her Majesties Servants" at the Phoenix playhouse. The title page ascribes the play to Shirley, but Alfred Harbage, "The Authorship of the Dramatic *Arcadia*," MP 35 (1938): 233-37, contends that "Shirley had nothing to do with it except as the victim of a bookseller's ruse." It is not included in the list of Shirley's plays that appeared in *Six New Playes* (1653). The play was, furthermore, printed for a publisher Shirley never used on any other occasion. G. E. Bentley does not accept Harbage's arguments as conclusive (III,A). There is a brief discussion of the play as a dramatization of Sidney in W. W. Greg, *Pastoral Poetry and Pastoral Drama* (1906).

C. CRITIQUE OF THE STANDARD EDITION

Gifford and Dyce's six-volume edition of Shirley's works was published in 1833 and is now hopelessly dated. There are no textual notes or textual apparatus, and the editors take great liberties with the text, rearranging, rewriting, and expurgating it at will and frequently without citation.

D. TEXTUAL STUDIES

There are no important textual studies of James Shirley's works with the exception of the commentary that accompanies the individual editions (see III,E). Much valuable textual work has, however, been done for the single editions of Shirley plays that have been produced as doctoral dissertations, and readers are recommended to survey these dissertation editions.

E. SINGLE-WORK EDITIONS

The most ambitious, textually correct, and generally complete edition of a Shirley play is Charles R. Forker's 1964 edition of *The Cardinal*. It contains much critical and textual introductory material as well as extensive explanatory footnotes. *The Traitor* has been edited by John Stewart Carter, *RRDS* (1965), and *The Gentleman of Venice* by Wilson E. Engel (1976). Both editors have provided readers with useful notes.

In *A Book of Masques: In Honour of Allardyce Nicoll* (1967), ed. T. J. B. Spencer and Stanley W. Wells, Clifford Leech has edited *The Triumph of Peace* and B. A. Harris *Cupid and Death*. Textual notes and a brief introduction accompany both editions.

F. EDITIONS OF NONDRAMATIC WORKS

The only modern edition of the poetry is *The Poems of James Shirley* edited by Ray Livingstone Armstrong in 1941. Six unpublished poems are printed in R. G. Howarth, "Some Unpublished Poems of James Shirley," *RES* 9 (1933): 24-29. Other previously unpublished poems have been found by modern scholars (see I, C). The Armstrong edition contains a general introduction, footnotes, and textual notes. Shirley's three school texts—*Via ad Latinam Linguam Complanata: The Way Made Plain to the Latin Tongue* (1649), *The Rudiments of Grammar: The Rules Composed in English Verse, For the Greater Benefit and Delight of Young Beginners* (1656), and *Manductio: or, A Leading of Children by the Hand through the Principles of Grammar* (1660)— have never been edited or reprinted since their original publication.

IV. SEE ALSO

A. GENERAL

Barber, C. L. *The Idea of Honour in the English Drama 1591-1700.* 1957.

Bas, Georges. "James Shirley, pasteur dans le Hertfordshire." *EA* 15 (1962): 266-68.

——. "James Shirley et *'Th' Untun'd* Kennell': Une petite guerre des theatres vers 1630." *EA* 16 (1963): 11-22.

Baugh, Albert C. "Some New Facts about Shirley." *MLR* 17 (1922): 228-35.

——. "Further Facts about James Shirley." *RES* 7 (1931): 62-66.

Bentley, Gerald Eades. *The Seventeenth-Century Stage.* 1968.

——. *The Profession of Dramatist in Shakespeare's Time.* 1971.

Boas, F. S. *Stuart Drama.* 1946.

Bowden, William R. *The English Dramatic Lyric, 1603-42.* 1951.

Bradbrook, M. C. *Themes and Conventions of Elizabethan Tragedy.* 1960.

Bridges-Adams, W. *The Irresistible Theatre.* 1957.

Bush, Douglas. *English Literature in the Earlier Seventeenth Century 1600-1660.* 1945; 2nd ed. 1962.

Cazamian, Louis. *The Development of English Humour.* 1952.

Davis, Joe Lee. *The Sons of Ben.* 1967.

Downer, Alan S. *The British Drama.* 1950.

Feil, J. P. "James Shirley's Years of Service." *RES* 8 (1957): 413-16.

Frost, David L. *The School of Shakespeare.* 1968.

Gurr, Andrew. *The Shakespearean Stage 1574-1642.* 1970.

Harbage, Alfred. *Thomas Killigrew.* 1930.

——. *Sir William Davenant.* 1935.

——. *Cavalier Drama.* 1936.

Heilman, Robert Bechtold. *Tragedy and Melodrama.* 1968.

Holzknecht, Karl J. *Outlines of Tudor and Stuart Plays, 1497-1642.* 1947. [*The Lady of Pleasure*; *The Cardinal*]

Howarth, R. G. *Literature of the Theatre: Marlowe to Shirley.* 1953.

Kirsch, Arthur C. *Dryden's Heroic Drama.* 1965.

——. *Jacobean Dramatic Perspectives.* 1972.

Leech, Clifford. *Shakespeare's Tragedies and Other Studies in Seventeenth Century Drama.* 1950.

——. *John Ford and the Drama of His Time.* 1957.

MacKenzie, Agnes Mure. *The Playgoer's Handbook to the English Renaissance Drama.* 1927.

Mehl, Dieter. "Beaumont und Fletchers *The Faithful Friend.*" *Anglia* 80 (1962): 417-24.

Miles, Josephine. *The Continuity of Poetic Language.* 1951.

Morillo, Marvin. "'Frier Sherley': James Shirley and Mercurius *Britanicus.*" *N&Q* 7 (1960): 338-39.

Nicoll, Allardyce. *British Drama.* 1925; rev. ed. 1962.

Parrott, Thomas Marc, and Ball, Robert Hamilton. *A Short View of Elizabethan Drama.* 1943.

Radtke, Stephen J. *James Shirley: His Catholic Philosophy of Life.* 1929.

Reed, Robert R. *The Occult on the Tudor and Stuart Stage.* 1965.

Ristine, Frank H. *English Tragicomedy.* 1910; rpt. 1963.

Smet, Robert de [Romain Sanvic]. *Le théâtre élizabéthain.* 1955.

Smith, John Harrington. *The Gay Couple in Restoration Comedy.* 1948.

Spencer, Theodore. *Death and Elizabethan Tragedy.* 1936.

Stiefel, A. L. "Die Nachahmung spanischer Komödien in England unter den ersten Stuarts." *Romanische Forschungen* 5 (1890): 193-220.
Taylor, Aline M. "James Shirley and 'Mr. Vincent Cane,' the Franciscan." *N&Q* 7 (1960): 31-33.
Waith, Eugene M. *The Pattern of Tragicomedy in Beaumont and Fletcher*. 1952.
———. *Ideas of Greatness*. 1971.
Wallis, Lawrence B. *Fletcher, Beaumont and Company*. 1947.
Wertheim, Albert. "James Shirley and the Caroline Masques of Ben Jonson." *Theatre Notebook* 27 (1973): 157-61.

B. INDIVIDUAL PLAYS

Bland, D. S. "A Word in Shirley's *The Cardinal*." *RES* 4 (1953): 358-59.
Gregory, George. *Two Studies in James Shirley* (1935). [*The Traitor*]
Legouis, Pierre. "Réflexions sur la recherche des sources a propos de *La Tragédie du Vengeur*." *EA* 12 (1959): 47-55. [*The Traitor*]

C. TEXTUAL STUDIES

Carter, Albert Howard. "Shirley's Return to London in 1639-40." *MLN* 58 (1943): 196-97. [*The Maid's Revenge*]
Fehrenbach, Robert J. "The Printing of James Shirley's *The Politician*." *SB* 24 (1971): 144-48.
Greg, W. W. "*The Triumph of Peace*: A Bibliographer's Nightmare." *Library* 1 (1947): 113-26.
Howarth, R. G. "A Manuscript of James Shirley's *The Court Secret*." *RES* 7 (1931): 203-13; *RES* 8 (1932): 203.
Huberman, Edward. "Bibliographical Note on James Shirley's *The Politician*." *Library* 18 (1938): 104-8.
King, T. J. "Shirley's *The Coronation* and *Love Will Find Out the Way*: Erroneous Title-Pages." *SB* 18 (1965): 265-69.
Stevenson, Allan H. "New Uses of Watermarks as Bibliographical Evidence." *SB* 1 (1948): 149-82. [*The Opportunity*]

D. EDITIONS

Anthologies

Baskervill, C. R., Heltzel, V. G., and Nethercot, A. H., eds. *Elizabethan and Stuart Plays*. 1934, rev. ed. in 2 vols., 1971. [*The Lady of Pleasure* and *The Cardinal*, both rpt. in vol. 2, *Stuart Plays*, 1971]
Brooke, C. F. Tucker, and Paradise, N. B., eds. *English Drama, 1580-1642*. 1933. [*The Cardinal*]
Chapman, Robin, and Grant, Allan, eds. *The City and the Court: Five Seventeenth-Century Comedies of London Life*. 1968. [*The Lady of Pleasure*]
Fraser, Russell A., and Rabkin, Norman, eds. *Drama of the English Renaissance*, Vol. 2, 1976. [*Hyde Park*]

Harrier, Richard C., ed. *An Anthology of Jacobean Drama*. Vol. 2. 1963. [*The Lady of Pleasure*]

Knowland, A. S., ed. *Six Caroline Plays*. 1962. [*The Wedding*]

Lawrence, Robert G., ed. *Jacobean and Caroline Tragedies*. 1974. [*The Cardinal*]

Neilson, William Allen, ed. *The Chief Elizabethan Dramatists, Excluding Shakespeare*. 1939. [*The Lady of Pleasure* and *The Cardinal*]

Parks, Edd W., and Beatty, R. C., eds. *The English Drama, An Anthology 900–1642*. 1935. [*The Cardinal*]

Schelling, Felix E., and Black, Matthew W., eds. *Typical Elizabethan Plays*. Rev. and enlgd., 1931. [*The Lady of Pleasure*]

Walley, Harold Reinoehl, and Wilson, John Harold., eds. *Early Seventeenth-Century Plays 1600-1642*. 1930. [*The Cardinal*]

RICHARD BROME

Ann Haaker

There is no standard edition of Brome's plays. Most of them are reprinted in John Pearson's *The Dramatic Works of Richard Brome: Containing Fifteen Comedies Now First Collected in Three Volumes* (1873; rpt. 1966). *The Antipodes* and *A Mad Couple Well Matched* are included in *Six Caroline Plays*, ed. A. S. Knowland (1962).

I. GENERAL

A. BIOGRAPHICAL

Scholars seem to agree on 1590 as Brome's probable birth date, yet his background, schooling, and the precise nature of his service to Ben Jonson remain matters of conjecture. Nineteenth-century biographical information came almost entirely from title pages, prologues, epilogues, prefaces, commendatory verses, contemporary references in Jonson's works, Sir Henry Herbert's *Office-book*, and early biographical sketches, such as Edward Phillips, *Theatrum Poetarum Anglicanorum* (1675), William Winstanly, *The Lives of the Most Famous English Poets* (1687), and Gerard Langbaine, *An Account of the English Dramatick Poets* (1691). Such material was also the basis of Edward Karl Richard Faust's early study *Richard Brome: Ein Beitrag zur Geschichte der Englischen Literatur* (1887; also in *Herrig's Archiv*, vol. 82, 1887).

Twentieth-century studies provided more factual and documentary evidence. George Brenner Tennant's "Jonson's 'Ode to Himself'" in the introduction to his edition of *The New Inn; or The Light Heart* (1908), pp. xxi–xxix, explains "Broom's sweepings" by dating the two versions of Jonson's ode. C. W. Wallace alerted scholars to the presence of a contract between Salisbury Court Theater and its playwright Richard Brome in "Shakspere and the Blackfriars," *The Century Magazine* 80 (1910): 742-52, and listed some of the terms of the agreement. Clarence

E. Andrews incorporates the Wallace information, including other facts from correspondence with Wallace, in the biographical section of his *Richard Brome: A Study of His Life and Works* (1913). He also adds a chronology and bibliography.

R. J. Kaufmann's introductory chapter, "On Being a Caroline Playwright," in *Richard Brome: Caroline Playwright* (1961), establishes Brome as a popular Caroline playwright "genuinely and deeply concerned to preserve the values of the older 'Tudor culture' which is being subverted before his eyes"; as a consequence, Brome's social comedies, according to Kaufmann, "form an intelligible and complex commentary on a central phase of an historical evolutionary process." Kaufmann includes evidence from G. E. Bentley's *The Jacobean and Caroline Stage*, 7 vols. (1941-68), and reviews past evidence in his chronological account of Brome's activities in the second chapter, "Biographical Anatomy," reserving for the third chapter, "Under the Seal of Ben," Brome's association with Jonson, "probably the most important and formative one of his whole life."

Most scholarship is about Brome's theatrical career. When Wallace died, the source of his information was unknown until Ann Haaker's rediscovery of two 1640 documents, the Salisbury Court Complaint against Brome and Brome's answer, complete transcripts of which are published in "The Plague, the Theater, and the Poet," *RenD* 1 (1968): 283-306. Haaker's accompanying article summarizes and explains the documents, which tell the complete story of Brome's activities from before his "first encounter with Salisbury Court up to his final break with the theater five years later in order to join William Beeston at the Cockpit theater." Wallace's 1910 transcript of the documents, found among his assorted manuscript papers at the Henry E. Huntington Library, led to the rediscovery of the originals at the London Public Record Office. These documents not only supply biographical evidence about Brome's theatrical activities but also offer pertinent evidence concerning the terms and conditions of early theatrical contracts. Gerald Eades Bentley includes this information in his discussion of Brome's dramatic career along with the careers of seven other even more prolific contemporaries— Heywood, Fletcher, Dekker, Massinger, Shakespeare, Shirley, and Rowley—in his *The Profession of Dramatist in Shakespeare's Time, 1590-1642* (1971). The book "is an explication of the normal working environment circumscribing the activities of those literary artists who are making their living by writing for the London theatres."

Alwin Thaler interprets the inclusion of the name "Richard Brome" among the Queen of Bohemia's players in a royal warrant for payment of court performances in "Was Richard Brome an Actor?" *MLN* 36 (1921): 88–91, as evidence that Brome, like Nathan Field, was an actor before he became a playwright and like Field was indebted to Jonson in both capacities. John Freehafer's "Brome, Suckling, and Davenant's Theater Project of 1639" *TSLL* 10 (1968): 367–83, illustrates the competitive and political threats attending professional pursuits in the theater. Because the theatrical ventures of William Davenant and the court influence of Sir John Suckling were a threat to Brome's own position as a playwright and to his friend William Beeston's management of the Cockpit theater at Drury Lane, Freehafer argues, Davenant and Suckling were satirized in Brome's *The Court Beggar* and in *A Jovial Crew*. Freehafer's article not only illustrates the shift in public taste from the style of Jonson, Middleton, and Brome to the courtly extravagances that Brome so consistently ridiculed, but also traces the slow but deliberate development of a modern theater. The new style of theater, "first projected about 1638," was "frustrated by powerful courtiers, ridiculed by Richard Brome, and delayed by a civil war, Puritan edicts, and a lack of funds." Finally, helpful to students will be Catherine Shaw's *Richard Brome*, TEAS, in press. Her introductory chapter, "The Man and His Time," offers a chronological updated account of what is known about Brome's life, along with some observations of her own, and a compendium of several previous studies, including some of the many unprinted dissertations.

B. GENERAL STUDIES OF THE PLAYS

The five major studies of Brome date from 1887 to a book still in press. Whereas most of the very early studies summarize the plots, discuss Jonsonian humours in the characters, and, as in the case of Faust (I,A), comment on genre and source, and on parallels to other plays in words, plot, and character, C. E. Andrews (I,A) classifies Brome's sixteen extant comedies according to type and takes into consideration the general structure, versification, and moral tone of the plays. Brome's lack of variety in character and in plot, which was critized by Faust, is explained by Andrews as a deliberate repetition of stock characters and stock situations which Brome found pleasing to Caroline audiences; the general weakening in moral tone and increasing demand for variety in plot and multiple intrigue, moreover, anticipates what was most popular in Restoration drama. Andrews concludes that in imitation of Jonson's structure, scenes, and portrayal of characters, Brome has gone further than the "Sons of Ben"; in fact in the imitation of satiric method, according to Andrews, Brome is practically the only follower of Jonson in that his plays most of the time adhere to a moral standard which "like his master, ridicules folly and vice, but never virtue." Herbert F. Allen, *A Study of the Comedies of Richard Brome, Especially as Representative of Dramatic Decadence* (1913), attempts to show that the most conspicuous features of dramatic decadence—"eclecticism, immorality, absorptive imitation, strain or forced 'originality,' and over-devotion to technique"—show, "in greater or less degree," in the comedies of Brome.

Professor Kaufmann (I,A) discusses Brome's plays in the context of his times and theater. The plays, whose alleged primary object is the creation of laughter, experiment in various "possible ways of digesting urgently needed corrections for social abuses." Using his Chapter 4, "The Caroline Editorial Page" as a buffer between the introductory section of the book and the more fully focused critical discussion of individual plays, Kaufmann illustrates how *The New Exchange*, *The Sparagus Garden*, *The City Wit*, and *The Antipodes* use the tableau device. The plays also "literalize," or "do the work of newspapers: they report, they advertize, they protest, they deplore, they frame social questions, they editorialize." In his chapter "Usury and Brotherhood," Kaufmann maintains that *Covent Garden Weeded*, *The English Moor*, and *The Damoiselle* translate a major economic and social question, usury, into the medium of drama by cleverly exploiting stereotyped prejudices against the usurer, who for the audience represented a type of social vice, an offense "against reason, love and humanity," in order to get the play under way. Brome structures the plays to explore parallel aspects of right and wrong, attitudes towards goods, and the varying effects on bonds of human relations; but in each case Brome makes clear that "goods cannot rightly take priority over the bonds of love."

Catherine M. Shaw's *Richard Brome* (I,A) aims "to provide the reader with a close analysis of each individual Brome play, both as literature and as theatrical composition, and to give a balanced and comprehensive view of the entire canon." Each play is discussed "in terms of stylistic techniques and prevailing moral attitudes and how these combine to achieve a dramatic totality." Play groupings in individual chapters offer interesting insights. For example, in Chapter 2, "The Ladies Take the Stage," she finds that *The Northern Lass*, *The*

Novella, and *The English Moor*, which focus upon a heroine, are less sharply satirical and socially geared than those of more masculine domination—*The Damoiselle*, *The City Wit*, and *The Court Beggar*, discussed in Chapter 3, "The Gentlemen: Fathers, Fools, and Fops." She credits Brome in *The Northern Lass* for his "ingenious and original plot with its intrigues and counter-intrigues and for his remarkable skill in characterization. Clearly superimposed upon the romantic triangles is the tri-leveling of the narrative and thematic concerns of the play. Then, in addition, are groups of character triads." Shaw finds similar tri-level structures in other plays by Brome. In Chapter 4, "Plays of Place-Realism," she discusses individually *The Weeding of the Covent Garden*, *The Sparagus Garden*, *The New Academy*, and *A Mad Couple Well Matched* as "comedies of manners, social satires in which particular 'humours' or the strivings of various characters for falsely affected pseudo-graces are exposed." Shaw explains how "in each of these plays of place-realism a particular location immediately identified initimately to the audience forms a central icon for the play." Chapter 6, "Plays of Generic Inversion," includes *The Lovesick Court*, a "parody on romantic tragicomedy", *The Antipodes*, "a satire within a satire", and *A Jovial Crew*, "an anti-romance"; "what links the three together is that each achieves its dramatic totality by Brome's turning of generic form upon itself." The final chapter, "Criticism and Revaluation," surveys "general critical attitudes taken during the late nineteenth and twentieth centuries" and considers "the justice of the various positions critics have taken toward what *kind* of dramatist Richard Brome was, what his technical strengths and weaknesses were, and what his contributions to his chosen literary form."

Not all criticisms are defensive. Theodore Miles marks the difference in realistic use of place in Brome's *The Weeding of the Covent Garden* and *The Sparagus Garden* and in plays by Marmion, Shirley, and Nabbes in "Place-Realism in a Group of Caroline Plays," *RES* 18 (1942): 428–40, and concludes that Shirley is more proficient than Brome in integrating place with plot and theme; Brome superimposes topographical scenes upon his act because of their timely interest: "The place advertizes the play." Frederick S. Boas's essay, "Richard Brome," in *An Introduction to Stuart Drama* (1946), censures Brome's craftsmanship. Choosing four plays which he considers "representative of Brome's best work for the theater at the beginning, middle, and close of his active career," Boas claims that the plot of *The Northern Lass* is "somewhat unpleasant" and "over-complicated by disguisings and impersonations"; that *The Sparagus Garden*, a comedy of Jonsonian humours, "centers mainly in technically subordinate characters"; that *The Antipodes* is "unduly dragged out" (its plot is overcomplicated and its play-within-the-play is an "acute observation . . . of the seamier side of London life" in inverted form); and finally that *A Jovial Crew* is a "merry, if somewhat overweighted, comedy." Boas attributes the popularity of the first two plays to exploiting "the contrast between town and country manners and speech," and in the case of *A Jovial Crew* to the luck, as is stated in the dedication, "to tumble last of all in the epidemical ruin of the scene," which "alone would give it a secure place in the history of Stuart drama."

Other studies ally Brome's plays to Restoration comedy. Kathleen M. Lynch, in *The Social Mode of Restoration Comedy* (1926), states that "Brome's plays exhibit a study of class relationships which is more detailed and more impressive than Middleton. . . . [Brome] habitually regards from the outside the manners of fashionable society, gaining his comic effects through their caricature and distortion when aped by curious citizens who perceive them only as mannerisms." Alfred Harbage, in *Cavalier Drama* (1936), considers Brome's disapproval of the court's invasion of the theater and of the current fad for the typical cavalier play; although "an uncompromising product of the old school," Brome effects his "high spirited jollity" by means of those very qualities in speech and dramatic situation which reveal much of the ground plan of Restoration comedy of manners. Elizabeth Cook's "The Plays of Richard Brome," *More Books: Bulletin of the Boston Public Library* 22 (1947): 285-301, first catalogues the canon and then discusses the plays; The Boston Public Library contains the first edition of each of Brome's plays except *The Northern Lass*. Although Cook sees an infiltration of Jonson and other Jacobean dramatists in Brome's plays, "the proportion of mixtures" is his own. Brome catches the trick of speech and the behavior which is true to the rising middle-class existence; he begins to work on a situation from its setting and social tone. Characters, often mouthpieces of topical fads and fancies, speak and act according to the circumstance and to their own breeding, and in this way Brome illustrates the temper of London life. According to Cook, "the comedy of manners is more securely grounded by the labours of Brome and Nabbes and Shirley than it would have been if the Killigrews and Carliles had written unrivalled."

Alfred Harbage, in "Elizabethan Restoration Palimpsest," *MLR* 35 (1940): 287-319 (rpt. in *Shakespeare Without Words and Other Essays*

(1972), pp. 170-218), hypothesizes: "Certain playwrights after 1660 secured, in manuscript, unprinted plays written before 1642, modernized them, and had them produced and published as their own; hence a number of Restoration plays hitherto considered original are actually adaptations of 'lost' Elizabethan plays." Harbage suggests that Brome's *Sparagus Garden* and *A Mad Couple Well Matched* suffered the like fate by becoming Dryden's early play *The Mistaken Husband*, which was unclaimed by the author, and his *The Wild Gallant*; the plays by Dryden follow what Harbage describes as the Brome formula in both materials and style—especially "the diction, the turn of phrase, the general atmosphere."

Miscellaneous studies such as Cicely Veronica Wedgwood's "Comedy in the Reign of Charles I" in *Studies in Social History*, ed. J. H. Plumb (1955), pp. 109-37, discuss Brome's topical plays, along with those of his contemporaries, which openly criticized "manners, morals, and even politics." Wedgwood claims that the Puritans used the plays as justification for the closure of the theaters as an act of policy: the players, as "the abstract and brief chronicles of the time, were far too dangerous to be left at liberty to utter what they would to excitable London audiences during the Civil War." "The beauty of these plays," comments Wedgwood, "is that they fix, in phrase after phrase, the vivid ephemeral details of that time . . . and a whole society with its petty pleasures and preoccupations starts into life from the pages of these comedies." Helen Kaufman's "The Influence of Italian Drama on Pre-Restoration English Comedy," *Italica* 31 (1954): 8-23, illustrates how Brome's *The Novella* and *A Mad Couple Well Matched* resemble Italian Renaissance comedy in temper, technique, and theme. Utterly gay in spirit, with no hint of didacticism, the plays exhibit salient characteristics of Italian comedy: "disguise, love intrigue, clever dialogue, confusion, buffoonery and the familiar stock characters," and a similarity of mood and purpose: "In those important formative years before 1660 . . . when Restoration comedy was slowly developing, English comedy was closer to the Italian than to that of any other country."

C. THE WORKS AT LARGE

Both Kaufmann and Andrews (I,A) list Brome's poems and songs, but there are no general studies of his nondramatic works. John Cutts, in "The Anonymous Masque-like Entertainment in Egerton MS. 1994, and Richard Brome," *CompD* 1 (1967): 277-87, argues that Richard

Brome wrote a mask-like entertainment called *Juno in Arcadia*, and its only song, "Hoy, boy, Hey, boy"; that it was performed at Oxford 5 August 1643 in honor of Queen Henrietta Maria, who arrived at Oxford in the middle of July 1643; and that it "might reasonably be listed as a 'lost' work of Richard Brome, and entered in the *Annals of English Drama* under the possible auspices of Oxford."

II. CRITICISM OF INDIVIDUAL PLAYS AND STATE OF SCHOLARSHIP

A. INDIVIDUAL PLAYS

The Antipodes

Andrews (I,A) appends a special study of *The Antipodes* to his *Richard Brome* "to give a more adequate idea of the character of Brome's work, and to show more fully to what extent he is a follower of Jonson in satire." He includes the sources of the play and of the term "Antipodes." G. P. Baker's introduction to his edition of the play (below, III, E) discusses Jonsonian influences and concludes that Brome was "no servile copyist" but achieved his effects in extremes rather than in Jonsonian-like essentials in moral consciousness: "Like Middleton, he works in a combination of the comedy of manners and the comedy of intrigue, developing a complicated story of a varied incident through numerous figures carefully studied from types of current London life." Joe Lee Davis, "Richard Brome's Neglected Contribution to Comic Theory." *SP* 40 (1943): 520–28, considers *The Antipodes* in advance of its time as an "anticipation of Gilbertian farce" and also as a "contribution to criticism and aesthetics." The play incorporates a theory of comic catharsis, inspired by Jonson and Randolph's *The Muses' Looking Glass* and also "what may be termed as an *extra*-realistic conception of the relationship between comedy and actuality." It is in the use of his play-within-a-play, according to Davis, that Brome achieves his comedic purpose of "psychological adjustment through engrossment in life's general incongruity rather than ethical correction through the exposure of specific deformities."

According to Kaufmann (I,A), "Brome's gay, imaginative, and spirited attempt to combine his instinct for theatrical pathos with a more generalized form of social satire in *The Antipodes*. . . is not quite successful, for there is an intellectual awkwardness, a loss of proper proportion that attacks Brome whenever he becomes too abstract or intellectual. He thought in terms of actable metaphors and his discursive or choral amplification of what he perceives is usually inferior to his direct presentation of it in stage action." Ann Haaker's introductory essay to *The Antipodes* (below, III,E), on the other hand, is in agreement with Davis and appraises the play as an ingenious demonstration of comic catharsis by means of the Letoy–Dr. Hughball team; their play-within-a-play provides a timely message and psychological therapy to three levels of audiences—Peregrine (who is ostensibly the patient), the play audience, and the theater audience—all of whom had recently suffered the effects of a plague and are suffering from other ills mentioned in the prologue and first act. The three-level cure, even as described in the play, takes the unsuspecting patients, the joyless ones, unawares, as it brings them to their "proper centers" by means of a series of ludicrous but "homebred" incongruities, with the concluding mask as the final antidote—"Wit against Folly, Love against Jealousy,/ Wine against Melancholy, and 'gainst Madness, Health." Thus, concludes Haaker, Brome demonstrates with originality, and yet in full accord with Jonson's comedic principles, how comedy assumes "its role as doctor of the age."

"To read *The Antipodes*," says Ian Donaldson in *The World Upside-Down* (1970) "is to feel in touch with a kind of mid-seventeenth-century folk humour" or with "another cluster of popular beliefs and superstitions which allowed for equally sharp comic contrasts between virtue and iniquity, normality and absurdity." Donaldson interprets the doctor in the play as symbolically representative of the dramatist, Blaze's house as Salisbury Court, Peregrine's antipodean obsession as a "central comic symbol highlighting the play's other reversals in social and domestic relationships," and the final mask, which will bring in harmony, as a reminder of the movement and purpose of the whole play. The inner play, according to Donaldson, has five rings of spectators, including the actors acting the actors; absurdity having dispelled absurdity, the various circles of characters are brought back to "this Hemisphere," for "reason in the little world of man must dominate over unreason, as in the greater world the upper hemisphere physically dominates the lower hemisphere," and "the very exaggeration of the reversals in that city reassure an audience that familiar ways are right ways." Shaw (I,A) rates *The Antipodes* as "the most sophisticated and ingenious of Brome's satires." She also affirms the play's comic catharsis: Brome's "satiric effect is gained by a duality of representations—one assumed to be firm and constant as the viewers' conception of what life is and the other the exaggerations, the opposites, or what they actually see in performance on stage. The catharsis comes through the ultimate realization that what they think and what they see are two distorted reflections of the same vision and thus comic catharsis within the interpolated performances on-stage becomes catharsis for the audience to the greater play."

A Jovial Crew

Kaufmann's "Utopian Epilogue" (I,A) perceives in *A Jovial Crew* "a touching partial capitulation by an ageing and tired Brome to the inevitability of a new order which he could neither condone nor ignore"; centering his play on beggars "who form a community within the community—small, cohesive, autarchical, and mutually interdependent under a patriarch . . . who rules by reasonable persuasion, not by invested power"—Brome creates a Utopia "in which his conservative values would have a chance for survival." John W. Crowther relates *A Jovial Crew* to the "variety of influences, themes, and techniques prominent in the dramatic history of the period as a whole" in "The Literary History of Richard Brome's *A Jovial Crew*," in *Studies in English Renaissance Literature* 12 (1962): 132–48, and concludes: "In writing this play Brome showed that he has assimilated the traditions of both romantic and realistic comedy, together with the social problem of beggary, and he shapes a variety of themes and characters, some of which bear interesting resemblances to earlier plays, in a strikingly imaginative way." According to Haaker (III,E) in her introductory essay to *A Jovial Crew*, Brome wrote his play against a "background of economic confusion" and, "ever sensitive to audience rapport," he recognized the need for homespun mirth and common sense. Using the same comedic formula applied in *The Antipodes*, Brome, the "age's doctor," first "supplies escape in the form of time-mellowed memories of the good old days; then, adding mirth, mixed reality with memories; and finally, . . . allows reality and mirth to displace escapism and pessimism." The play becomes "a study in contrasts" and in subtle shades of escapism contesting responsibility; "eventually what were only dreams of happiness become realities to those who have learned to enjoy happiness" by recognizing and facing their fate in the true comic vein. Shaw (I,A) says that "the deliberate undercutting of generic expectancy casts a sombre mood over romance in *A Jovial Crew* and shifts it away from the usual moral reassessments found in green world comedy. . . . It would appear that one by one each of the expected triumphs of the green world over the wasteland is undercut by intruding a kind of harsh reality into the merry beggar world. Equally as skillfully as he undercuts romantic notion, Brome shows the obverse side of the coin." According to Shaw, *The Antipodes* and *A Jovial Crew* "outrank all but the best of Jonson."

The Court Beggar

The Court Beggar uses the stage "to register a sharp political protest through detailed personal satire of specific public figures"—the court favorites, Sir John Suckling and Sir William Davenant, whose theatrical aspirations were threats to the careers of both Brome and his friend William Beeston, according to R. J. Kaufmann's "Suckling and Davenant Satirized by Brome," *MLR* 55 (1960): 332–44; also printed as "Suckling's New Strain of Wit" in *Richard Brome* (I,A). "The destructive fun Brome makes of these two," says Kaufmann, "is related to the 'second war of the theaters' being waged between the courtiers and the professional dramatists, as well as to the rising anti-Cavalier sentiment which was one of the unapprehended tremors of the coming Rebellion." Infused in the play are major social problems in the years leading up to the revolution, such as "monopolists, projectors and self-interested court favourites." In addition, Kaufmann concludes: "*The Court Beggar*, we can now say, constitutes a substantial addition to our limited knowledge of Suckling's biography; it furnishes through satiric criticism of Davenant's threatened ambitions some formative notes for the history of the Caroline theatre; by its manifest and angry attack on 'favouritism' it can cause us to modify our opinions about the docility of Stuart playwrights under censorship." Shaw (I,A) concurs that *The Court Beggar* is "a political satire in which the whole ethic of unmerited and irresponsible preferment is attacked." The main plot, "concerned with the folly and ultimate defeat of Mendicant's striving for court position and influence," exposes "the viciousness of a system which allows for a total disregard of personal feeling or moral ethic." The ultimate triumph of virtue over "illicit opportunity gained by favoritism of birth or rank is part of the strong morality we have seen underlying all of the Bromean canon."

The Weeding of the Covent Garden

In "Paternalism, Puritanism, and Sociological Comedy" (I,A), R. J. Kaufmann claims that Brome in *The Weeding of the Covent Garden* "argued for an ethic of restricted paternalistic state interference in a society rapidly being polarized into militant and mutually intolerant factions." With "minute exactness and contemporaneity of place realism and architectural allusions" in the opening scenes, Brome prepares us for a dramatic exposé of local abuses relating to "housing, licensing, soap, price-fixing, monopolies, and other items of interest to the paternalistic state." The play also satirizes the Puritans and develops a "basic plea for a moderation between extremes of moral conduct." Shaw (I,A) suggests that the character Rooksbill may be identified with Inigo Jones, adding "a further dimension to the place realism . . . than has previously been realized."

The Lovesick Court

Kaufmann's "Court Drama and Commonsense" (I,A) demonstrates, by analysis of the "structure, tone, and producing context," that Brome intended to satirize in *The Lovesick Court* "the silly distortion of human motive and conduct becoming conventionalized in the new courtier drama." The play burlesques the excessive posturing of friend and lover and such issues as "love and honor," "idealized chastity," "friendship, and self-renunciation." Structural burlesque in the comic subplot directly parallels the main action and obviously is intended to debase the "stature" and to ridicule the "motives of the principals of the main plot." "The play," concludes Kaufmann, "stands as a capable instance of criticism as mimesis, or, put more modestly, it reminds us again that effective parody and thoughtful burlesque are complex critical acts creating as they destroy."

The Queen and Concubine

Kaufmann's essay "Parable and Hagiography" (I,A) illustrates how Brome's *The Queen and Concubine* once again gives dramatic expression to a general ethic that through a process of reeducation and regeneration people can be made to realize that "virtue is the true nobility." Brome, however, organizes and gives new life to standard patterns of moral commonplaces. He proves himself "one of the last masters of the art of analogical thinking"; the characters denote "extra-personal significance," and "there is meant to be a constant cross reference between the presented action and the moral values which underlie it." Queen Eulalia, for example, who "acts throughout as a repository of virtue and as a nearly allegorical embodiment of patience and wisdom," transcends the function of a virtuous wife to that of St. Eulalia, "Queen

of a mystical Sicily, a realm where divine Providence becomes ob-
servably functional and the extremes of unexplained virtue and un-
motivated vice gain a new kind of detached and distant acceptability."
In this manner, continues Kaufmann, "thematic strands of selfishness
versus disinterested devotion to the public interest and the general
contrast of appearance and reality are brought together." Shaw (I,A) is
in agreement with Kaufmann and mentions the similarity of the play to
As You Like It in its movement from court world and all its attendant
ills to "a green world dominated by nature and the desire for spiritual
growth and moral advancement." She believes the play "deserves
recognition for the Elizabethan quality of high moral tone which
Brome achieves well within the bounds of tragicomic form and for the
implementation of fine character diversity and thematic unity to support that tone."

The Sparagus Garden

Most studies include *Sparagus Garden* in reference to the fad for
place-realism (see I,B). Leroy L. Panek, "Asparagus and Brome's *The
Asparagus Garden*," *MP* 68 (1971): 362-63, notes that asparagus, the
potent "speciality of the establishment," so effusively praised by
Moneylack during his catalogue of aphrodisiacs, is really, according to
the herbalists in Brome's time, nothing more than a potential salad
and diuretic. The plant "is part of Sir Hugh's shell game" and also a
device to exploit humorous characters.

The Novella

According to Robert Boies Sharpe in "The Sources of Richard
Brome's *The Novella*," *SP* 30 (1933): 69-85, Brome "has expanded the
main plot of *The Novella* from a manuscript source [Part 4 of Fynes
Moryson's *Itinerary*] to which his access is biographically probable; . . .
the playwright's creative methods display themselves interestingly in
this expanding process, as he complicates and idealizes the action and
fills in the details of manners and social and local background from the
recognized contemporary authority [*Itinerary* and *Crudities of Thomas
Coryat*] on the picturesque life of the twenty thousand Venetian courte-
sans."

B. OVER-ALL STATE OF CRITICISM

"Of the many Tudor and Stuart dramatists, perhaps Richard Brome
has been the most neglected." While recent scholarship has somewhat

improved the situation described by Catherine Shaw (I,A), few people know that a Richard Brome ever existed. There are several reasons for his neglect. Harbage's comment in *Cavalier Drama* (I,B) directs attention to social and intellectual snobbery: "He has suffered too much from a kind of critical snobbery, which has stigmatized him as the base imitator of a greater man whose groom he had formerly been." The social stigma of having been a servant, "the Broome's sweepings," in addition to an equally unimpressive fate—"*Poor* he came into th' world, and *poor* went out"—has influenced the scholarship of each successive era. And, paradoxically, what should have been a propellant to fame, his having served his apprenticeship to Ben Jonson in playwriting, too often has proven in the past to be a deterrent; critics, even when admitting that Brome was not a servile imitator of Jonson, condemned him for lack of Jonsonian luster, especially in poetic skills and force of satiric thrust. Only Lynch (I,B) recognized that "Brome's lesser individuality than Jonson's enabled him to present a greater verisimilitude than the more literary or artful aspect."

The critical assessment of Brome's works in early histories of English literature often revealed more of the age and perhaps of the critic than of Brome. J. A. Symonds, "Review of *The Dramatic Works of Richard Brome, 1873*" in *The Academy* 5 (1874): 304-5, is a case in point: "In this age of exhaustive study and antiquarian scholarship, . . . perhaps there is sufficient reason for reprinting . . . the rubbish heap of Brome's plays . . . [in which] all the coarse and gross and seamy side of human life . . . [is] shown . . . with prosaic ruthlessness. . . . His view of the world is that of a groom, rather than of a gentleman; and the scenes and characters . . . [are] drawn from the experience of a flunky." Rev. Ronald Bayne, "Lesser Jacobean and Caroline Dramatists," *Cambridge History of English Literature*, vol. 6 (1910), pp. 224-32, is more charitable: finding Brome's plays a picture of London "full of interest and value," he yet wishes for a broader outlook. In other studies such expressions as "decadence," "immoral enjoyment of the vulgar and the vicious," and "decidedly coarser style and outlook" recur. Ashly H. Thorndike, for example, in *English Comedy* (1927), writes: "Though very vulgar he does not dare to be immoral. . . . Still he does present a broad and varied view of his Englishmen," and Andrews (I,A) finds interest in Brome to be historic rather than intrinsic. Kathleen Lynch, on the other hand, (I,B) admits: "We may turn with confidence to Brome for a full commentary on the social discontent of the citizen class in the London of his time." To most, however, Brome "twinkles in a constellation of lesser dramatists who prepare for the Restoration stars" (Cook, I,B).

What is needed is a greater consideration of some of the attributes for which Brome was recognized by his contemporaries or near contemporaries. Seventeenth- and eighteenth-century critics saw fit to praise Brome for the naturalness with which he depicted men and their manners: "In them we see ourselves, in them we find/ Whatever Time or Custom taught Mankind" (T.S., 1659); "But all so plain . . . he made/ T' inform the understanding, not invade it" (Alexander Brome, 1653). The age that Brome depicts in his comedies, it is well to remember, spanned the turbulent era of changing values and judgments from the last years of Queen Elizabeth's reign, through the reigns of James I and Charles I, through the unprecedented beheading of a king, into the first year of the Commonwealth under Oliver Cromwell. The shifts in moral, social, spiritual, and aesthetic standards are reflected in the Brome canon. Brome's contemporaries also praised him for his craftsmanship in the structure of his plays, for his showmanship, and also for his originality of plot and character: "the offspring of his own Judgment and Experience" (David Erskin Baker, *Companion to the Play-House*, 2 vols., 1764); "Whose excellency in Comical Wit has been sufficiently proved" (H.B., 1657); "you do them well . . . By observation of those Comick Lawes," (Ben Jonson, 1632); and "the design so probable" (Alexander Brome, 1653). They lauded his gentle and medicinal satire: "Thy Hearbs are physical and do more good/ In purging Humors, then some's letting blood" (C. G., 1640); "Thou'rt th' Ages Doctor now" (Alexander Brome, 1652); "the World's Mad . . . Thy well wrought Piece,/ May bring it Cure" (Jo. Tatham, 1652). They praised him for his message: "This witty pen, this mirthfull Comick style, . . . Wraps serious truths in fablous mysteries/ And thereby makes us merry, and yet wise" (Alexander Brome, 1653). Finally they praised him for his popularity: "In a word, his Plays in general are good ones, met with great Applause when first acted, and . . . were thought by the Players worthy to be revived, to their own Profit and the Author's Honour, in that critical age which he himself lived in. . . . Nay, we have had a proof even in our own time, of the merit of one of his Comedies; which, with a very little alteration, has been lately revived and with great success, vis. *The Jovial Crew*, which for no less than three Seasons past has brought crowded audiences to the theatre-Royal in Covent-Garden, at all the frequent Repitions of its Performances" (Baker, above). In our reassessment of Brome, we may do well to heed a humbling, if not sobering, bit of seventeenth-century advice: "For there's no other standard but Opinion" (Alexander Brome).

Major modern studies once again relate Brome to his own time and theater and are more objective in their appraisals than those of the late nineteenth and early twentieth century. To Kaufmann (I,A), "Brome is a good minor artist, sensitive to his own limitations and with a gifted sense of social proportion"; his "socially engaged" plays are "less self repetitive" than Shirley's and more versatile in comic invention than Fletcher's. He concludes that "Brome's work in the theater forms a kind of reduced but undistorted model of what the serious writer of critical comedy must do. He must sense, project, and test the social preoccupations of his time." Shaw (I,A) says: "Though these works are not without flaw, Brome was, nonetheless, a highly artistic and individualistic dramatist, remarkably eclectic, and one whose stature and influence in the seventeenth century was considerable."

A gradual accretion of documentary and factual evidence has brought to light more about Brome's theater, but much about his life and career is still conjectural. More published critical editions of the plays are needed; information from ten unpublished dissertations needs to be made more available. Much still remains to be said from the point of view of the audiences that first saw these plays. More bibliographical studies are needed, especially since Brome himself edited and oversaw the publication of some of his own plays. All in all, Brome remains neglected. Typical of this neglect is T. S. Eliot's treatment of him in *The Sacred Wood: Essays on Poetry and Criticism* (1923). Though he says that "Brome deserves to be more read than he is, and first of all to be more accessible than he is," Eliot saw fit to write only six sentences alluding to Brome, and five of those are directed toward the imperfect criticism of Swinburne's justification of Brome's plays.

III. CANON

A. PLAYS IN CHRONOLOGICAL ORDER

This list follows Alfred Harbage's *Annals of English Drama, 975-1700*, rev. S. Schoenbaum (1964), which is also the source for the type of play, the acting date (in italics preceding semicolon), and the original date of publication. For a further description of early editions, see W. W. Greg, *A Bibliography of the English Printed Drama to the Restoration*, 4 vols. (1939-59); for a discussion of the canon and lost plays, see G. E. Bentley, *The Jacobean and Caroline Stage*, vol. 3 (1956).

The Northern Lass, comedy (*1629;* 1632)

The City Wit, or The Woman Wears the Breeches, comedy (*1629–37;* 1653)

The Queen's Exchange, tragicomedy (ca. *1629–32 (?);* 1657)

The Novella, comedy (*1632–33;* 1653)

The Weeding of the Covent Garden, or the Middlesex Justice of Peace, comedy (*1632;* 1659)

The Late Lancashire Witches, topical play (*1634;* 1634)

C. E. Andrews, "The Authorship of *The Late Lancashire Witches,*" *MLN* 28 (1913): 163–66, concurs with Fleay "that this is an old play of Heywood's revised by Brome to make it timely in its contemporary allusions for a revival in 1634." Andrews assigns to Brome only nine pages out of a play of eighty-nine, "passages that are undoubtedly based on the evidence gathered at the second trial for witchcraft in Lancashire in 1633" during the examination of Edmund Robinson and the confession of Margaret Johnson, and concludes: "Brome's reworking here has resulted in making a worse play out of a very poor one, merely to be up-to-date." On the other hand, Robert Grant Martin in "Is *The Late Lancashire Witches* a Revision?" *MP* 13 (1915): 253–65, in agreement with Wallace Notestein in *A History of Witchcraft in England, 1558–1718* (1911), after reconsidering the question of authorship and date and after reviewing the deposition and charges of witchcraft, concludes: "*The Late Lancashire Witches* was an entirely new play, the product of joint authorship of Heywood and Brome, written in 1634." R. J. Kaufmann (I,A) agrees that the play was a collaborative effort but says that it was not completed before the end of August 1634. Catherine Shaw (I,A) attributes to Brome the Seely plot, "which provides the most vivid topsy-turvydom in the play and the most startling incongruities" and which later "provides whatever harmony and order are restored at the end of the play." She adds: "The unity of this play is based on connections inherent within cyclical changing tempos, thematic repetitions on various levels, and comic reversals. It is obvious that the various plot reversals are cleverly paralleled as each is suited to a particular level of the plot."

The New Academy, or The New Exchange, comedy (*1623-40;* 1659)

The Queen and Concubine, tragicomedy (*1635-39;* 1659)

The Sparagus Garden (Tom Hoydon o' Tanton Deane), comedy (*1635;* 1640)

The English Moor, or The Mock Marriage, comedy (*1637;* 1659 & MS)

The Antipodes, comedy (*1638;* 1640)

The Damoiselle, or The New Ordinary, comedy (*1637-38 (?);* 1653)

The Lovesick Court, or The Ambitious Politic, tragicomedy (ca. *1639-40;* 1659)

A Mad Couple Well Matched, comedy (*1637*(?)*-39;* 1653)

The Court Beggar, comedy (*1639-40;* 1653)

A Jovial Crew, or The Merry Beggars, comedy (*1641;* 1652)

B. UNCERTAIN ASCRIPTIONS; APOCRYPHA

A Fault in Friendship, with Jonson and "Young," comedy (*1623;* lost)

A Lovesick Maid, or The Honour of Young Ladies, comedy (*1629;* lost)

Christianetta, or Marriage and Hanging Go by Destiny, with Chapman, comedy (ca. *1623-34;* lost)

The Apprentice's Prize, with T. Heywood (?), comedy (?) (ca. *1633-41;* lost)

Sir Martin Skink, with T. Heywood, history (ca. *1633-41;* lost)

Wit in a Madness, comedy (?) (ca. *1635-40;* lost)

The Jewish Gentleman, comedy (?) (*1640;* lost)

C. CRITIQUE OF THE STANDARD EDITION

John Pearson's *The Dramatic Works of Richard Brome*, 3 vols. (1873), reprinted in 1966 without benefit of modern bibliographical scholarship, duplicates many of the errors of the early editions.

D. TEXTUAL STUDIES

Harvey Fried, "The Early Quartos of Brome's *Northern Lasse*," *PBSA* 54 (1960): 179-81, lists variant readings in six copies of *The Northern Lass* and concludes that the second quarto of 1633 is "a straight resetting of the 1632 quarto" and that "a first quarto similar to the Harvard and Folger copies was used as copy-text for the third quarto of 1684." Most of the textual information, however, remains in introductions to unpublished dissertations of individual old-spelling editions.

E. SINGLE-WORK EDITIONS

George Pierce Baker first edited *The Antipodes*, including a brief introduction and explanatory notes, in C. M. Gayley's *Representative English Comedies*, vol. 3 (1914). A. S. Knowland includes *The Antipodes* and *A Mad Couple Well Matched* in his *Six Caroline Plays* (1962), which has a brief general introduction to the six plays and comments on the texts, but no explanatory notes. His text of *The Antipodes* is based on a copy of the 1640 edition in the Brotherton Collection in the Library of the University of Leeds, with consultation of the Baker edition; *A Mad Couple* is based on a 1653 edition of *Five New Plays* at the Bodleian Library. Ann Haaker edited *The Antipodes* (1966) and *A Jovial Crew* (1968) for the Regents Renaissance Drama Series. Each edition has an informative introduction, discussing date, source, criticism of the play, stage history, and text; a chronology; and both textual and explanatory notes. *The Antipodes* is based on a collation of twenty-two copies of the 1640 edition, with consultation of the Baker edition; *A Jovial Crew* is based on a collation of eight copies of the 1652 edition; in addition, copies of the 1661 Q2 and 1684 Q3 were taken into consideration, as was the Giles Roberts Floyd unpublished thesis, 1943.

F. EDITIONS OF NONDRAMATIC WORKS

There is no edition of Brome's nondramatic works.

IV. SEE ALSO

Adams, Joseph Quincy. "Hill's List of Early Plays in Manuscript." *Library* 20 (1939): 73.

Albright, Evelyn May. *Dramatic Publications in England, 1580-1640: A Study of Conditions Affecting Content and Form of Drama.* 1927.

Aronstein, Philipp. *Das englische Renaissancedrama.* 1929.

Babb, Lawrence. *The Elizabethan Malady: A Study of Melancholia in English Literature from 1580 to 1642.* 1951.

Barbar, Laird H. Jr. "*The Late Lancashire Witches.*" *N&Q* 9 (1962): 29.

Bradley, Jesse F., and Adams, J. Q., eds. *The Jonson Allusion-Book.* 1922.

Cawley, Robert Ralston. *Unpathed Waters: Studies in the Influence of the Voyagers in Elizabethan Literature.* 1940.

Clark, Arthur Melville. *Thomas Heywood: Playwright and Miscellanist.* 1931.

Eckhardt, Eduard. *Das englische Drama im Zeitalter der Reformation und der Hochrenaissance.* 1928.

Fletcher, Jefferson Butler. "Precieuse at the Court of Charles I." *Journal of Comparative Literature* 1 (1903): 120-53.

Friedland, Louis Sigmund. "The Dramatic Unities in England." *JEGP* 10 (1911): 56-89.

Holzknecht, Karl J. *Outlines of Tudor and Stuart Plays, 1497-1642.* 1963. [*A Jovial Crew*]

Knight, G. Wilson. "*Timon of Athens* and Its Dramatic Descendants." *Stratford Papers on Shakespeare.* 1963. Pp. 99-109.

Koch, Max. "Review of E. K. R. Faust, *Richard Brome.*" *Englische Studien* 12 (1889): 97.

Koeppel, E. "Brome's *Queen and Concubine.*" *Quellen und Forschungen* 82 (1897): 209-18.

Latham, Robert Clifford, and Mathews, William, eds. *The Diary of Samuel Pepys.* Vol. 2, 1970, p. 141.

Nicoll, Allardyce. *British Drama: An Historical Survey from the Beginnings to the Present Time.* 1925; rev. ed. 1963.

———. *A History of the Restoration Drama.* 1923.

Oliphant, E. H. C. "Problems of Authorship in Elizabethan Dramatic Literature," *MP* 8 (1911): 411-59.

Perkinson, Richard H. "Topographical Comedy in the Seventeenth Century." *ELH* 3 (1936): 270-90.

Schelling, Felix E. *Elizabethan Playwrights: A Short History of the English Drama from Medieval Times to the Closing of the Theaters in 1642.* 1925.

Stonex, Arthur Bivins. "The Usurer in Elizabethan Drama." *PMLA* 31 (1916): 190-210.

Swinburne, A. C. "Richard Brome." *Fortnightly Review* 57 (1892): 500-507.

Thompson, Elbert N. S. *The Controversy between the Puritans and the Stage.* 1903.

Tieck, L. "Die Hexen in Lancashire." In *Shakesperes Vorschule* 1 (1823): xxxviii-xlii and 251-620 [?]. [Not seen]

Wagner, B. M. "Manuscript Plays of the Seventeenth Century." *TLS*, 4 Oct. 1934, p. 675.

WILLIAM DAVENANT

Michael V. DePorte

The standard edition of the plays is *The Dramatic Works of Sir William D'Avenant*, ed. James Maidment and W. H. Logan, 5 vols. (1872-74). *Gondibert* had been edited by David F. Gladish (1971), the poems and songs by A. M. Gibbs (1972).

I. GENERAL

A. BIOGRAPHICAL

Alfred Harbage's *Sir William Davenant: Poet Venturer, 1606–1668* (1935) and Arthur H. Nethercot's *Sir William D'Avenant: Poet Laureate and Playwright-Manager* (1938) remain the standard biographies, though objections to certain of the new evidence they introduced about Davenant's early life have recently been raised by J. P. Feil, "Davenant Exonerated," *MLR* 58 (1963): 335-42. Feil questions whether Davenant was in fact married by 1624, whether he ever served in Buckingham's campaigns abroad, and whether he was guilty of murdering the tapster, Thomas Warren. Feil's argument is based on his discovery of another William Davenant, a distant cousin, who he thinks may have been the Davenant listed on the 1624 baptismal document, who was probably the Davenant that fought with Buckingham in 1628, and who, as a notoriously violent, quarrelsome man, was certainly the Davenant who stabbed Warren. Had the poet been the murderer, why, Feil asks, would that fact not have been exploited in one or another of the many attacks made on him? A. M. Gibbs, in his introduction to Davenant's poems (below, III,E), finds Feil's case for exoneration conclusive, but accepts Harbage and Nethercot's account of Davenant's military service, and suggests that the conflicting evidence regarding his marital status points to the "strong possibility that Davenant was twice married before 1650."

Davenant's career as a theater manager, always of central concern in studies of his life, continues to receive attention. R. J. Kaufmann, "Suckling and Davenant Satirized by Brome," *MLR* 55 (1960): 332-44, notes that in *The Country Beggar* Davenant is mocked as an arrogant, inept court favorite, and that this attack was in part motivated by Davenant's efforts to replace Beeston as manager of the Cockpit. John Freehafer, "Brome, Suckling, and Davenant's Theater Project of 1639," *TSLL* 10 (1968): 367-83, on the other hand, argues that Brome did not attack Davenant for "inexperience and lack of ability," but because his projected new playhouse would "add to the courtly influences upon the theater that had already threatened Brome's position as a playwright." Davenant's theater, with its proposed facilities for movable scenery and lavish spectacles, promised the kind of novelty which Brome, "a writer of old-fashioned rough-and-tumble comedies, had reason to fear." Freehafer observes that though Davenant's plans for a new theater were blocked by his enemies, they were eventually realized after the Restoration in the theater he built in Lincoln's Inn Fields, a theater which Nethercot has described as "perhaps the most influential single playhouse in English stage history." Davenant's original theater project is considered briefly by Gerald Eades Bentley, *The Jacobean and Caroline Stage*, vol. 6 (1968).

In "The Rights of the Restoration Theatrical Companies," *Studia Neophilologica* 35 (1965): 174-89, Gunnar Sorelius discusses the complicated question of Davenant and Killigrew's rights to prewar plays and explores the reasons why the King's Company gained rights to so many more of the old plays than did the Duke's. In "The Formation of the London Patent Companies in 1660," *Theatre Notebook* 20 (1965): 6-30, John Freehafer modifies the widely held theory that the King's and Duke's Men were created by dividing the players who performed at the Cockpit between 8 October and 3 November 1660. Freehafer sees this troupe not as a dual company under the joint patronage of the king and duke of York, but as a single group raised in the king's name and directed by Killigrew alone. Davenant, he suggests, was allowed a share of the profits, and used the four weeks to train the young, inexperienced company he had already assembled, and to secure rights to plays for them to act. Freehafer observes further: "Among the numerous commentators who have denounced Davenant for 'improving' Shakespeare, not one seems to have noted the crucial fact that Davenant was legally obliged to 'reform' those plays, as a prescribed condition for obtaining the right to perform them."

It is unlikely that any new light will ever be shed on Davenant's personal relationship with Shakespeare, but Paulina Palmer, "Carew: An Unnoticed Allusion to Davenant's Illegitimacy," *N&Q* 10 (1963): 61-62, finds evidence in Carew's commendatory verses for *Madagascar* (1638) to indicate that Davenant may have been telling his tale of illustrious parentage far earlier than has previously been thought. Davenant's relationship with Milton also remains a matter for discussion. W. Arthur Turner, "Milton's Aid to Davenant," *MLN* 66 (1948): 538-39, reviews the sources for the story that Milton's intervention with Parliament saved Davenant's life, and concludes that while Milton did not "save" Davenant—he was never brought to trial for his life— there is reason to believe that Milton assisted him in gaining his liberty. William R. Parker, *Milton: A Biography* (1968), vol. 2, also doubts that Milton played any part in saving Davenant, but submits that "we are probably justified in believing that Milton spoke up on his behalf before reasons of state actually saved his life, and that he procured him some relief as a prisoner afterwards."

B. GENERAL STUDIES OF THE PLAYS

Though Harbage's critical biography (I,A) is still the best introduction to Davenant, Howard S. Collins, *The Comedy of William Davenant* (1967), offers the only full-length assessment of the plays in English. Collins's aim is "to study Davenant's dramaturgic treatment of the Comic Spirit in its relationship to the other drama of the time and to the life of that age." In light of his notion of "Comic Spirit," a term he derives from Meredith and defines as "that which produces an elation of the mental faculties, tending towards laughter," Collins provides substantial discussions of *The Wits*, *News from Plymouth*, and *The Playhouse to Be Let*, and shorter analyses of the comic elements he finds present in all of Davenant's other plays except *The Siege of Rhodes* and the masks. That Davenant's comedies have been so long neglected is owing, Collins thinks, to one of their great strengths—richness of topical allusion—as well as to their emphasis on "the physical rather than the mental qualities of comedy": "Combine these two features, topicality and external comedy, and one produces comedy that has only an ephemeral value." At the same time, Collins regards Davenant as the "most comprehensive comic dramatist of his age," a writer who worked easily with the conventions of the comedies of intrigue, humours, and manners; who, though usually a follower of dramatic trends, is to be credited with an important comic innovation, the introduction of burlesque to the Restoration stage; and who is to be especially valued for his diversity.

In *The Sons of Ben: Comedy in Caroline England* (1963), Joe Lee Davis discusses *The Wits*, *News from Plymouth*, and *The Platonic Lovers* as contributions to the development of a comedy of wit. He concludes that had Davenant "injected his satire into a comedy of London life and held in check his rampageous penchant for farce, he might have worn the sophisticated sock more impressively than any of his colleagues."

Lothar Honnighausen's *Der Stilwandel im dramatischen Werk Sir William Davenants* (1965) ignores Davenant's comedies. Honnighausen is concerned with the evolution of Davenant's serious plays and distinguishes three stages: an early period in which Davenant was under the influence of Beaumont and Fletcher, a transitional period in which his plays show the influence of the queen and court, and a final period in which the courtly themes of love and honor prevail. Richard Southern, "Davenant, Father of English Scenery," *Life and Letters Today* 32 (1942): 114-26, stresses the importance of court influence in a different way: Davenant introduced the scenery of royal masks into the public theater and was the first dramatist to write plays "expressly conceived for presentation with scenery." Philip Parsons, "Restoration Tragedy as Total Theatre," in *Restoration Literature: Critical Approaches*, ed. Harold Love (1972), pp. 27-68, contends that while Davenant's first plays show the influence of Fletcher in their preoccupation with ideas rather than character, his later works go beyond Fletcher: "Given that a play is not to be like life but like a discussion of it, there is no point in picturing even such limited personality as Fletcher's characters present. Ideas are best worked out with moral and emotional counters; the presence of more than one or two qualities in a character merely confuses the pattern."

Davenant's contribution to the development of dramatic opera is assessed by Eugene Haun, *But Hark! More Harmony: The Libretti of Restoration Opera in English* (1971), while his diction is the subject of close study in Rudolf Stamm's "Sir William Davenant and Shakespeare's Imagery," *ES* 24 (1942): 65-79, 97-116. Like Hazelton Spencer, *Shakespeare Improved* (1927), Stamm maintains that Davenant's revisions of Shakespeare were dictated by a concern for clarity and elegance of language that is characteristic of the Restoration. He shows how, in *The Law against Lovers* and *Macbeth*, Davenant consistently seeks to "normalize" Shakespeare's metaphors, to make them more logical, precise, immediately intelligible, and, in the process, less richly connotative. Because Davenant required that there be a "clear intellectual link between primary idea and image," he excluded "images introduced for the sake of their emotional aura only, as well as those attempting to express experiences altogether beyond the reach of conventional language."

C. WORKS AT LARGE

A book has yet to be written on Davenant's nondramatic work, but the recent introductions to A. M. Gibbs's edition of the poems and David F. Gladish's edition of *Gondibert* (below, III,E), are helpful. Gibbs sees Davenant as a transitional figure between the metaphysical and Augustan poets; his poetry reveals "an exceptionally wide experience of seventeenth-century life and society." He was, Gibbs maintains, both "a vigorous early experimenter in mock-heroic and burlesque forms," and a versatile lyric poet: "to the characteristic Cavalier virtues of elegance and poise, there is sometimes added in Davenant's writing an intellectual weight and gravity of love not often found in the secular poetry of the time." Douglas Bush has similar praise for Davenant in the prefatory note to his edition of Davenant's poetry (below, III,E). At their best, Bush remarks, Davenant's poems have a "distinctive vein of thoughtful sobriety and a large masculine vigor of imagination." Gladish finds this intellectuality especially conspicuous in *Gondibert*, which he describes as a "poetic museum of seventeenth-century literature and theory, written with an anti-scholastic slant." In it Davenant defends the "new philosophy" of Bacon, preaches the deism of Hobbes, and attacks the barbarities of war and the abuses of the priesthood. *Gondibert* is a kind of poetic "hybrid," a mixture of romance, drama, epic, and lyric which, by attempting in some measure to deal "with domestic and material realities . . . anticipates more modern forms of narrative and drama." Gladish leaves open the question of whether the poem is or is not an allegory: it may well be a "veiled allegorical discussion of current issues, but if so the allusions are vague and hard to pin down." Keith Thomas, "Social Origins of Hobbes's Political Thought," *Hobbes Studies*, ed. Keith Brown (1965), pp. 185–236, observes that the influence between Hobbes and Davenant was reciprocal: Hobbes, moved by Davenant's remarks in the *Preface to "Gondibert"* on the didactic function of heroic poetry, came to regard "the moral and political education of the aristocracy as the essential task of government."

II. CRITICISM OF INDIVIDUAL PLAYS AND STATE OF SCHOLARSHIP

A. INDIVIDUAL PLAYS

1 and 2 The Siege of Rhodes

The historical importance of *The Seige of Rhodes* is reconsidered by Philip Parsons (I,B), who thinks that the special impact it had for audiences of the day derived from the way Davenant applied the principles of the mask to traditional drama: "His characters are presented as people, but in behaviour each runs through a series of masque absolutes, chiefly Love, Jealousy and Magnanimity." Parsons holds that this new heroic form is "at once more flamboyant and more austere than its precursor," and that what gives the form its "baroque excitement" is "the paradoxical combination of wildness and discipline." He goes on to suggest that because the characters lack depth and credibility a "total theatrical assault" was needed for the production to succeed. Accordingly Davenant heightened the artificiality of his material to make it a wholly self-contained stage piece "inviting no direct reference to a world of ordinary life." Whereas earlier plays "addressed the mind directly, chiefly by verbal means, *The Siege of Rhodes* does not address the mind directly; it assaults it by way of the senses in a coordinated appeal—sculptural, painterly, musical, balletic, rhetorical." Anne Righter, "Heroic Tragedy," in *Restoration Theatre*, SuAs 6 (1965), pp. 135-57, argues that the air of "fantasy" in the play sets a precedent of escapism which Restoration tragedy would follow: "Faced with the new science and the doctrines of Hobbes, with the split between faith and reason, appearance and reality, it retreated in confusion to a land of rhetorical make-believe." In the introduction to her edition of the play (1973), however, Ann-Mari Hedbäck observes that the political implications are Hobbesian and that Davenant's treatment of the love-honor conflict places greater emphasis on the need to subordinate such passions to reason than does later heroic drama. Hedbäck also reviews the question of sources. In addition to those proposed by Killis Campbell, "The Sources of Davenant's *The Siege of Rhodes*," *MLN* 13 (1898): 177-82, C. G. Child, "The Rise of the Heroic Play," *MLN* 19

(1904): 166-73, and Alwin Thaler, "Thomas Heywood, D'Avenant, and *The Siege of Rhodes*," *PMLA* 39 (1924): 624-41, she contends that Davenant was probably indebted to certain French plays dealing with the Turks which precede Mlle. Scudéry's romance, *Ibrahim*, to Thomas Artus's *Continuation de l'historie des Turcs* (1612), and to Italian opera. She further contends that Alphonso and Ianthe may be modeled on Charles I and Henrietta Maria.

The Wits

Robert Blattès, "Elements parodiques dans *The Wits* de Sir William Davenant," *Caliban* 10 (1974): 127-40, takes issue with the assertion Kathleen Lynch made in *The Social Mode of Restoration Comedy* (1926) that for reasons of expediency comedies of the 1630s contain little satire of the *préciosité* in vogue at court. He gives examples of the way Davenant parodied the literary taste of the queen and her courtiers throughout the play, and argues that such parody is essential to its comic effect. Collins (I,B) follows earlier critics in seeing *The Wits* as Davenant's most successful and influential comedy. He suggests that Davenant anticipated Restoration comedy not only in his ridicule of the country, but also in his creation of a strong, unsentimental, witty heroine: "Lady Ample represents the Restoration ideal of a woman being the equal to a man in all respects."

The Platonic Lovers

Charles L. Squier, "Davenant's Comic Assault on *Préciosité: The Platonic Lovers*," *University of Colorado Studies*, Series in Language and Literature, vol. 10 (1966): 57-72, considers the play a neglected "minor masterpiece," a pointed, artful burlesque of court Platonism which is both less serious and less ambiguous than has been thought. Many of the speeches praising Platonic love have been taken seriously, he suggests, because Davenant's parody is too close to the original to be recognized for what it is, whereas the ambiguities which have so often perplexed readers are "integral to the play's satiric attack on the absurdities of the Platonic cult." Clifford Leech, *Shakespeare's Tragedies and Other Studies in Seventeenth-Century Drama* (1950), contends that though the burlesque of court fashion is marred by the introduction of Fredeline—"a feeble villain . . . whose machinations blunt the satire's edge"—the play still deserves to be better known as it contains "some of the best topical satire of Caroline years." Davenant's aim, according to Leech, is to expose the snobbery of Platonic love, its assumption that "fine people are of different stuff from the common."

Macbeth

Christopher Spencer, in his introduction to *Five Restoration Adaptations of Shakespeare* (1965), takes a more sympathetic view of Davenant's revision than have most previous scholars. He submits that *Macbeth*, like other Restoration adaptations of Shakespeare, is best understood if seen as a new play; so regarded it will rank among the better plays of the period. Revisers of Shakespeare were, Spencer thinks, primarily concerned with moral clarity: "they were interested in the sense of harmony and pattern and consistency and order that they felt art should offer"; they stressed poetic justice because it was believed to reveal the natural order of things, rather than the freakish exceptions; and they emphasized the "permanent patterns of human relationships" more than the "depths of individual experience." In *Macbeth* the cuts and additions work to underscore the theme of ambition. Spencer grants that the tragedy is thus rendered less profound and the poetry more pedestrian, but insists that Davenant's *Macbeth* is nonetheless "a coherent and forceful presentation of his chosen theme." Catherine Itzin, "*Macbeth* in the Restoration," *Theatre Quarterly* 1 (1971): 14-18, agrees with Freehafer (I,A) that Davenant was legally bound to revise *Macbeth* before presenting it, but notes that other factors determined the way he revised the play: the political climate, which dictated increased attention to the crime of usurpation; the taste of his audience for rhetorical language, which resulted in changing the play "from a study of the developing evil emerging from the character of Macbeth, to a study of ambition and an emphasis on *discussion* of the subject and *showing* its effects on characters' actions"; the use of actresses, which led to enlarged roles for Lady Macduff and the witches. Dennis Bartholomeusz, "The Davenant-Betterton *Macbeth*," *Komos* 1 (1967): 41-48, studies Davenant's text with an eye to discovering how Betterton played Macbeth. He concludes that, given the way Davenant attempts to reduce the complexity of Macbeth's character and to make his speeches more refined and rational, Betterton "could not have created a fully tragic Macbeth." The influence of Davenant's adaptation on subsequent productions is indicated by G. Blakemore Evans in his introduction to *Shakespearean Prompt-Books of the Seventeenth Century*, vol. 5: *The Smock Alley "Macbeth"* (1970). Evans discusses the extent to which the Smock Alley prompt-book reflects Davenant's revisions.

The Tempest, or The Enchanted Island

Norman N. Holland, *The First Modern Comedies: The Significance of Etherege, Wycherley, and Congreve* (1959), and Christopher Spencer (above) both find that the Davenant-Dryden *Tempest* affords a less sanguine view of Prospero's world than had Shakespeare's. Holland argues that Davenant saw in the play a "study of the 'natural man,'" and that his adaptation is "based on one continued joke—the contrast implied between the 'enchanted island' of the play and 'the Town' of his Restoration audience." Davenant prefers the knowledge and sophistication of "the Town" to the naivete and innocence of the island because such knowledge, though "disruptive in its first effects" leads finally to wisdom: "Civilization has its discontents, but it is worth them, for society regulated passions toward peace." Robert D. Hume, *The Development of English Drama in the Late Seventeenth Century* (1976), remarks that though the general effect of Davenant's changes is to "lower the tone of the original," yet the "subtle use of a three-level hierarchy plot and some telling thematic interconnections make this adaptation far more than a prostituting of Shakespeare." W. Moelwyn Merchant, "Shakespeare 'Made Fit,'" in *Restoration Theatre*, SuAS, no. 6 (1965), pp. 195-219, finds in Dryden's preface of 1670 indications that he was uneasy about some of Davenant's additions to the play. Aline MacKenzie Taylor, "Dryden's *Enchanted Isle* and Shadwell's *Dominion*," *Essays in English Literature of the Classical Period Presented to Dougald MacMillan*, ed. Daniel W. Patterson and Albrecht B. Strauss (1967), pp. 39-53, suggests that the new version of the play was prompted by public interest in the West Indies and that Davenant and Dryden envisioned Prospero's Island as Barbados; John W. Loofbourow, "Robinson Crusoe's Island and the Restoration *Tempest*," *Enlightenment Essays* 2 (1971): 201-7, indicates that the setting of the play may have been the prototype for the landscape of Crusoe's island.

The First Day's Entertainment at Rutland House

Jackson I. Cope, "Rhetorical Genres in Davenant's *First Day's Entertainment at Rutland House*," *Quarterly Journal of Speech* 45 (1959): 191-94, discusses Davenant's use of two distinct rhetorical modes: the speeches of Diogenes and Aristophanes are written in the tradition of the mock encomium, those of the Parisian and Londoner in the tradition of the character.

The Man's the Master

James U. Rundle, "D'Avenant's *The Man's the Master* and the Spanish Source," *MLN* 65 (1950): 194-96, contends that parallels between *The Man's the Master* and Rojas Zorilla's *Donde hay agravios no hay zelos* (the play on which Scarron's *Jodelet* was based) indicate that Davenant may have borrowed directly from Rojas. John Loftis, *The Spanish Plays of Neoclassical England* (1973), finds Rundle's evidence "less than conclusive."

B. STATE OF SCHOLARSHIP

Davenant has been well served by his biographers, by students of theatrical history, by reassessments of his role as an adaptor of Shakespeare, and most recently by the editors of *The Siege of Rhodes*, *Macbeth*, *The Tempest* (below, III,D), and of his poetry (below III,E). But the emphasis of scholarship continues to be on his historical importance. Critics of his plays stress the influences to which he was subject, and the influence he in turn had, oftener than they do the character of the plays themselves. More of his plays need to receive serious attention in their own right, attention of the sort that would be invited were more of them to appear in modern editions.

III. CANON

A. PLAYS IN CHRONOLOGICAL ORDER

This list follows the chronology of Alfred Harbage, *Annals of English Drama, 975-1700*, rev. S. Schoenbaum (1964). The acting date is in italics preceding the semicolon; the second date is that of the earliest edition. Further discussion of the canon may be found in Harbage and Nethercot (I,A), and in Bentley, *The Jacobean and Caroline Stage*, vol. 3 (1956). For bibliographical descriptions of the early editions see W. W. Greg, *A Bibliography of the English Printed Drama to the Restoration*, 4 vols (1939-59).

The Cruel Brother, tragedy (*licensed 12 Jan. 1627;* 1630)

Albovine, King of the Lombards, tragedy (*1626-29;* 1629)

Bentley, vol. 3, and Nethercot (I,A) believe *Albovine* to have been Davenant's first play. Harbage's arguments (I,A) for thinking it written after *The Cruel Brother*—that *Albovine* is superior, and that Davenant would have preferred to publish his best play first—Bentley finds unconvincing.

The Just Italian, comedy (*licensed 2 Oct. 1629;* 1630)

The Siege, tragicomedy (*1629?;* 1673)

Harbage speculates that this is the same play as *The Colonel* (licensed 22 July 1629). Bentley tentatively accepts the identification, but thinks the evidence for it "incomplete." He notes further that while the text of the 1673 folio is commonly regarded as a revision, "not much evidence has been cited besides its brevity and the prominence of the comic plot."

Love and Honour, or *The Courage of Love,* or *The Nonpareilles,* or *The Matchless Maids,* tragicomedy (*licensed 20 Nov. 1634;* 1649)

Scenes from the subplot of *Love and Honour,* together with scenes from *Twelfth Night* and *Henry V,* were adapted in the eighteenth century by Charles Molloy as *The Half-Pay Officers* (1720).

The Wits, comedy (*licensed 19 Jan. 1634;* 1636)

News from Plymouth, comedy (*licensed 1 Aug. 1635;* 1673)

Bentley, vol. 3, rejects the conjecture of Frederick G. Fleay, *A Biographical Chronicle of the English Drama* (1891), vol. 1, that Davenant based *News from Plymouth* on a superior play (now lost), the setting for which had been Portsmouth.

The Platonic Lovers, comedy (*licensed 16 Nov. 1635;* 1636)

The Temple of Love, mask (*10 Feb. 1635;* 1635)

The Triumphs of the Prince d'Amour, mask (*23 or 24 Feb. 1636;* 1636)

Britannia Triumphans, mask (*licensed 8 Jan. 1638;* 1638)

The Fair Favourite, tragicomedy (*licensed 17 Nov. 1638;* 1673)

Luminalia, or The Festival of Light, mask (*6 Feb. 1638;* 1638)

Bentley, vol. 3, agrees with Enid Welsford, *The Court Masque: A Study in the Relationship between Poetry and the Revels* (1927), that Davenant's part in *Luminalia* was smaller than in his other masks. Davenant was responsible for the songs, and perhaps for the prose descriptions, but the action and argument were plagiarized from Italian sources by Inigo Jones.

The Unfortunate Lovers, tragedy (*licensed 16 April 1638;* 1643)

MacD. P. Jackson, "Three Unidentified Play Titles of the Early Seventeenth Century," *N&Q* 20 (1973): 465-66, argues that *The Tragedy of Heildebrand,* which appears in Supplementary List II,f, of the *Annals* as an annonymous play not known to have been printed, is an alternate title for *The Unfortunate Lovers.*

The Spanish Lovers, comedy (*licensed 30 March 1639;* 1673)

Harbage accepts the theory, first put forward by Edmund Malone, that *The Spanish Lovers* of 1639 is *The Distresses* of the 1673 folio.

Salmacida Spolia, mask (*21 Jan. 1640;* 1640)

The Athenians' Reception of Phocion, entertainment (*1656-57;* lost)

The First Day's Entertainment at Rutland House, disputation (*23 May 1656;* 1657)

Satirical Declamations, disputations (*1656-57;* lost?)

Harbage speculates that this may be an alternate title for *The First Day's Entertainment.*

1 The Siege of Rhodes, tragicomedy (*Sept. 1656;* 1656)

The printing history of the early editions is discussed by Ann-Mari Hedbäck, "The Printing of *The Siege of Rhodes,*" *Studia Neophilologica* 45 (1973): 68-79. Hedbäck finds Greg's account of the first quarto "not quite accurate," and notes that "there is no critical edition of Part 1 of the play based on the first quarto," the only edition of the play set up from manuscript. Hedbäck's own edition of the play (1973) supplies the need for such a text.

The Cruelty of the Spaniards in Peru, operatic show (*1658;* 1658)

Included as Act IV of *The Playhouse to Be Let* (1663). Harbage speculates that this may be the same as *2 Sir Francis Drake.*

1 Sir Francis Drake, pseudo-history (*1658-59;* 1659)

Included as Act III of *The Playhouse to Be Let* (1663).

2 Siege of Rhodes, tragicomedy (*1657*-ca. *1659;* 1663)

The Law against Lovers, comedy (*10 Feb. 1662;* 1673)

Adaptation of Shakespeare's *Measure for Measure* and *Much Ado about Nothing.*

The Playhouse to Be Let, comic medley (ca. *Aug. 1663;* 1673)

Act II is from Molière's *Sganarelle;* see listings for *The Cruelty of the Spaniards in Peru* and *1 Sir Francis Drake.* André de Mandach, *Molière et la comédie de moeurs en Angleterre (1660-68)* (1946), argues that the play was first staged in the autumn of 1662. More recently, in "The First Translator of Molière: Sir William Davenant or Colonel Henry Howard," *MLN* 66 (1951): 513-18, Mandach has tried to prove that the play, which is listed among those performed by Killigrew and which until the late eighteenth century was attributed to Colonel Henry Howard, should no longer be considered Davenant's. Mandach does not, however, make clear how much of the play should be assigned to Howard, since he evidently accepts Davenant as the author of *1 Sir Francis Drake* and *The Cruelties of the Spaniards in Peru.*

Macbeth, dramatic opera (*5 Nov. 1664;* 1674 and MS)

Adapted from Shakespeare. Christopher Spencer, "*Macbeth* and Davenant's *The Rivals,*" *SQ* 20 (1969): 225-29, suggests that the frequent echoes of Davenant's *Macbeth* in the first scene of *The Rivals* indicate that he revised *Macbeth* shortly before, probably by "late autumn of 1663." In the introduction to his edition of *Macbeth* (1961), Spencer contends that Davenant based his adaptation on a pre-Restoration manuscript of the play independent of the first folio, and that the opening ten lines of the witches' song added near the beginning of II.v may have been written by Shakespeare. J. G. McManaway, "The Year's Contribution to Shakesperian Studies," *ShS* 16 (1963): 172-81, finds both suppositions unconvincing. John P. Cutts, "The Original Music to Middleton's *The Witch*," *SQ* 7 (1956): 203-10, discusses Davenant's recovery of two Middleton songs—"Come away Hecate" and "Black spiritts and white"—for use in his adaptation of *Macbeth*. In "Lost Lore in *Macbeth*," *SQ* 24 (1973): 223-26, however, James O. Wood argues, largely on the basis of Spencer's evidence, that several of the songs Davenant "introduced" may well have been Shakespeare's and that at least one of the two songs found in *The Witch* may have originally come from *Macbeth*.

The Rivals, comedy, (*1664;* 1668)

Adaptation of Shakespeare and Fletcher's *The Two Noble Kinsmen*. Jackson, "Three Unidentified Play Titles" (above *The Unfortunate Lovers*), thinks that *Love Yields to Honour*, referred to in Supplementary List II,f, of the *Annals* as an anonymous play not known to have been printed, is possibly an alternate title for *The Rivals*.

Greene's Tu Quoque, comedy (*12 Sept. 1667;* lost)

Adaptation of John Cooke's *Greene's Tu Quoque*.

The Tempest, or The Enchanted Island, with Dryden, comedy (*7 Nov. 1667;* 1670)

Adapted from Shakespeare.

The Man's the Master, comedy (*26 March 1668;* 1669)

Translation of Scarron's *Jodelet, ou le maître valet*.

B. UNCERTAIN ASCRIPTIONS; APOCRYPHA

Christopher Spencer, "'Count Paris's Wife': *Romeo and Juliet* on the Early Restoration Stage," *TSLL* 7 (1966): 309-16, has recently argued that Davenant probably revised *Romeo and Juliet* some time before James Howard made it into a tragicomedy.

The Countryman, unknown (*5 Nov. 1657?;* lost)

According to the *Annals* this is probably the same play as *The Countryman,* entered in the Stationers' Register by Humphrey Moseley as one of a group of anonymous plays dating between 1600 and 1642. In *Cavalier Drama: An Historical and Critical Supplement to the Study of the Elizabethan and Restoration Stage* (1936), Harbage conjectures that the play was a droll based on *The Wits.* Bentley finds no evidence either that the play was a droll or that it was Davenant's.

Hamlet, tragedy (*1661?;* 1676)

Adapted from Shakespeare.

C. CRITIQUE OF THE STANDARD EDITION

A new edition of the complete dramatic works is badly needed. James Maidment and W. H. Logan's *The Dramatic Works of Sir William D'Avenant,* 5 vols. (1872-74), prints all of the plays except *Luminalia* and *The Tempest* (Shadwell's version is given instead), but the commentary is neglible and the texts fall far short of modern editorial standards.

D. SINGLE WORK EDITIONS

The Siege of Rhodes is available in an old spelling edition prepared by Ann-Mari Hedbäck: *Sir William Davenant, "The Siege of Rhodes": A Critical Edition,* Acta Universitatis Upsaliensis, Studia Anglistica Upsaliensia, no. 14 (1973). The text of Part I is based on all known extant copies of the first quarto (1656); Hedbäck has based the text of Part II on the 1663 edition, but has also consulted the transcript of the play in the Douai Bibliotheque Municipale. Another excellent critical edition is Christopher Spencer's *Davenant's "Macbeth" from the Yale Manuscript: An Edition with a Discussion of the Relation of Davenant's Text to Shakespeare's* (1961). Spencer reprints this text, as well as the 1670 text of *The Tempest,* in his *Five Restoration Adaptations of Shakespeare* (1965). A. S. Knowland edited *The Wits* for the World's Classics series anthology *Six Caroline Plays* (1962); his text is based on the first edition of 1636. T. J. B. Spencer's edition of *Salmacida Spolia* (based on the quarto of 1640) is included in *A Book of Masques: In Honour of Allardyce Nicoll,* ed. T. J. B. Spencer and Stanley Wells (1967), pp. 339-70. Texts of *The Triumph of the Prince d'Amour* and of *Britannia*

Triumphans appear (in English) in *Trois masques a la cour de Charles 1ᵉʳ d'Angleterre*, ed. Murray Lefkowitz (1970). *News from Plymouth* has been printed with a parallel Italian text in *"News from Plymouth"*: *Commedia*, ed. and trans. Anna Maria Crinò (1972).

The text of the Dryden-Davenant *Tempest* is carefully distinguished from that of the 1674 operatic version by George Robert Guffey in the introduction to his fascimile edition of four versions of Shakespeare's play, *After the Tempest: "The Tempest, or The Enchanted Island" (1670)*; *"The Tempest, or The Enchanted Island" (1674)*; *"The Mock-Tempest, or The Enchanted Castle" (1675)*; *"The Tempest: An Opera" (1756)* (1970). In addition to another fascimile edition of the Dryden-Davenant *Tempest* (1969), there are fascimile texts of the following: *The Law Against Lovers* (1970); *Macbeth* (1969); *The Rivals* (1970); and *The Half-Pay Officers* (1969)—Charles Molloy's 1720 adaptation of *Love and Honour* with added scenes from *Twelfth Night* and *Henry V*.

E. NONDRAMATIC WORKS

The Clarendon Press has recently issued the definitive edition of Davenant's poetry. Vol. 1, *The Shorter Poems, and Songs from the Plays and Masques*, ed. A. M. Gibbs (1972), contains all the known songs and poems except *Gondibert*, including five new poems from manuscript sources. Three of these poems were printed earlier by Herbert Berry, "Three New Poems by Davenant," *PQ* 31 (1952): 70-74, the fourth by Gibbs himself, "A Davenant Imitation of Donne?"*RES* 18 (1967): 45-48. Gibbs's edition has a general critical introduction, extensive discussions of text and canon, detailed commentary on individual poems, and an appendix, prepared by Judy Bleezard, giving the seventeenth-century musical settings which survive for fifteen of the songs. Volume 2, *Gondibert* (1971), ed. David F. Gladish, offers a scrupulously edited text of the poem based on the quarto of 1651 containing numerous corrections in Davenant's hand. Gladish also prints Davenant's *Preface* and Hobbes's *Answer*, as well as *The Seventh Canto of the Third Book*, which was not published until 1685, and which was generally regarded as a spurious continuation before the studies of J. G. McManaway, "The 'Lost Canto' of *Gondibert*," *MLQ* 1 (1940): 63-78, and Alvin I. Dust, "*The Seventh and Last Canto of Gondibert* and Two Dedicatory Poems," *JEGP* 60 (1961): 282-85. There is also a fascimile edition of the first quarto of *Gondibert* which includes *The Seventh Canto*, and two poems from the 1673 edition of his works thought to be fragments of *Gondibert* (1970). Douglas Bush has edited a brief collection of Davenant's verse: *Selected Poems of Sir William Davenant* (1943); and extracts of Davenant's *Preface to Gondibert* appear in *Neo-Classical Criticism 1660-1800*, ed. Irene Simon (1971).

IV. SEE ALSO

Adams, H. M. "The Shakespeare Collection in the Library of Trinity College, Cambridge." *ShS* 5 (1952): 50–54. [*The Tempest*]

Baier, Lee. "An Early Instance of 'Daydreams.'" *N&Q* 17 (1970): 409.

Blackburn, Thomas H. "Edmund Bolton's *London, King Charles His Augusta, or City Royal*." *HLQ* 25 (1962): 315–23.

Bonnard, Georges A. "Shakespeare in the Biblioteca Bodmeriana." *ShS* 9 (1956): 81–85. [*Macbeth* and *The Tempest*]

Francis, F. C. "The Shakespeare Collection in the British Museum." *ShS* 3 (1950): 43–57.

Haywood, Charles. "*The Songs and Masque in the New Tempest:* An Incident in the Battle of the Two Theaters, 1674." *HLQ* 19 (1955): 39–56.

Hobbs, Mary. "Robert and Thomas Ellice, Friends of Ford and Davenant." *N&Q* 21 (1974): 292–93.

Hoffman, D. S. "Some Shakespearian Music, 1660-1900." *ShS* 18 (1965): 94–101. [*Macbeth* and *The Tempest*]

James, E. Nelson. "Drums and Trumpets." *Restoration and Eighteenth-Century Theatre Research* 9 (1970): 46–55; 10 (1971): 54–57.

McElroy, D. "The 'Artificial Sea' in Jonson's *Masque of Blacknesse*." *N&Q* 7 (1960): 419–21.

Macey, Samuel L. "Duffet's *Mock Tempest* and the Assimilation of Shakespeare during the Restoration and Eighteenth Century." *Restoration and Eighteenth-Century Theatre Research* 7 (1968): 44–52.

McGee, Arthur R. "*Macbeth* and the Furies." *ShS* 19 (1966): 55–67.

Maxwell, J. C. "William Davenant." *TLS*, 25 Aug. 1972, p. 997. [Gloss on "Written when Collonell Goring was beleev'd slaine, at the siege of Breda."]

Muir, Kenneth. "Shakespeare's Imagery—Then and Now." *ShS* 18 (1965): 46–57.

Nethercot, Arthur H. "Scribblings in a Copy of D'avenant's *Gondibert*." *N&Q* 17 (1970): 249–51.

Olive, W. J. "Davenant and Davenport." *N&Q* 194 (1949): 320.

Ram, Tulsi. *The Neo-Classical Epic, 1660-1720*. 1971.

Riewald, J. G. "Laureates in Elysium: Sir William Davenant and Robert Southey." *ES* 37 (1956): 133–40.

Roberts, Peter. "Theatrical Cavalier." *Plays and Players* 5 (1959): 7.

Sen, Sailendra Kumar. "Adaptations of Shakespeare and His Critics, 1660-1790." *Indian Journal of English Studies* 3 (1962): 44–60.

Sorelius, Gunnar. "*The Giant Race Before the Flood*": *Pre-Restoration Drama on the Stage and in the Criticism of the Restoration*. 1974.

Stroup, Thomas B. *Type Characters in the Serious Drama of the Restoration, with Special Attention to the Plays of Davenant, Dryden, Lee, and Others*. Kentucky Microcards, Series A, no. 5. 1956.

Summers, Vivian, comp. *"The Tempest": A Performing Script from Shakespeare's Play and the 1674 Adaptation*. 1974.

Van Lennep, William. "The Smock Alley Players of Dublin." *ELH* 13 (1946): 216–22. [Rejects claims that Davenant had a share in adapting Shakespeare's *Julius Caesar*]

Waddell, David. "The Writing of Charles Davenant (1656-1713)." *Library* 11 (1956): 206–12.

Waith, Eugene M. *Ideas of Greatness: Heroic Drama in England*. 1971.

Wickham, Glynne. *Early English Stages 1300 to 1660*. Vol. 2: *1576-1660*. 1972.

Woodward, D. H. "The Manuscript Corrections and Printed Variants in the Quarto Edition of *Gondibert* (1651)." *Library* 20 (1965): 298–309.

ANONYMOUS PLAYS

Richard B. Davidson

Books and articles consulted date from 1941, the publication date of the early volumes of G. E. Bentley, The Jacobean and Caroline Stage, *7 vols. (1941–68), to the end of 1973. Some important earlier studies are included, as is some material after 1973, primarily new editions. Only those plays with some published scholarship since 1941 are included. For additional information, see Bentley; W. W. Greg,* A Bibliography of the English Printed Drama to the Restoration, *4 vols. (1939–59); Alfred Harbage,* Annals of English Drama, *rev. Samuel Schoenbaum (1964), and the first* Supplement *by Schoenbaum (1966). The dates following play titles indicate the preferred date of first performance, or range of dates in which first performance is most likely (in italics), and the date of the first edition, where there has been one, from the* Annals *and the first* Supplement; *type classifications are from the* Annals.

Swetnam the Woman-Hater Arraigned by Women, **comedy** (*1615–19*; 1620)

Editions

Since A. B. Grosart's edition of 1880 in *Occasional Issues*, vol. 14, there have been two published editions: Coryl Crandall's University of Illinois dissertation, "*Swetnam the Woman-Hater*; A Critical Edition" (1966), which is the basis for his *Swetnam the Woman-Hater: The Controversy and the Play* (1969), and a Tudor fascimile text (1914). Crandall's introduction discusses the feminist literature and controversy which form the background of the play, its sources, stage history and authorship, and its relationship to the dramatic literature of its time.

Sources and Background

Langbaine, according to Crandall, was the first to attribute the play's source to Juan de Flores's *Historia de Aurelio e Isabella* (a translated and slightly modified version of Flores's *Grisel y Mirabella*) written about 1495, and published five times in England between 1556 and 1586. Barbara Matulka, *The Novels of Juan de Flores and Their European Diffusion* (1931), discusses the relationships between these two sources.

Crandall argues that the play is a culmination of works connected to a controversy which began with the publication of *The Arraignment of Lewd, Idle, Froward, and Unconstant Women,* 1615, by Joseph Swetnam. Daniel Tuvil's *Asylum Veneris*, both a debate-book and courtesy book, may or may not be a response to Swetnam's antifeminine pamphlets, but three pamphlets of 1617 clearly are responses which attest to the prevailing interest in the feminist controversy from which the play draws its subject matter. Rachel Speght, *A Mouzell for Melastomus*, Ester Sowerman, *Ester hath hang'd Haman*, and Constantia Munda, *The Worming of a Mad Dogge*, respond in varying tones, from mild and polite to heated and aggressive, to Swetnam's pamphlet; these tones form the parameters for debate on the degree of anger implied by the play, which comprises a final, public statement. Crandall maintains that the play is the most calm, as well as the most accomplished, of the documents in the antifeminist controversies, and that its overriding theme is a concern for justice for both sexes. Matulka, *The Novels of Juan de Flores*, and Jean Elisabeth Gagen, *The New Woman: Her Emergence in English Drama, 1600-1730* (1954), argue that the play is profeminist.

In addition to the novel of de Flores and the background of controversy and pamphlet war, there are suggested sources for specific parts of the play. Allan Holaday, "Shakespeare, Richard Edwards, and the Virtues Reconciled," *JEGP* 66 (1967): 200-206, argues for a conscious allusion to the Parliament in Heaven motif from Lyly's *Endymion* and Peele's *The Arraignment of Paris*.

Stage History

The title page of the 1620 edition says that *Swetnam* was "Acted at the Red Bull by the late Queenes Servants." Crandall argues for a first performance sometime in 1618 or 1619, after Munda's *Worming*, which was entered 29 April 1617, as the last of the "answers" to Swetnam's pamphlet. G. E. Bentley, *The Jacobean and Caroline Stage*, vol. 5 (1956), says that 1617 is the earliest possible date, his argument centering on "spight" (V.ii.322) which, he says, is based on "Speght," whose *Mouzell for Melastomus* was entered 14 November 1616. George F. Reynolds, *The Staging of Elizabethan Plays at the Red Bull Theater*,

1605-1625 (1941), cites Felix E. Schelling, *Elizabethan Drama, 1558-1642* (1908), who places the performance in 1618 or 1619.

The likelihood, according to Crandall, is that the closing of the theaters between the queen's death on 2 March and her funeral on 13 May 1619 would suggest a production in late 1618. The play then went into dormancy until performed again, according to Bentley, around 1633, when an allusion to it occurs in Thomas Nabbes's *Tottenham Court*.

Authorship

There is no external evidence pointing to authorship. On the basis of internal evidence, Grosart, in his 1880 edition, speculated on the possibility of Dekker's or Heywood's authorship: both were associated with the Red Bull Theater. Bentley suggests Thomas Drewe the actor, whose name appears on the performance lists, but acknowledges that the actor may not be the same person as that minor writer.

On the basis of verbal parallels, Grosart seems to favor Heywood: the use of "odure" in *Swetnam* is similar to Heywood's in his *Golden Age*. Louis B. Wright, *Middle-Class Culture in Elizabethan England* (1935), comes close to assigning Heywood: he was with the company at the time of the play; he used similar situations wherein romance between boy and girl troubles the family peace; and the play looks as if it were written with the source immediately in front of the writer, in haste, as was Heywood's habit. Wright concludes that "the language, dialogue, and clownery are all patterned after Heywood."

See Also

Camden, Charles. *The Elizabethan Woman*. 1952.
Crandall, Coryl. "Cultural Implications of the Swetnam Anti-Feminist Controversy in the Seventeenth Century." *Journal of Popular Culture* 2 (1968): 136–48.
Harbage, Alfred. *Cavalier Drama: An Historical Supplement to the Study of the Elizabethan and Restoration Stage*. 1936.

The Costly Whore, **pseudo-history (ca.** *1619-32*; **1633)**

Edition

Since A. H. Bullen's edition in *A Collection of Old English Plays*, vol. 4 (1885), there has been no new edition.

Date

The date of first performance is a matter of some debate: G. E. Bentley, *The Jacobean and Caroline Stage*, vol. 5 (1956), mentions that the title page of the 1633 edition, which says that the play was "Acted by the Company of the Revels", has suggested to some, notably Fleay, that the "revels" in question were the King's rather than the Red Bull's, which would put the date of performance between 1629 and 1636, rather than 1619 and 1623. But Bentley notes that "the play seems much too crude and primitive for the time of Charles I, and is quite unlike other plays of the King's Revels company in this respect, though not very different from one or two in the Red Bull Revels company." He goes on to suggest that while not conclusive in itself, the fact that Augustine Matthews printed *The Heir*, "an undoubted Red Bull Revels play," with *The Costly Whore* might well be corroborative material to argue for a performance in the earlier period.

Authorship

Debate about authorship is confined to an early exchange between W. J. Lawrence and Walter Worral in *MLR* 17 (1922). Lawrence, "The Authorship of *The Costelie Whore*," pp. 167-68, claims authorship for Henry Martin on the basis of a bookseller's note appended to *Free Parliament Quaeries*, wherein Henry Martin, Seargeant Trumpeter to the King, is so named. In his answer of the same title, p. 411, Worral points out that the document in question is a series of gibes at "the Late Rump," gibes couched in obviously rhetorical, hyperbolical, and absurd questions (e.g., was it not Sir Arthur Haslerigg who wrote *Orlando Furioso?*), which makes it an unlikely piece of evidentiary material for claims to Martin's authorship of *The Costly Whore*.

The Two Noble Ladies and the Converted Conjurer, tragicomedy (*1619–23*; MS)

Editions

After Bullen, *Old English Plays*, vol. 4 (1885), the play has been edited by Rebecca G. Rhoads for the Malone Society (1930). There is a facsimile and transcript of Act III, scene 3, in W. W. Greg, *Dramatic Documents from the Elizabethan Playhouses*, vol. 2 (1931).

Date

Rhoads suggests in her introduction to the Malone Society edition that "perhaps it would be unwise to say more than that it is less likely that this was written before 1600 or after 1630 than between those dates." But she and others tentatively narrow the range to between 1619 and 1623, with a likelihood of performance in late 1622 or early 1623. G. E. Bentley, *The Jacobean and Caroline Stage*, vol. 5 (1956), quotes the title page, which states that the play was acted at the Red Bull by the Company of Revels. This company, formed from remnants of Queen Anne's men in 1619, continued to act at the Red Bull until the first half of 1623. While the company was not officially named "Children of the Revels" until 1622—a fact which would further narrow down the play's date to between 1622 and 1623—it was retrospectively so known, and thus both Bentley and Rhoads conclude that 1619 and 1623 are the limits.

Description of Manuscript; Implications

F. S. Boas, *Shakespeare and the Universities* (1923), notes the interlacing of abbreviations of minor actors' names in the stage directions, which suggests to him that this play and the others in the 'Repertoire" he is discussing were for the same company. Boas suggests the possibility that a London company was touring provincial areas. W. J. Lawrence, reviewing Greg's *Dramatic Documents* (above) in *RES* 8 (1932): 224-28, notes, in support of this hypothesis, that none of the manuscripts bears the censor's license. In a rejoinder, Greg, "Elizabethan Dramatic Documents," *RES* 8 (1932): 457-58, argues that, without certain knowledge that plays in the country did not need official licensing, Lawrence's evidence is inconclusive.

Certain inferences can, however, be made from the manuscript. Greg's opinion of the British Museum manuscript is that it is the author's copy containing many alterations and corrections; furthermore, the insertion of six actors' names in different hands at various points in the text would suggest that it is also a prompt copy. Rhoads (above) suggests the likelihood that author and prompter were working on the manuscript at the same time. If so, the performances alluded to on the title page were probably the first the play had. Again, the evidence, while not conclusive, strongly suggests a date between 1619 and 1623.

Sources

Bentley discounts Fleay's claim that the play is founded on Calderon's *Magico Prodigioso*, a claim reiterated by W. C. Hazlitt, *A Manual for the Collector and Amateur of Old English Plays* (1892). Most of the scenes, says Bentley, are unrelated. Furthermore, Calderon did not write his play until 1637. Perhaps the two plays have a common ancestor.

Nero, tragedy (*1624 [published]*; 1624 & MSS)

Editions

A. H. Bullen, *Old English Plays*, vol. 1 (1882), and H. P. Horne, *"Nero" and Other Plays*, Mermaid series (1888), are the last published editions; Stephen J. Teller did an edition for his 1968 University of Illinois dissertation. Teller presents an old-spelling text based on a collation of eleven extant copies of Q1 (1624) and Q2 (1633) and Egerton MS 1994 "which is probably earlier than Q1." In his critical introduction he considers the genre of the Roman history play and relates *Nero* to it. He discusses sources, attempting for the first time to discriminate where the author of *Nero* borrowed directly from original sources from where he borrowed from translations such as Greneway's 1598 translation of Tacitus's *Annals*. The last part of the introduction takes up questions of authorship, date of composition, structure, and style.

Date

Wilfred P. Mustard, "Notes on *The Tragedy of Nero*," *PQ* 1 (1922): 173-78, points to the initial printing of the play in 1624. The performance date, however, is somewhat more problematical. G. Blakemore Evans, "Note on Fletcher and Massinger's *Little French Lawyer*," *MLN* 52 (1937): 406-7, says that Fletcher's and Massinger's character La-Writ, IV.iv. 12-16, is drawn from *Nero*, III.ii.83-85, "I love a dire revenge. . . . " Evans says that this would argue against the opinion of Horne (above) and F. E. Schmid, ed., *The Tragedy of Julia Agrippina, Empresse of Rome*, in *Materialen zur Kunde des älteren Englischen Dramas*, 43 (1914): 155-56, that *Nero* was not known in its time. Bentley, vol. 5, . agrees that Fletcher alludes to *Nero* in *The Little French Lawyer*. If so, a date between May 1619 and May 1623 would be suggested, *Nero* and *The Little French Lawyer* both being performed by the King's Company, with *Nero* first. Evans dates *Nero* as before *Little French Lawyer* (1619).

Authorship

Bentley argues against early attributions, F. G. Fleay's *Biographical Chronicle* (vol. 2, 1891) to May on the basis of May's *The Heir* being transferred to the *Stationers' Register* simultaneously with *Nero* in 1633, Schmid's (above) and Alan Griffith Chester's (*Thomas May*, 1932) to Massinger on the basis of alleged manuscript attribution in an old hand and on the binder's grouping of old plays.

Sources

In *The Poems of Thomas Carew* (1949), Rhodes Dunlap claims that thirty-one lines of Carew's "Rapture" employ the same figures and sequences as those in *Nero*, IV.vii, the speech of Petronius. Dunlap inclines to believe that the playwright followed Carew.

See Also

Babb, Lawrence. *The Elizabethan Malady: A Study of Melancholia in English Literature from 1580–1642.* 1951.

The Partial Law, tragicomedy (ca. *1615–30?*; MS)

Editions

After Bertram Dobell's limited edition of 1908 there has been no other. T. M. Parrott, "Two Late Dramatic Versions of the Slandered Bride Theme," in *Joseph Quincy Adams Memorial Studies*, ed. James G. McManaway, et al. (1948), pp. 537–51, provides a scene-by-scene synopsis. The manuscript is now in the Folger Shakespeare Library.

Date

Dobell dates the play between 1605 and 1630. W. W. Greg, reviewing Dobell's edition in *MLR* 4 (1908): 118–19, suggests a date sometime in the reign of Charles I.

Authorship

Dobell rejects the attribution to Henry Glapthorne as well as to Massinger. Greg (above) suggests a courtly amateur, albeit a very skilled one. Parrott (above) adds that on the basis of internal evidence the author seems to have been a gentleman at court and a connoisseur of contemporary drama. G. E. Bentley, *The Jacobean and Caroline Stage*, vol. 5 (1956), agrees with the attribution to an amateur, observing that "if the tragi-comedy was ever produced, the text shows no sign of it. . . . Probably *The Partial Law* is closet drama."

Sources

There is agreement that the Ariodante and Ginerva story is from *Orlando Furioso*. Rinaldo's denunciation of "the partial law" which demands death for unchastity unless a defending champion appears is found in Ariosto. It is tempting to speculate that the play's title derives from this specific scene, but Parrott's review of the combined thematic motifs gives pause: ocular proof, the slandered bride, and her supposed unchastity go back to Chariton's *Chaereas and Callirhoe*, ca. 150 A.D., and are included in Arthurian and continental literature; the persistence and breadth of these motifs would suggest, for *The Partial Law*, combined sources.

Parrott concludes his essay with an assessment of the play's aesthetic qualities and a discussion of its place in the tragicomic convention, borrowed from the Italian, which Parrott finds to be on the wane: "As a whole the play is a striking example of the decadence of Elizabethan drama under the prevailing convention of its later years."

See Also

Winslow, Ola Elizabeth. *Low Comedy as a Structural Element in English Drama from the Beginnings to 1642*. 1926.

Dick of Devonshire, tragicomedy (*1626*; MS)

Editions

First published by A. H. Bullen, *A Collection of Old English Plays*, vol. 2 (1883), the play was most recently edited by James G. and Mary R. McManaway for the Malone Society (1955).

Date and Source

A limiting early date for this play, of which there is no record of performance or contemporary publication, is 18 July 1626—if the assumption that the plot of the play is based on Richard Peeke's pamphlet entered to J. Trundle on that date is correct. Scholars seem to agree on this assumption, although Louis B. Wright, *Middle-Class Culture in Elizabethan England* (1935), suggests that Richard Pike of Tavistock had made such a name for himself in single combat against the Spaniards that he could have been directly transposed into a dramatic hero. Felix E. Schelling indirectly supports this possibility, in *Elizabethan Playwrights* (1925), when he describes *Dick of Devonshire* as in the "journalistic spirit" of Daborne's *A Christian Turned Turk* and Heywood's *Fortune By Land and Sea*; Schelling finds the play, however, "a belated specimen of this class." Whether the play is based on the pamphlet or is a direct response to the historical events which generated the pamphlet, the difference in a limiting early date is only three months; Richard Pike landed at Fowley in Cornwall, 23 April 1626.

Authorship

G. E. Bentley, *The Jacobean and Caroline Stage*, vol. 5 (1956), follows A. M. Clark, *Thomas Heywood: Playwright and Miscellanist* (1931), and Mowbray Velte, *The Bourgeois Elements in the Dramas of Thomas Heywood* (1922), and assigns the play to Heywood: "only the warning of the chaos created by Fleay's attributions restrains me from listing *Dick of Devonshire* as a Heywood play without more ado." All would follow Bullen's original suggestion, that attitudes in the play toward England, Catholicism, and the bourgeoisie resemble Heywood's. F. S. Boas, *Thomas Heywood* (1950), says that "Bullen's tentative ascription has found general acceptance."

But in fact it has not. There are other candidates. In his "Latin Title-Page Mottoes as a Clue to Dramatic Authorship," *Library* 26 (1945): 28–36, James G. McManaway says that Heywood used the same few Latin mottoes repeatedly, insofar as we have records of them; since the motto on this play is different, Heywood is not a possibility. Having rejected Heywood, McManaway assigns the play to Davenport, arguing that the motto on *Dick of Devonshire* is Davenport's because it is the same as the one found on *The Bloody Banquet*, a play by "T. D.," whom he takes to be Thomas Davenport. (F. S. Boas, *Shakespeare & the Universities* [1923], is helpful in regard to the history of the manuscript of *Dick of Devonshire* and the possible identities of the people behind its initials.) In the introduction to the Malone Society edition, McManaway amplifies his argument on behalf of Davenport's authorship: Davenport, he says, is harder to dismiss than Heywood or Shirley, and there are resemblances between the character of Buzzano in *Dick of Devonshire* and that of Pambo in Davenport's *The City Nightcap*, in the device of the priest-disguise in both plays, and in the protestations of Eleanora in the former play, Abstemia in the latter. Finally, McManaway points to similar turns and twists in the trial scenes of the two plays. Having argued on the basis of these structural similarities, McManaway concludes with stylistic parallels—the sententiousness in the speeches, and the interruption of dialogue with moralizing couplets. Shirley, once one of the candidates for authorship, is dismissed by McManaway on the basis that IV.ii, wherein two Irish-born priests try to persuade Peeke to confess and seek absolution, "could hardly be the invention of Shirley."

See Also

Ribner, Irving. *The Elizabethan History Play in the Age of Shakespeare.* 1957; rev. ed. 1965.

Philander King of Thrace, tragicomedy (*after 1627*; MS "author-plot")

Editions

There is no record that this "author-plot," or outline guide for the playwright, was ever written out or, in fact, conceptually completed. The manuscript, in the Folger Library, is reproduced by J. Q. Adams in "The Author-Plot of an Early Seventeenth Century Play," *Library* 26 (1945-46): 17-27.

Description

The manuscript contains a scenario and notes for three acts of an untitled tragicomedy. Adams provides details about ink color, the nature of the hand, and so on. Acquired in 1923, the dealer's catalogue had incorrectly described the plot as a tragedy, and had, as well, supplied the title by which it is now known, but which is evidently apocryphal.

See Also

Freeman, Arthur, "The Argument of *Meleager.*" *English Literary Renaissance* 1 (1971): 122-31.

Hierarchomachia, or The Anti-Bishop, "comic-satire" (*1629?*; MS)

The playwright is assigned the pseudonym "Reverardus," a contemporary attribution with apparently satiric and probably obfuscatory intent. Suzanne Gossett, "Drama in the English College, Rome, 1591–1660," *English Literary Renaissance* 3 (1973): 60-93, points out that Jesuit regulations required plays to be in Latin, but that these rules were, as with this play, regularly transgressed. She describes *Hierarchomachia* as a "dense and precise allegory of the quarrel between seculars and regulars over the appointment of the bishop of Calcedon." The manuscript contains no corrections or production directions, and was, according to Gossett, probably not written or produced at the English College, Rome, where it is kept. The play has not been edited.

See Also

Murtaugh, Cyril. "*Hierarchomachia*." *The Venerabile* 17 (1955): 164-68. [Not seen]

The Wasp, "comical history" (ca. *1630-38?*; MS)

Editions

The Wasp has not been edited or published; it resides, in manuscript, in Alnwick Castle, Northumberland, MS 507.

Date and Authorship

W. W. Greg, *Dramatic Documents from the Elizabethan Playhouses*, vol. 1 (1931), assigned a date of ca. 1630. Bentley, *The Jacobean and Caroline Stage*, vol. 5 (1956), assumes that Greg did so on the basis of the principal hand. Both Greg and Bentley believe that there is no conclusive evidence concerning authorship. J. J. Gourlay, however, ascribes the play to Thomas Jordan; in a letter, *TLS*, 17 Aug. 1933, p. 549, Gourlay reports that he is transcribing a manuscript which he believes to be Jordan's. Ten years later Gourlay is certain he is correct: in another letter, *TLS*, 5 June 1943, p. 271, he asserts that Jordan wrote the play in 1638. He goes on to describe the auspices: the play was acted by the amalgamated Kings Revels—Queen Henrietta's Company. Bentley, vol. 5, argues against these assumptions, maintaining that there is no evidence Jordan ever acted with Queen Henrietta's Company, or that any of his plays was written for it. Greg (above) reports that prompt notes "show that the manuscript has been used in the playhouse for performance."

Love's Changelings' Change, pastoral (ca. *1630*–ca. *1640?*; MS)

This pastoral play, which has not been edited or published, is the fourteenth manuscript play in B.M. MS Egerton 1994. W. W. Greg conjectures a date between 1630 and 1640, based on analysis of the literary hand (*Dramatic Documents*, vol. 1 [1931], p. 342). In *Pastoral Poetry and Pastoral Drama* (1906), Greg proceeds from a description of the hand and the paper to a discussion of the pastoral elements, which are drawn directly from Sidney's *Arcadia*. He concludes by stating his agreement with Bullen that this is a dull play.

Alfred Harbage, *Cavalier Drama* (1936), lists this play among undated dramatizations of Sidney's *Arcadia*, and points out that it contains both a main plot used in *The Arcadia* (1632), a dramatized romance, and episodes of the capture of the princesses by Cecropia and Amphialus. Harbage concurs with most previous readers: the play is "a very long and very dull treatment of Sidney's *Arcadia*."

G. E. Bentley, *The Jacobean and Caroline Stage*, vol. 5 (1956), states that other than Greg's dating of the hand, no other evidence has been adduced to date the play. There is no evidence of censorship or use in a playhouse.

Wit's Triumvirate, or the Philosopher, comedy (*1635 MS date*; MS)

Like *Hierarchomachia* (above), this play is not recorded in any of the usual sources. Samuel Schoenbaum, "*Wit's Triumvirate*: A Caroline Comedy Recovered," *SEL* 4 (1964): 227-37, announces the discovery of a previously unknown five-act play "written, produced, and presented at Court in the year 1635." Schoenbaum discusses the manuscript, presented to the British Museum in 1942, and speculates on reasons why it had gone unnoticed. He provides a full description of the manuscript. In his discussion of the content of the play, he acknowledges that *Wit's Triumvirate* is "by no means successful as a play"; it is talky, Jonsonian in tone, and broadly topical. One of the topical references helps to confirm speculations about the date: there is a reference to Davenant's *The Platonic Lovers*, licensed 16 November 1635.

Wit's Triumvirate is modeled on *The Alchemist*: the triumvirate have Jonson-like names, Clyster, Silence, and Bond, and they comprise, says Schoenbaum, "the Caroline analogue to the 'indenture tripartite.'" Schoenbaum provides a detailed synopsis with continuous commentary, and ends with speculations about the author, whom he takes to be "one of the 'modish scholars'—the apt phrase is Alfred Harbage's—who invaded the professional theater in the 1630's."

The Valiant Scot, by "J. W.", tragedy (*1637 [published]* ; 1637)

Date

The play was entered for publication by John Waterson 26 April 1637; its date of composition is not known. The play has not been edited since its first publication. There is no record of stage production in 1637 or 1638; apparently it had a run of five days in 1639 after the players of the Fortune Playhouse were jailed and fined for a production of *The Cardinal's Conspiracy*. Unfortunately, immediate records of that event are sketchy, and the detailed account in *Vox Borealis, or The Northern Discoverie*, "the yeare coming on, 1641," is suspect because it is nearly two years after the fact, and because of the probability that it was altered to suit the purposes of antiepiscopal propaganda. See Leslie Hotson, *The Commonwealth and Restoration Stage* (1928), and G. E. Bentley, *The Jacobean and Caroline Stage* vol. 5 (1956).

Authorship

John Linton Carver, "*The Valiant Scot*, By 'J. W.'," in Allison Gaw, ed., *Studies in English Drama*, 1st series (1917), pp. 75–104, suggests two possibilities: that "J. W." is the printer John Waterson, or else William Boyer, who, in a letter of dedication to the Marquis of Hamilton, speaks of a play ("what I have") which he is giving ("I bestow upon you . . . "). Bentley (above) dismisses both attributions: of the first, he says that coincidence of like initials is not a substantial reason for an attribution; if the second, he argues that Boyer's letter could equally well be construed as announcing a gift of a manuscript in his ownership rather than one which he had written.

Type and Source

The play is an old-fashioned chronicle history in the late form of Ford's *Perkin Warbeck* and Glapthorne's *Albertus Wallenstein*. It is based on Henry the minstrel's old Scottish poem about Wallace, *The Lyfe and Actis of W. Wallace*, which went through five seventeenth-century editions (see Bentley, vol. 5, and Carver). It contains regular Scots dialect in the part of Peggie, and some in the part of Wallace. Alfred Harbage, *Cavalier Drama* (1936), considers the play "a belated (and well written) chronicle drama." Irving J. Ribner, *The Elizabethan History Play in the Age of Shakespeare* (1957; rev. ed. 1965), sees it as a good example of the declining episodic history play.

The Fairy Knight, or Oberon the Second, comedy (*1637?-58?*; MS)

Manuscript and Edition

The manuscript, Folger Shakespeare Library 46.1, was edited by Fredson Thayer Bowers, *"The Fary Knight or Oberon the Second": A Manuscript Play* (1942). In the typography Bowers has maintained line- and word-division from the original manuscript.

Authorship and Date

While there is general agreement on the poor dramatic quality of the play, questions of authorship and date have produced significant differences of opinion. Bowers suggests in "Ben Jonson, Thomas Randolph, and *The Drinking Academy*," *N&Q* 173 (1937): 166-68, that a problem of interpretation in the Prologue of *The Drinking Academy* may be solved if otherwise oblique allusions to witches and devils are taken as references to Randolph's "own" *The Fairy Knight*.

In the introduction to his edition of the play, Bowers develops his argument for Randolph's authorship in more detail, and with an additional thesis concerning the history of the text: he posits a play, *The Fairy Knight*, written by Randolph for performance at Westminster School about 1623/4, at about the same time as *The Drinking Academy*. Both plays, Bowers says, were transcribed in the same hand. The Folger manuscript of *The Fairy Knight* "represents an augmented transcription by an unknown writer of an early lost play by Thomas Randolph" made about 1657-58. In a review, Cyrus Day, *JEGP* 42 (1943): 440-41, agrees with Bowers.

But in another review, J. B. Leishman, *RES* 20 (1944): 321-22, does not; neither does G. E. Bentley, *The Jacobean and Caroline Stage*, vol. 5 (1956). Leishman finds Bowers's evidence "neither separately nor collectively convincing" and questions Bowers concerning the change from blank verse to prose in the "augmentation"; he believes that Bowers's thesis suffers from failure to consider the implications of this change. Bentley answers Bowers's thesis point by point, and suggests that since the play shows no evidence of major revision, it must date after *The Traitor* (1631) and *The Young Admiral* (1633), to both of which it is indebted. Bentley suggests an upper limit date of 1658 for original composition, and bases the suggestion on the epitaph for Frances Monson (1658) included in the manuscript. Bentley is cautious even here, noting that the manuscript was broken up and it is thus not certain that the epitaph postdates the play.

A question arises concerning a play of the same title: there is Sir Henry Herbert's license of 11 June 1624 of "A new play, called *The Fairy Knight*: written by Forde, and Decker." Bentley summarizes all arguments made against Randolph, the 1624 date, and adds, simply, that "nothing in the manuscript sounds like Ford or Dekker. . . ."

The Telltale, tragicomedy (*1605*–ca. *1640*; MS [IV incomplete])

Edition

The Telltale was edited by R. A. Foakes and J. C. Gibson for the Malone Society (1960 for 1959). George F. Warner, *Catalogue of the Manuscripts and Muniments . . . at Dulwich* (1881), prints a short synopsis of the play. Kenneth L. Wheeler, "A Critical View of *The Telltale*, an Anonymous Play," *ESRS* 15 (1966): 34-48, includes a detailed synopsis.

Date

Foakes and Gibson suggest a date after 1605 because of similarities between *The Telltale* and *Law Tricks*, *The Phoenix*, *The Malcontent*, and *Measure for Measure*. W. W. Greg, *Dramatic Documents from the Elizabethan Playhouses*, vol. 1 (1931), narrows the dates to 1630-40. The *Annals* allows for both views. Wheeler (above) makes a rather thorough case for affinities between this play and some plays of the period 1597-1604. G. E. Bentley, *The Jacobean and Caroline Stage*, vol. 5 (1956), follows Greg. There is no consensus, although an upper limit date would be 1658, in which year Nathaniel Brook advertised *TellTale: A Comedy* as intended for publication. There is no evidence that it was ever in fact published.

Authorship

A. H. Bullen, *A Collection of Old English Plays*, vol. 2 (1883), and Alfred Harbage, "Elizabethan and Seventeenth-Century Play Manuscripts," *PMLA* 50 (1935): 698, suggest William Rowley as author, but their surmise has not found favor. The Malone editors argue for multiple authorship. A monogram at the end of the play has suggested to Greg (above) as well as to Bentley (above), the possibility of John Nichols or Nicholas, who may have written a lost unnamed comedy performed at Trinity College, Cambridge, in 1639 or 1640. Arthur Freeman, "The Authorship of *The Tell-Tale*," *JEGP* 62 (1963): 288-92, asserts that there is no doubt: the play is chiefly, if not entirely, by Thomas Dekker. The evidence is entirely internal, Freeman says; resemblance to plots and incidentals of *Match Me in London*, *The Wonder of a Kingdom*, and *If This Be Not a Good Play, the Devil Is In It* leave no doubts.

The Play

The play is divided into acts, with no scene divisions (the Malone editors supply suggested scene divisions). Greg, *Dramatic Documents*, vol. 1 (1931), describes the manuscript. While he finds no evidence of censorship or prompt notes, the Malone editors believe that "wine" (line 1971) and "A Cry wthin" (line 738) are evidence of a prompter's hand.

The play is a comedy of intrigue; its author was well versed in beast fables and proverb lore. Wheeler (above) points out that the oriental pelican fable also is used in *King Lear*, III.iv.77.

Three motifs—the disguised duke, the usurper, and the "purge"—are used in Marston's *Malcontent* (1604), Middleton's *The Phoenix* (1603-4), Day's *Law Tricks* (1604), and Shakespeare's *Measure for Measure*. Wheeler surmises that this affinity strengthens the suggestion that the *Telltale*'s author was intimately familiar with the Elizabethan drama of the early 1600s.

The Ghost, or The Woman Wears the Breeches, comedy (*1640?*; 1653)

The title page of the play says it was written in 1653; G. E. Bentley, *The Jacobean and Caroline Stage*, vol. 5 (1956), points out that the play seems too crude for private theaters, and that lines in the prologue and epilogue do not apply to performances at a public theater. He raises the question as to whether this play might have been prepared for surreptitious performance after the closing of the theaters, and then published with a careful disclaimer on the title page.

Alfred Harbage, *Cavalier Drama* (1936), calls it one of the most "repulsive" plays of the period which "goes out of its way to make an issue with the Puritans." He contrasts its "dark and embittered caricature" with Sir William Davenant's "good natured and honestly amusing foolery" in *News from Plymouth*.

Read and Wonder, political dialogue (*1641*; 1641)

Alfred Harbage, *Cavalier Drama* (1936), mentions this "play" as being like *Canterbury His Change of Diet* (1641): both are pamphlets in dialogue form, satirizing Archbishop Laud. Harbage describes the resistance in this period to the closing of the theaters, wherein most plays became avowed instruments of partisanship on the side of the king. Three exceptions exist, among which is *Read and Wonder*.

The Dictionary of Anonymous and Pseudonymous Literature, vol. 5 (1929), assigns *Read and Wonder* to George Wither, an attribution also made by Charles S. Hensley, *The Later Career of George Wither* (1969), who lists the play but does not discuss it.

Andromana, or the Merchant's Wife, tragedy (*1642-60*; 1660)

Editions

Since Dodsley's edition, in *Old English Plays*, vol. 14 (1875), there has been no new edition.

Authorship

While the 1660 Stationers' Register entry attributes the play to James Shirley, the title page of the 1660 quarto merely carries the initials "J.S." G. E. Bentley, however, in *The Jacobean and Caroline Stage*, vol. 5 (1956), says that the Burtonian melancholy of the play is not characteristic of Shirley. Bentley cites W. R. Chetwood, *The British Theatre* (1752), who says the play was revived in 1671, with a prologue claiming that it was Shirley's muse "that laboured for its Birth." But Bentley also cites Greg's remark that we have only Chetwood's authority and says that "even if Chetwood was right, a Restoration prologue is of little value in establishing the authorship of an early play."

Source

The debate concerning sources is not whether the Plangus story in the *Arcadia* is the source, but whether or not it comes to this play by way of Beaumont and Fletcher's *Cupid's Revenge*. Michael C. Andrews, "The Sources of *Andromana*," *RES* 19 (1968): 295-300, notes that W. W. Greg, in *Pastoral Poetry and Pastoral Drama* (1906), had asserted that *Andromana* came directly from the *Arcadia*, a conclusion that "no subsequent writer has questioned." S. Blaine Ewing, Jr., "Burton, Ford, and *Andromana*," *PMLA* 54 (1939): 1007-17, does not fundamentally question Greg's description of the source, but says that the play reflects the influence of Ford's studies of abnormal psychology, which are modeled on case histories from Burton's *Anatomy of Melancholy*. Ewing goes on to suggest that Beaumont and Fletcher's *Cupid's Revenge* partakes of this concern with abnormal psychology. He rejects Ford on the basis of style.

Andrews (above) examines features common to the *Arcadia* and *Andromana* but not to *Cupid's Revenge*, and common to *Andromana* and *Cupid's Revenge* but not the *Arcadia*. In so doing, he concludes that the influence of *Cupid's Revenge* upon *Andromana* is more extensive and pervasive than the influence of the *Arcadia*; thus he establishes the opposite case from Greg's contention of 1906.

Fredson Bowers, *Elizabethan Revenge Tragedy* (1940), says that the play was written about 1642. The author tried, he says, to write a villain play, but the prominence of Plangus (*Arcadia* II.15) and interest in his character led to "a fatal compromise between the villain play and revenge tragedy." Bowers provides a broad plot summary in conjunction with his explication and evaluation.

The Cyprian Conqueror, or The Faithless Relict, comedy (*before 1642;* MS)

Alfred Harbage, *Cavalier Drama* (1936), describes this play as "a crude comic treatment of Petronius Arbiter's tale of the Roman matron." The plot derives from a popular story, "The Matron of Ephesus." John Quincy Adams, "*The Cyprian Conqueror, or The Faithless Relict,*" *MLN* 23 (1908): 65–67, suggests that the subplot comes from the *Decameron,* xii. 2.

W. W. Greg, *Dramatic Documents from the Elizabethan Playhouses,* vol. 1 (1931), dates the play ca. 1640. Alfred Harbage, "Elizabethan Acting," *PMLA* 54 (1939): 685–708, dates it shortly after 1633 because of allusions to Prynne's *Histriomastix*.

The author is unknown; Greg says the play was copied by a nearly illiterate scribe who, according to Adams, was not the author. Adams describes stage directions and speculates that the play was performed in one of the regular playhouses and acted more than once.

Harbage, "Elizabethan Acting," considers this play in the context of debates concerning whether Elizabethan acting was "formal" or "natural"; the preface to *Cyprian Conqueror* suggests the former. Greg (above) says that while "both prologue and epilogue contemplate performance, . . . the manuscript is purely literary."

OTHER DRAMATISTS

Terence P. Logan—Denzell S. Smith

The figures included here were active at the same time as the major playwrights treated in this volume; they are included because their plays have been the subject of some recent scholarship. Articles and books dealing exclusively or primarily with their nondramatic works are not included. For additional information see: G. E. Bentley, The Jacobean and Caroline Stage, 7 vols. (1941-68), W. W. Greg, A Bibliography of the English Printed Drama to the Restoration, 4 vols. (1939-59), Alfred Harbage, Annals of English Drama, 975-1700, rev. Samuel Schoenbaum (1964), and the Supplements by Schoenbaum (1966, 1970). William Van Lennep, ed., The London Stage 1660-1800: Part I, 1660-1700 (1965), supplies a record of Restoration productions of plays by many of the dramatists named in this chapter, and includes selected contemporary critical comments. The essays on anonymous plays and on appropriate major authors in this volume and the three others in the series include more extensive treatments of the plays of uncertain authorship and the collaborative plays that are dealt with here. Playwrights are discussed in alphabetical order. Entries are listed in chronological order for each playwright and include items listed in the source bibliographies from the publication date of the initial volumes of The Jacobean and Caroline Stage *(1941) to those available by mid-1976; the title of each work is followed by a brief summary of its contents.*

SIMON BAYLIE

De Vocht, Henry, ed. *The Wizard.* 1930. In this edition for Materials for the Study of the Old English Drama, De Vocht discusses the few known facts about Baylie's life, sources, and influence, and speculates on possible later changes by another hand. Composition of the play is dated between 1614 and 1625, partly on the basis of allusions by Massinger and Fletcher.

ANTHONY BREWER

Dent, Robert W. "*The Love-Sick King*: Turk Turned Dane." *MLR* 56 (1961): 555-57. The play "has too little artistic value to deserve attention for its own sake, but as a late species of English chronicle play it does merit some consideration." Although usually dated 1607-17, "Brewer's handling of the catastrophe may well imply some time a decade or more later."

LODOWICK CARLELL

Nicoll, Allardyce, ed. *The Fool Would Be a Favourite, or The Discreet Lover (1657).* 1926. The play's historical interest partially compensates for Carlell's limited dramatic talent.

———, ed. *The Tragedy of Osmond the Great Turk, or the Noble Servant (1657).* 1926. The play is an interesting early example of heroic tragedy written in prose and establishes Carlell as "one of the chief intermediaries between Beaumont and Fletcher, and Dryden and Settle."

Harbage, Alfred. *Cavalier Drama: An Historical and Critical Supplement to the Study of the Elizabethan and Restoration Stage.* 1936. Carlell's life is summarized and there is brief critical comment on each of his plays. The overall assessment is strongly negative: "His interest now is purely historical; his plays call for silence, or for compassion."

Ruoff, James E. "A 'Lost' Manuscript of Lodowick Carlell's *Arviragus and Philicia*." *N&Q* 2 (1955): 21-22. Previous critics, including Harbage, have assumed that the Petworth MS became the Bodleian MS and that there was only a single extant MS version. The two are actually quite different.

Toynbee, Margaret, and Gyles Isham. "Lodowick Carlell." *N&Q* 2 (1955): 204. The Petworth MS of *Arviragus and Philicia* may have been Carlell's gift to Lucy, Countless of Carlisle, and he may have sheltered her during the interregnum.

———. "The Family Connections of Joan Carlisle." *N&Q* 2 (1955): 515-21. Several *D.N.B.* errors about Lodowick and his family are corrected.

Ruoff, James E. "The Dating of Carlell's *Passionate Lovers.*" *N&Q* 3 (1956): 68-70. Internal evidence suggests that the play was written ca. 1629-34; the prologue claim that it is Carlell's last play and the accepted dating of 1638 are both wrong.

———. "Lodowick Carlell after 1660." *N&Q* 4 (1957): 35-37. New information about Carlell's activities and relations, especially with the court, is provided to supplement the biographical material given in the articles by Toynbee and Isham (above).

Duncan-Jones, E. E. "The Two *Osmond* Plays." *N&Q* 8 (1961): 128-29. Bentley and others who suggest that Carlell's *Osmond the Great Turk, or The Noble Servant*, published in 1657, is the same play as *Osmond the Great Turk*, licensed in 1622 (lost), are in error. Carlell's play is about a Tartar, not a Turk, and "the earlier play was one wholly distinct from Carlell's."

Maxwell, J. C. "Lodowick Carlell: An Echo of Webster," *N&Q* 16 (1969): 288. Carlell's *Osmond the Great Turk* has "a clear recollection of *The White Devil*, V, vi, 240-41."

WILLIAM CARTWRIGHT

Evans, Willa McClung. *Henry Lawes: Musician and Friend of Poets.* 1941. Lawes's association with Cartwright began while both were students at Oxford. Lawes contributed at least one song to *The Ordinary* and suggested improvements to *The Royal Slave*.

Danton, J. Periam. "William Cartwright and His *Comedies, Tragi-Comedies, with Other Poems . . .* 1651." *Library Quarterly* 12 (1942): 438-56. Individual copies of the edition have an unusually large number of variant readings.

Evans, Gwynne B. "*Comedies, Tragi-Comedies, with Other Poems, by Mr. William Cartwright 1651*: A Bibliographical Study." *Library* 22 (1942): 12-22. The arrangement of the preliminary quires is especially complex and the publisher may have cancelled an index to save expense.

Evans, G. Blakemore, ed. *The Plays and Poems of William Cartwright.* 1951. This is a generous definitive edition. The introduction establishes the canon and chronology, gives a biography, and critically analyzes each title.

Ruoff, James E. "Cartwright's Human Sacrifice Scene in *The Royal Slave*." *N&Q* 4 (1957): 295-96. The sacrifice scene, V.iii, probably derives from a similar scene in Carlell's *Arviragus and Philicia*.

Davis, Joe Lee. *The Sons of Ben: Jonsonian Comedy in Caroline England*. 1967. A brief biography of Cartwright, one of the eleven Sons of Ben, is given. *The Ordinary* is a "partially effective experiment in a type of comic eclecticism" which helped "transmit to the Restoration a lesser but lusty tradition of citizen buffoonery."

Evans, Willa McClung. "Cartwright's Debt to Lawes." In *Music in English Renaissance Drama*, ed. John H. Long (1968), pp. 103-16. The two collaborated from before 1635 until Cartwright's death in 1643; Lawes made a significant contribution to Cartwright's understanding of dramaturgy.

Foxon, D. F. "The Varieties of Early Proof: Cartwright's *Royal Slave*, 1639, 1640." *Library* 25 (1970): 51-54. "The primary significance of the proofs of sheet A of 1639 and sheet B of 1640 is that they were undoubtedly made before the formes were on the press ready to be printed off, and thus correspond to what Moxon calls 'proof' rather than 'revise'. Their freedom from obvious error suggests that they may be 'second proofs.'"

WILLIAM CAVENDISH

Mandach, André Bernard de. *Molière et la comédie de mœurs en Angleterre (1660-68): Essai de littérature comparée*. "La part de Dryden dans la composition de cette comédie [*Sir Martin Mar-all*] semble négligeable." The play is "une œuvre authentique" of Cavendish who "était un des premiers moliéristes du monde."

Davis, Joe Lee. *The Sons of Ben: Jonsonian Comedy in Caroline England*. 1967. A biographical summary of Cavendish, one of the eleven Sons of Ben, is given. With Killigrew, Cavendish marks the climax of "the efforts of the Sons of Ben to wear the sophisticated sock." However, "too servile imitation of Jonson's technique in his 'dotages' may account for Cavendish's inability to sustain sophistication."

JOHN CLAVELL

Lawless, Donald S., and J. H. P. Pafford. "John Clavell, 1603-42. Highwayman, Author, and Quack Doctor." *N&Q* 4 (1957): 9. New biographical information is given and the Greg and Pafford attribution of *The Soddered Citizen* to Clavell (in their Malone society edition, 1936) is supported with new arguments. Materials found in the Public Records Office also suggest that Bentley's "1629 or 1630" date for the play (vol. 3, 1956) is correct, rather than the 1632-33 date given by Greg and Pafford.

ASTON COKAIN

Mathews, Ernst G. "Cokain's *The Obstinate Lady* and the *Araucana*." *MLN* 57 (1942): 57-58. Much of Cokain's plot is an adaptation of the plot of Massinger's *A Very Woman*; a Spanish speech spoken by the hero is from Alonso de Ercilla y Zúñiga's *La Araucana*.

ROBERT DAVENPORT

McManaway, James G. "Latin Title-Page Mottoes as a Clue to Dramatic Authorship." *Library* 26 (1946): 28-36. The manuscript of *Dick of Devonshire* is in the same scribal hand as *Blurt, Master Constable*. The title-page motto for *Dick* differs from the one Thomas Heywood always used, but is found on the anonymous *Bloody Banquet*, usually attributed to Thomas Drue. This, and internal evidence, suggest that these last two plays are by Davenport.

Olive, W. J. "Davenant and Davenport." *N&Q* 194 (1949): 320. Davenport's name is incorrectly cited on the title page of *King John and Matilda*, "his single extant tragedy," by Washington Irving in *Bracebridge Hall*, and by the *Shakespere Allusion Book* (vol. 2, p. 31).

——. "Davenport's Debt to Shakespeare in *The City-Night-Cap*." *JEGP* 49 (1950): 333-44. Davenport's heavy borrowing from Shakespeare's plays and poems seems to reflect the publication of the first folio the year before *The City Night Cap* was licensed.

——. "Shakespeare Parody in Davenport's *A New Tricke to Cheat the Divell*." *MLN* 66 (1951): 478-80. Falstaff's catechism of honor in *1 Henry IV*, V.i, is paraphrased in I.ii of *A New Trick*.

McManaway, James G. and Mary R., ed. *Dick of Devonshire*. 1955. The editors of this Malone Society edition argue that the manuscript is in the hand of a playhouse scribe. It is not the hand of Thomas Heywood, James Shirley, or Robert Davenport, to whom the play has been attributed. Shirley cannot be the author, and a summary of the arguments for Heywood and Davenport concludes that the author is unknown. The date is probably 1626. The play is not entered in the Stationers' Register, there is no contemporary edition, and the play might not have reached the stage. Its source is the pamphlet published by the play's titular hero, Richard Pike, soon after his return from the Cadiz expedition. There is no known source for the secondary plot.

Ribner, Irving. *The English History Play in the Age of Shakespeare*. 1957; rev. ed. 1965. Davenport was familiar with the historical drama of the sixteenth century; his interest is in it and not in the chronicles. In *King John and Matilda*, his "concern was to write a tragedy of passion, and his primary didactic purpose was to eulogize female virtue." The political lesson is traditional: "civil chaos . . . is created by kings who are governed by their lust." The play exemplifies what happened to the history play, "a genre which had come to be dominated by essentially non-historical concerns," by 1625.

Armstrong, W. A., ed. *Elizabethan History Plays*. 1965. The introduction briefly discusses the political ideas in *King John and Matilda*, and mentions its source (*The Downfall of Robert Earl of Huntingdon*) and Fletcher's influence on plot and character.

Dean, James S., Jr. "Borrowings from Robert Greene's *Philomela* in Robert Davenport's *The City-Night Cap*." *N&Q* 13 (1966): 302-3. Davenport borrowed names, phrases, and one part of the plot.

Maxwell, J. C. "Notes on Davenport's *King John and Matilda*." *N&Q* 14 (1967): 215-17. A long list of errors, failures in modernization, questionable emendations, acceptances of 1662 quarto readings, and punctuation provides evidence for Maxwell's charge that Armstrong's edition of *King John* is a "slovenly piece of work."

Leggatt, Alexander. *Citizen Comedy in the Age of Shakespeare*. 1973. In *A New Trick to Cheat the Devil*, the restored prodigal is not criticized as severely as the mean-spirited characters. The basic lesson is the importance of charity, a higher value than financial good sense. The play is set in the context of other comic plots treating the story of the prodigal.

JOHN DENHAM

O Hehir, Brendan. "The Early Acquaintance of Denham and Waller." *N&Q* 13 (1966): 19–23. Close analysis of literary and historical evidence yields two conclusions: that by 1642 at the latest Denham had read one Waller poem, and that speculation about the early acquaintance of the two has no support.

———. *Harmony from Discords: A Life of Sir John Denham.* 1968. This well-documented and soundly argued full-scale biography replaces earlier inaccurate accounts of Denham's life. It connects his "poetic canon with the episodes of his experience." Political events in 1641 and 1642 suggest that *The Sophy* was not performed in those years; little evidence exists to support the often-repeated notion of its immediate success. Supposed correspondences between the plot and current political events are evaluated in the light of Denham's known political moderation and views of the law. His completion of Katherine Phillips's translation of Corneille's *Horace* is treated briefly.

Banks, Theodore H., ed. *The Poetical Works of Sir John Denham.* 1928; 2nd ed. 1969. The edition includes Denham's only play, *The Sophy*. The introduction contains a biography and critical appraisal of his work, and briefly discusses the play, its source (Thomas Herbert, *Some Yeares Travels into Divers Parts of Asia and Afrique*, 1634), the influence of contemporaries (Shakespeare and Fletcher on theme and verse), and its success and topicality.

Steiner, Thomas R. "Precursors to Dryden: English and French Theories of Translation in the Seventeenth Century." *Comparative Literature Studies* 7 (1970): 50–81. Denham reinvigorated Chapman's ideals of literary translation: to open the "entire artistic world of the original author" by means of "spiritual commerce" between the translator and the author.

Legouis, Pierre. "Une biographie de Sir John Denham (avec un supplement)." *EA* 24 (1971): 292–97. Corrects details in O Hehir's book (above).

Berry, Herbert. "Sir John Denham at Law." *MP* 71 (1974): 266–76. O Hehir (book, above) did not consult the extensive legal records about Denham's life. Berry describes Denham's legal involvements in detail.

KENELM DIGBY

Gabrieli, Vittorio. "La missione di Sir Kenelm Digby alla corte di Innocenzo X (1645–1648)." *EM* 5 (1954): 247–88. Unpublished material, including Digby holographs in the Vatican Library, provides information about Digby's service as Henrietta Maria's representative to the papal court. While Digby's earlier vacillations between the Catholic and Protestant faiths may have been motivated by opportunism, his service in Rome was selflessly idealistic; "gli interressi che egli stavano a curoe erano solo quelli delli Regina e della religione." He could not, however, cope with "le tergiversazione a gli intrighi della Corte romana," and Innocent X was determined to sacrifice the interests of English Catholics and the Stuarts to other papal diplomatic interests.

Petersson, R. T. *Sir Kenelm Digby: The Ornament of England, 1603–1665.* 1956. This detailed biography also contains a bibliography of Digby's writings.

Gabrieli, Vittorio. *Sir Kenelm Digby: Un inglese italianato nell' età della controriforma.* 1957. This life reprints in an appendix twenty letters and two meditations from the period after Venetia Stanley's death.

Davis, Joe Lee. *The Sons of Ben: Jonsonian Comedy in Caroline England.* 1967. That court Platonism was more conducive to romance than comedy is exemplified in the real-life attachment of Digby to Venetia Stanley, and in his prose romance "exalting their mutual fidelities," *Loose Fantasies*.

Bodemer, Charles W. "Embryological Thought in Seventeenth Century England." In *Medical Investigation in Seventeenth Century England*, ed. Charles W. Bodemer and Lester S. King (1968), pp. 3–25. Digby's *Nature of Bodies* is a "bold attempt to explain embryonic development in terms commensurate with his time"; his is an optimistic belief that man's reason and logical faculties can make accessible the mechanism of embryogenesis.

THOMAS DRUE

McManaway, James G. "Latin Title-Page Mottoes as a Clue to Dramatic Authorship." *Library* 26 (1946): 28-36. The manuscript of *Dick of Devonshire* is in the same scribal hand as *Blurt, Master Constable*. The title-page motto for *Dick* differs from the one Thomas Heywood always used, but is found on the anonymous *Bloody Banquet*, usually attributed to Drue. Internal evidence as well as the title-page mottoes suggest that these last two plays are by Robert Davenport.

Bacon, Wallace A., ed. *William Warner's "Syrinx, or A Sevenfold History."* 1950. The author of *The Bloody Banquet* "borrowed liberally" from four of these seven tales for his narrative, but altered "motivation, personality, and detail." The source and play are compared at length.

Oliver, Leslie Mahin. "Thomas Drue's *Duchess of Suffolk*: A Protestant Drama." *SB* 3 (1950-51): 241-46. This play, among others, represents a minor tendency from 1590 on to appeal to the religious-minded in the community. There is a strong vein of local interest in the play and in its production in 1623. Places and characters in the play were closely associated with the locality of the Fortune, the place of production. The source is John Foxe, *Acts and Monuments*, and a ballad by Thomas Deloney from 1602.

Ribner, Irving. *The English History Play in the Age of Shakespeare.* 1957; rev. ed. 1965. Drue's *The Duchess of Suffolk* (licensed 1624, printed 1631), a melodramatic biographical play, is a belated example of a kind of drama popular about 1600. It has a "crude episodic" plot, and "little to recommend [it] either as drama or history."

Schoenbaum, S., ed. *The Bloody Banquet.* 1962. This Malone Society reprint collates ten copies of the 1639 quarto; no significant variants are listed. Insufficient evidence exists to establish a date of composition. The authorship arguments are summarized and the scholarship cited; the question is still open. Schoenbaum agrees with Bacon (above) about the play's source, but disagrees with McManaway (above) that the text is a "bad quarto."

NATHAN FIELD

Peery, William. "Lady Perfect and Sir John Loveall." *N&Q* 189 (1945): 192. The name Sir John Loveall, used but once in *Amends for*

Ladies, is not the name of Lady Perfect's husband. Collier (1829) made the mistake, and other editors and critics have continued it.

Boas, Frederick S. *An Introduction to Stuart Drama.* 1946. The merits of Field's unaided plays (*A Woman Is a Weathercock* and *Amends for Ladies*) lie in "sprightly dialogue and in a slickness of plot management natural to Field from his experience as an actor." Massinger was the "predominant partner" in their collaborative *Fatal Dowry*.

Peery, William. "Who 'Thrusts the Boy Out'?" *N&Q* 190 (1946): 11-12. Modern editors designate the character Proudly to perform the function of thrusting the "boy" (a disguised maid) offstage after the duel in Act. IV; the first quarto prints "Fr.", the second "Pr." Peery argues that the brother, Frank, would have been the most logical choice to do it.

Mabbott, Thomas Olive. "Who 'Thrusts the Boy Out' in Field's *Amends for Ladies*?" *N&Q* 190 (1946): 86. The stage direction abbreviation "Fr." may be either "Frank" or "frater," so Peery's argument (above, "Who Thrusts . . . , " *N&Q* 190 [1946] : 11-12) is strengthened.

Peery, William. "Nathan and Nathaniel Field Again." *N&Q* 190 (1946): 121. Corrects the *N&Q* editor's change of "Nathan" to "Nathaniel" in his article "Who 'Thrusts the Boy Out'?" in *N&Q* 190 (1946): 11-12.

——. "Frank vs. Frater in *Amends for Ladies*." *N&Q* 190 (1946): 173. Mabbott (above) is wrong; Field used Latin for stage directions only once, except for "exit" and "exeunt."

——. "*The Curious Impertinent* in *Amends for Ladies*." *Hispanic Review* 14 (1946): 344-53. Only three plot elements in *Amends* suggest the influence of Cervantes; the extent of the influence has been exaggerated.

——. "Field's *A Woman Is a Weathercock*, III,iii." *Expl* 4 (1946): Item 43. A confusing passage about the basilisk's glance is clarified by seventeenth-century lore.

——. "Four Misassigned Speeches in *A Woman Is a Weathercock*." *N&Q* 191 (1946): 230-31. Collier misassigned them and other editors followed. The quarto assigns them to Lucida; further, they are appropriate to her.

——. "The Influence of Ben Jonson on Nathan Field." *SP* 43 (1946): 482-97. The influence of Jonson on Field has been exaggerated by critics discussing subject, satiric tone, realism, characterization, plot construction, and stage devices. Chapman and Middleton were as strongly influential as Jonson.

——. "A Latin Quotation in *Wonder of Women* and *Woman Is a Weathercock.*" *N&Q* 191 (1946): 33-34. Identifies the source, Persius, in Marston's *Wonder of Women*. Field translated it in his play.

——. "Nathan Field's Dates." *MLR* 41 (1946): 409-10. Some earlier erroneous citations of dates are noted and corrected.

——. "Nid Field Was Whose Scholar?" *SAB* 21 (1946): 80-86. Drummond's remarks about Field and Jonson have been embellished by the critics. Field's debt to Jonson "stands in need of careful appraisal based primarily upon the internal evidence."

——. "Note on a Commonplace: The Three Souls." *PQ* 25 (1946): 382-83. The Aristotelian notion of the three souls clarifies a quarto reading in *Amends for Ladies*.

——. "The Portrayal of Woman in the Comedies of Nathan Field." *ShAB* 21 (1946): 129-41. "Field's literary treatment of women is not to be connected with his biography." The accepted view that the anti-feminism of one play is equalized by the feminism of the other is not supported by the plays, which are on the feminist side, but chiefly "portray in humorous fashion the war between the sexes." Field is neither feminist nor antifeminist.

——. "Proverbs and Proverbial Elements in the Plays of Nathan Field." *SFQ* 10 (1946): 1-16. *A Woman Is a Weathercock* and *Amends for Ladies* contain fifty-four proverbs and proverbial phrases; Field uses them for characterization, to promote audience acceptance of a line of argument or conduct, and for stylistic embellishment.

——. "The Quarto of Field's *Weather-Cocke.*" *Library* 1 (1946): 62-64. Four of the formes of the 1612 quarto exist in two states, one superior to the other.

———. "Six Confused Exits and Entrances in the Plays of Nathan Field." *N&Q* 191 (1946): 53-56. In both of Field's plays, the seventeenth-century editions and modern editors leave the designated exits and entrances confused. Peery gives explanatory notes.

———. "Three Contented Widows." *Comparative Literature Studies* 21-22 (1946): 29. The widow's defense of her state in *Amends for Ladies* is similar to two earlier defenses, one English, one German.

———. "*A Woman Is a Weathercock*." *TLS*, 16 Feb. 1946, p. 84. A cryptic stage direction which received varying interpretations by earlier editors and critics probably refers to two characters in the play.

Verhasselt, Eliane. "A Biography of Nathan Field, Dramatist and Actor." *Revue belge de philologie et d'histoire* 25 (1946-47): 485-508. Earlier authorities from Langbaine (1671) to Chambers (1923) are confused about Field because they did not distinguish between Nathan, the dramatist and actor (1587-1620), and his brother Nathaniel (1581-1633). Nathan's father, a Puritan preacher, died in 1587; in 1600 Nathan was kidnapped to be educated as an actor for the Children of the Chapel. The facts of his subsequent career as an actor are traced in detail.

Kermode, J. Frank. "A Note on the History of Massinger's *The Fatal Dowry* in the Eighteenth Century." *N&Q* 192 (1947): 186-87. The play is a source for Nicholas Rowe's *The Fair Penitent* and Aaron Hill's *The Insolvent*.

Peery, William. "*Eastward Ho!* and *A Woman Is a Weathercock*." *MLN* 62 (1947): 131-32. A passage in *Eastward Ho!* is echoed by Field; it has not been noticed previously.

———. "Nineteenth-Century Editorial Practice as Illustrated in the Descent of the Text of Nathan Field." *Studies in English* (Univ. of Texas) 26 (1947): 3-17. Collier's editions (1829) of Field's two plays introduce 270 readings which depart from the copy text, but Collier acknowledges only 15 of them. Hazlitt's editions (1875) depend on Collier rather than the quartos; he adopts 254 of Collier's readings and introduces 120 of his own. Verity's edition (1888) uses all 254 of Collier's readings followed by Hazlitt and adopts 104 of Hazlitt's. Nineteenth-century editors of Elizabethan plays used inadequate editorial methods. They failed to select a copy text, collate copies, and acknowledge departures from the copy text. Textual degeneration resulted.

Scott, Florence R. "Teg—the Stage Irishman." *MLR* 42 (1947): 314-20. The Irish footboy in *Amends for Ladies* is one of many sham Irishmen in comedies of the period.

Peery, William. "The Roaring Boy Again." *ShAB* 23 (1948): 12-16, 78-86. *Amends for Ladies*, III.iv, and Middleton and Rowley's *A Fair Quarrel* (among others) contain descriptions of "roaring boys" that seem to limit the dates during which such activities had a contemporary interest.

———. "The 1618 Quarto of Field's *Amends for Ladies*." *Library* 2 (1948): 53-59. While the 1618 text is relatively correct, "no single copy contains all . . . formes in their corrected states."

Baldini, Gabriele. "La farsa Giacobina di Nathan Field." *Nuovo Antologia* 84 (1949): 281-307. Not seen.

Peery, William. "Shakespeare and Nathan Field." *Neophil* 34 (1950): 238-45. A review of the evidence suggests that while Field did not act with the King's Men during Shakespeare's lifetime, he "knew Shakespeare's plays and drew upon them in his own writing."

———. ed. *The Plays of Nathan Field*. 1950. The editor provides an extended biography, an estimate of Field's relationship to his contemporaries (Jonson, Chapman, Fletcher, Middleton), and a critical estimate of the comedies (technically good but basically insincere). The edition contains *A Woman Is a Weathercock* and *Amends for Ladies*, with explanatory and textual notes and a bibliography of previous scholarship.

Gerritsen, J., ed. *The Honest Man's Fortune: A Critical Edition of Ms. Dyce 9 (1625)*. 1952. The edition is based on the promptbook. The editor discusses previous editions, the manuscript, the scribe and his handwriting, the relationship between the manuscript and its printing in the Beaumont and Fletcher 1647 Folio, authorship (Tourneur, Field, and Fletcher), and sources (no single source). Full explanatory notes are provided.

Sherbo, Arthur. "*The Knight of Malta* and Boccaccio's *Filocolo*." *ES* 33 (1952): 254-57. Sherbo believes the play is Fletcher's. The portion titled "The Thirteen Questions of Love" in *Filocolo* is the source of the play, not two stories in Painter's *Palace of Pleasure*.

Waith, E. M. "'Controversia' in the English Drama: Medwall and Massinger." *PMLA* 68 (1953): 286-303. In its plot, *The Fatal Dowry* works out the situation presented in a *controversia* (a form of declamation) of Seneca the Elder. The play also follows the *controversia* in structure, character, and style, and like other Tudor-Stuart plays, reflects a rhetorical tradition which helped shape that drama early and late.

Blayney, Glenn H. "Field's Parody of a Murder Play." *N&Q* 2 (1955): 19-20. In *A Woman Is a Weathercock* Field parodies the dramatic excesses of murder plays of the time (*Arden of Feversham*, *A Warning for Fair Women*, and especially *The Miseries of Enforced Marriage*). "Not every one saw these plays without some amusement."

———. "Nathan Field and the *Faerie Queene*." *N&Q* 2 (1955): 59-60. The character Scudmore and his successful romantic love in Field's *A Woman Is a Weathercock* perhaps was suggested by Spenser's theme of romantic love in marriage in the story of Amoret and Sir Scudamour in Book III of the *Fairie Queene*.

Hoy, Cyrus. "The Shares of Fletcher and His Collaborators in the Beaumont and Fletcher Canon (IV)." *SB* 12 (1959): 91-116. Field and Fletcher collaborated on *Four Plays, or Moral Representations, in One*. Field, Fletcher, and Massinger collaborated on *The Knight of Malta* and *The Queen of Corinth*. *The Honest Man's Fortune* is "basically Field's own work," with scenes by Fletcher and Massinger. Linguistic forms in Field's two unaided plays (*A Woman Is a Weathercock* and *Amends for Ladies*) are analyzed, and that evidence used to establish Field's shares.

Dunn, T. A., ed. *The Fatal Dowry*. 1969. This Fountainwell edition contains critical introduction, textual introduction, textual notes, and commentary. The shares of Field and Massinger are easily distinguished on stylistic grounds; 1619 is probably the date of composition. Two compositors set the 1632 quarto from a manuscript in two hands (probably authorial) with a third hand evident in the stage directions. "Loyalty and trust, and their opposites, form the antithetical themes of the play. To express these themes, the play centers round the idea of courtesy."

THOMAS FULLER

Addison, William. *Worthy Dr. Fuller.* 1951. This discussion of Fuller's life and work is meant for the general reader. It does not mention *Andronicus*.

Wood, James O. "Thomas Fuller's Oxford Interlude." *HLQ* 17 (1954): 185-208. The anonymous *Andronicus, a Tragedy*, printed in 1661, was written by Fuller in 1643. A detailed discussion of Fuller's life, loyalties, and literary production during the 1640s, and the relationship of the play to Fuller's known historical biography *Life of Andronicus* (1646) establish his authorship. The play is not an early draft by John Wilson of his *Andronicus Comnenius* (1664); Wilson's play is based on Fuller's biography. Biographical-historical information is presented in full.

Roberts, S. C. *Doctor Johnson and Others.* 1958. The chapter on Fuller surveys his life and work.

HENRY GLAPTHORNE

Leech, Clifford. *Shakespeare's Tragedies and Other Studies in Seventeenth Century Drama.* 1950. Glapthorne's plays are mentioned in an essay treating "Love as a Dramatic Theme" in the drama of the time.

Cutts, John P. "William Lawes' Writing for the Theatre and the Court." *Library* 7 (1952): 225-34. The setting for the song "Loves a Child" in *Argalus and Parthenia* is identified in Lawes's autograph manuscript.

Brown, Arthur, ed. *The Lady Mother.* 1959, for 1958. A. H. Bullen's ascription of the play (in *Old English Plays*, vol. 2, 1883) to Glapthorne has not been questioned, although there is no contemporary evidence for it. This Malone Society edition reprints the manuscript, which was revised by both scribe and author. The date is probably 1633-35. There are no contemporary records of performance, although the play was licensed in 1635. Earlier scholarship is cited.

Davis, Joe Lee. *The Sons of Ben: Jonsonian Comedy in Caroline England*. 1967. An "eclectic" comedy, *The Hollander* caters to the courtly interest in Platonism, and links it to the "sentimental theme of the reformed rake": with others which are not true comedies of witty amorous intrigue, it established a tradition of citizen comedies continued into the Restoration. *Wit in a Constable* is also "eclectic" and "Bromesque" in its preoccupation with citizens, but looks ahead to a new use of the forms of Jonson, Beaumont and Fletcher, and Shirley. Both plays are analyzed.

THOMAS GOFFE

O'Donnell, Norbert F. "Shakespeare, Marston, and the University: The Sources of Thomas Goffe's *Orestes*." *SP* 50 (1953): 476-84. Unlike writers and producers of academic drama in his time, Goffe was not contemptuous of the popular theater. *Orestes* is indebted in scenes and lines to *Hamlet* and *Antonio's Revenge*, and in over-all conception to the tragedy of revenge.

——. "A Lost Jacobean *Phoenissae?*" *MLN* 69 (1954): 163-64. Goffe plausibly might have written the play Jonson refers to.

——. "The Authorship of *The Careless Shepherdess*." *PQ* 33 (1954): 43-47. While external evidence supports Thomas Goffe's authorship, other reasons suggest John Gough, author of *The Strange Discovery*.

Cutts, John P. "Thomas Goffe's *The Courageous Turke*." *N&Q* 2 (1955): 333-35. The effect of the death of Menthe on her wedding night is heightened by the use of music. Variant texts of the song exist, and the musical setting is preserved.

Armstrong, William A. "The Audience of the Elizabethan Private Theaters." In *The Seventeenth Century Stage: A Collection of Critical Essays*, ed. Gerald Eades Bentley (1968), pp. 215-34. Characters in the Praeludium to *The Careless Shepherdess* provide evidence for the nature of the audience.

Carnegie, David. "The Identification of the Hand of Thomas Goffe, Academic Dramatist and Actor." *Library* 26 (1971): 161-65. Contemporary records establish Goffe's hand as that found in a Harvard manuscript which contains actors' parts for plays performed at Christ Church. Goffe wrote one of the plays, and acted two of the roles.

———, ed. *The Raging Turke.* 1974 for 1968. This Malone Society edition provides a facsimile reprint of the first and authoritative edition, the quarto of 1631, with lists of variant readings by forme and of irregular and doubtful readings from all thirty-three known extant copies. The introduction gives a bibliographical description of the quarto.

WILLIAM HABINGTON

Combs, Homer C. "Habington's *Castara* and the Date of His Marriage." *MLN* 63 (1948): 182-83. The marriage occurred in the spring of 1633.

Allott, Kenneth, ed. *The Poems of William Habington.* 1969. This standard edition includes the prologues, epilogues, and songs for *The Queen of Arragon*, and an extended biography, with Habington's contemporary and later reputation.

PETER HAUSTED

Mills, Laurens J. *Peter Hausted: Playwright, Poet, and Preacher.* 1944. The study considers in separate sections Hausted's life, his rivalry as a playwright with Thomas Randolph, his poetry (briefly), and his work as preacher and chaplain. The occasion of the first performances of Hausted's *The Rival Friends* and Randolph's *The Jealous Lovers* is discussed at length.

———, ed. and trans. *Senile Odium.* 1949. This edition reproduces the Latin text of the 1633 edition and gives an English translation. The brief introduction argues for 1631 as a performance date, and comments on the satire of Euphuism and the success of the comic and realistic scenes and characters.

Elmen, Paul. "The Death of Peter Hausted." *N&Q* 195 (1950): 16-17. Since the date (20 July 1644) and the place (Banbury Castle) of death are known from a contemporary historian, in likelihood Hausted "was one of twenty-nine victims of the plague which decimated the castle during the month of July."

Mills, Laurens J., ed. *Peter Hausted's "The Rival Friends."* 1951. A six-page critical essay and explanatory and textual notes accompany the text, which is based on a collation of nine copies of the only previous edition of 1632. Mills defends the play against its detractors from Hausted's day to ours.

———, ed. and trans. *Senilis Amor.* 1952. "Specific, tangible details" in the Latin style of this play and *Senile Odium* suggest that this play is not by Hausted but by an unknown "university man who was imitating . . . title and . . . situation in *Senile Odium*." This edition prints the Latin manuscript and gives an English translation.

Davis, Joe Lee. *The Sons of Ben: Jonsonian Comedy in Caroline England.* 1967. *The Rival Friends* has the "invidious distinction of being one of the most chaotic hybrids among Caroline comedies." It combines pastoral romance, tragicomedy, and comedy of humours, yet it anticipates the sophistication of the comedy of manners.

BARTEN HOLIDAY

Cavanaugh, Mary Jean Carmel, ed. *"Technogamia," by Barten Holyday: A Critical Edition.* 1942. This printed dissertation (Catholic Univ.) provides an introduction, a photographic reproduction of the first (1618) edition, and explanatory and textual notes. The seventy-seven page introduction contains a biography and describes the play's much-publicized reception in its 1617 and 1621 performances, its academic milieu, literary affiliations, and early editions.

THOMAS JORDAN

Gourlay, James J. "Caroline Play, *The Wasp*." *TLS,* 5 June 1943, p. 271. The play, which Gourlay attributes to Jordan, is dated 1638 and was "presumably acted by the amalgamated King's Revels–Queen Henrietta's Company at Salisbury Court in Fleet Street."

McManaway, James G. "A *Hamlet* Reminiscence in 1660." *N&Q* 8 (1961): 388. The origin of some lines in Jordan's poem, *A Speech Made to His Excellency The Lord General Monk . . . ,* "is patently the Ghost's speeches to Hamlet."

THOMAS KILLIGREW

Harbage, Alfred B. *Thomas Killigrew, Cavalier Dramatist, 1612-1683.* 1930. This is the standard study of the life and works. The final assessment is strongly qualified: at times the reader "can glimpse, through the haze of his rhetoric, the foothills of poetry."

Boas, F. S. "Killigrew's *Claracilla.*" *TLS*, 18 March 1944, p. 144. The manuscript in the Castle Howard Library has variants from the published texts of 1641 and 1664. It "was either a presentation copy or specially valued by an owner" and is an independent authority for the establishment of a final text.

Van Lennep, William. "Thomas Killigrew Prepares His Plays for Production." In *Joseph Quincy Adams Memorial Studies*, ed. James G. McManaway, et al. (1948), pp. 803-8. Markings in Killigrew's copy of the 1664 folio edition of his plays reveal considerable information about his staging plans.

Stoye, J. W. "The Whereabouts of Thomas Killigrew 1639-41." *RES* 25 (1949): 245-48. Killigrew traveled to Paris, Geneva, and Italy; while in Rome, he twice visited the English College of Jesuits.

Keast, William R. "Killigrew's Use of Donne in *The Parson's Wedding*," *MLR* 45 (1950): 512-15. Some of the dialogue in the play is prose settings of Donne's verse; Killigrew probably intended his audience to catch the borrowings as part of an added level of wit.

Knowland, A. S., comp. *Six Caroline Plays.* 1962. A text of *The Parson's Wedding*, with a brief introduction, is included in this volume in the Oxford University Press World Classics series.

Freehafer, John. "The Formation of the London Patent Companies of 1660." *Theatre Notebook* 20 (1965): 6-30. This closely documented account of Killigrew and Davenant's attempts to impose their monopoly on existing companies provides new information on the theatrical situation just prior to the Restoration and corrects errors in several standard sources.

Davis, Joe Lee. *The Sons of Ben: Jonsonian Comedy in Caroline England.* 1967. A brief biography is given of Killigrew, one of the eleven Sons of Ben. The satire of *The Parson's Wedding* is "directed primarily at Puritan extremism and Court Platonism, the two chief enemies of the Caroline comic spirit."

Killigrew, Thomas. *Comedies and Tragedies (1664)*. 1967. This is a facsimile reprint of the original edition.

Wertheim, Albert. "Fraternity and the Catches in Two Restoration Theater Productions." *Journal of the Catch Society of America* 1 (1969): 14-19. Catches were used in productions of *The Knight of Malta* and Killigrew's *The Princess* "to evoke a spirit of manly camaraderie"; the texts of two catches are reproduced.

———. "Production Notes for Three Plays by Thomas Killigrew." *Theatre Survey* 10 (1969): 105-13. Killigrew's elaborate stage directions for productions of *The Princess*, *Claracilla*, and *The Parson's Wedding* provide "a nice basis for general speculations about Restoration acting and production."

———. "A New Light on the Dramatic Works of Thomas Killigrew." *SB* 24 (1971): 149-52. Killigrew's eight extant plays are each considered; a chronology is advanced which differs from that in Harbage's *Thomas Killigrew* (above).

JOHN KIRKE

Freehafer, John. "Shakespeare's *Tempest* and *The Seven Champions*." *SP* 66 (1969): 87-103. Bentley's date of 1634-38, based on his reading of topical allusions, is wrong. Allusions, theme, source, and publishing history support a date for the play as being written and acted in 1613 or 1614. Wentworth Smith, who also wrote *The Hector of Germany*, is the author, not John Kirke. *Seven Champions* is a contemporary burlesque of *The Tempest*.

MARTIN LLEWELLYN

Cutts, John P. "The Dramatic Writings of Martin Llewellyn." *PQ* 47 (1968): 16-29. Llewellyn is known as a minor Cavalier poet; "now it becomes necessary to add his name to the list of English dramatic writers, for one of these pieces, 'The Wake,' comprises the same songs in exactly the same sequence as are to be found in *The King Found at Southwell*, the last dramatic entertainment for the Cavaliers at Oxford,

May 5, 1646, before the city's capitulation to parliamentary forces, June 22-24." The name "Lloyd" on the title page may be one Llewellyn is "deliberately hiding behind." Seven pages of the first edition (1646) are reproduced. The *Second Supplement* (1970) to the *Annals* adds an entry for the title.

JAMES MABBE

Secord, Arthur W. "I.M. of the First Folio Shakespeare and Other Mabbe Problems." *JEGP* 47 (1948): 374-81. Presents the evidence for Mabbe as the author of verses signed "I.M." in the Folio and particulars about Mabbes's life and work.

Lacalle, Guadalupe Martínez. "A Manuscript Version of Mabbe's *Celistina*." *RLC* 39 (1965): 78-91. The manuscript, in Alnwick Castle, differs from the printed version in the location of marginal notes and is a fair copy of a first draft of the translation.

SHAKERLY MARMION

Miles, Theodore. "Place-Realism in a Group of Caroline Plays." *RES* 18 (1942): 428-40. Place-realism was introduced for "intrinsic appeal rather than for its effectiveness as setting" in six plays dated 1631-35; all were popular. Marmion's *Holland's Leaguer* is among these plays which reveal the influence of topical, extraliterary influences on drama.

Maxwell, Sue. "A Misprint in Marmion's *Holland's Leaguer*." *MLR* 39 (1944): 179-80. Corrects the reading "bezor" (antidote) to "bever" (beaver) in V.iii.

Nearing, Alice J. *"Cupid and Psyche," by Shakerly Marmion: A Critical Edition with an Account of Marmion's Life and Works*. 1944. The introduction to the poem contains facts about Marmion's life and the three plays definitely ascribed to him.

Leech, Clifford. *Shakespeare's Tragedies and Other Studies in Seventeenth Century Drama*. 1950. Marmion's plays are mentioned in an essay treating "Love as a Dramatic Theme" in Jacobean and Caroline drama.

Davis, Joe Lee. *The Sons of Ben: Jonsonian Comedy in Caroline England*. 1967. *Holland's Leaguer* "transcends the world of citizen comedy" in its use of verse, foreign names, and allusions to the court. The lovers, adherents of court Platonism, are used as "critics and purgers of pretenders to wit and gentility," but they fall short of the wit of the gay couple in Restoration comedy. *A Fine Companion* "surpasses *Holland's Leaguer* in sophisticated eclecticism." Contrasted pairs of lovers are norm characters, but the "counterpointing of the sexes" is not a major concern. *The Antiquary*, also eclectic, is remote from the world of London citizen comedy. The conflict of wit and witty woman is developed in two of the norm characters, but the play falls short in its "effort toward complexity."

Gair, W. R. "The Politics of Scholarship: A Dramatic Comment on the Autocracy of Charles I." In *The Elizabethan Theatre III*, ed. David Galloway (1973), pp. 100-118. The central incident of the Duke taking the antiquary's collection in *The Antiquary* reflects the contemporary sensation of Charles I and his privy council's autocratic plan to confiscate the collection of the famous antiquary Charles Cotton in 1629.

THOMAS MAY

Gabrieli, Vittorio, ed. *The Tragedie of Cleopatra Queene of Aegypt.* 1962. Not seen.

Davies, H. Neville. "Dryden's *All for Love* and Thomas May's *The Tragedie of Cleopatra, Queen of Egypt.*" *N&Q* 12 (1965): 139-44. Dryden preferred for sources the English dramatic versions of the Antony and Cleopatra story; May's is the source for the beginning and ending of Dryden's play and for Antony's melancholy.

Berry, J. Wilkes. "Thomas May's *The Tragedy of Cleopatra.*" *Discourse* 11 (1968): 67-75. "Impressive to the modern reader" is May's characterization of Cleopatra, his knowledge of psychology, and his emphasis on the justness of Antony's war against Octavius.

JASPER MAYNE

Davis, Joe Lee. *The Sons of Ben: Jonsonian Comedy in Caroline England.* 1967. A biographical note on Mayne, one of the Sons, is included along with a brief critical appreciation of the "penetrating satire" and sophistication of *The City Match.*

THOMAS NABBES

Miles, Theodore. "Place-Realism in a Group of Caroline Plays." *RES* 18 (1942): 428-40. Place-realism was introduced for "intrinsic appeal rather than for its effectiveness as setting" in six plays dated 1631-35; all were popular. Nabbes's *Covent Garden* and *Tottenham Court* were among these plays which reveal the influence of topical, extraliterary influences on drama.

Cutts, John P. "Thomas Nabbes's *Hannibal and Scipio.*" *EM* 14 (1963): 73-81. While the estimate of Nabbes as a dramatist has never been high, *Hannibal and Scipio* invites association with Nabbes's masks rather than his plays because of its considerable use of music, song, and dance. Cutts transcribes a seventeenth-century musical setting for the last song of the play, "On bravely on."

Brown, John Russell, ed. *The Spring's Glory*. In *A Book of Masques: In Honour of Allardyce Nicoll*, ed. T. J. B. Spencer and Stanley Wells (1967), pp. 317-36. Unperformed (but published in 1638), the mask may have been meant as a "blank" mask, "to be adapted to almost any occasion as required," or it may have been intended as an entertainment in a public theater, like other contemporary experiments of this sort.

Davis, Joe Lee. *The Sons of Ben: Jonsonian Comedy in Caroline England*. 1967. The framework plot in *Tottenham Court* creates an "enveloping conventional 'delight' to make more palatable the sentimental 'teaching' that is Nabbes's real end," namely a "single standard of sexual morality" and the "wit and virtue of ordinary folk." *The Bride* clearly shows the "religious motivation of Caroline sentimental comedy." *Covent Garden* defends court Platonism. The plays receive detailed analysis.

Vince, R. W. "Thomas Nabbes's *Hannibal and Scipio*: Sources and Theme." *SEL* 11 (1971): 327-43. The source is Livy, although Nabbes also used North's Plutarch. The treatment of the "historical material resembles that of Petrarch" in his *Africa*, and the theme—"the Ciceronian distinction between political and contemplative virtues"—is also used by Petrarch.

———. "Morality and Masque: The Context for Thomas Nabbes's *Microcosmus.*" *ES* 53 (1972): 328-34. The pattern of the morality plot and the elements of the mask are integrated in the play, which presents the "conflict in man's soul as he wanders from the path of righteousness and is eventually redeemed."

Freehafer, John. "Perspective Scenery and the Caroline Playhouses." *Theatre Notebook* 27 (1973): 98-113. Thomas Nabbes's "statements show that [his] *Hannibal and Scipio* was produced at the Cockpit in Drury Lane in 1635 with five sets of perspective scenery which were changed between the acts."

THOMAS NEALE

Mitchell, John A., ed. *The Warde*. 1937. The introduction speculates that the play may be based on events in Neale's own life; it is so amateurish that it is doubtful it was ever performed.

THOMAS RANDOLPH

Eagle, R. L. "Thomas Randolph and Francis Bacon." *Baconiana* 25 (1941): 149-50. Not seen.

Bowers, Fredson Thayer. "Thomas Randolph's *Salting.*" *MP* 39 (1942): 275-80. A commonplace book contains a hitherto unnoticed monologue written by Randolph in the summer or fall of 1627; it probably belonged to one of Randolph's fellow students at Trinity College, Cambridge.

———, ed. *"The Fary Knight or Oberon the Second": A Manuscript Play Attributed to Thomas Randolph.* 1942. This is a meticulous edition which, in the Introduction, presents virtually all the facts known about the play. The attribution to Randolph, however, has not been generally accepted. Alfred Harbage's review, *MLN* 59 (1944): 130-31, for example, charges that Bowers is "too easily satisfied with verbal parallels;" the play could as easily be "a Shirley *juvenilia* revised by a reader of Randolph . . . or the work of some Commonwealth juvenile who had read both Shirley and Randolph."

Davis, Joe Lee. "The Case for Comedy in Caroline Theatrical Apologetics." *PMLA* 58 (1942): 353-71. *The Muses' Looking Glass* is an effective answer to Prynne's *Histrio-Mastix* and deserves "a more important place in the history of seventeenth century drama and dramatic theory than it has hitherto received."

Mills, Laurens J. *Peter Hausted: Playwright, Poet, and Preacher*. 1944. Mills discusses the literary feud occasioned by performance on the same day of Randolph's *Jealous Lovers* and Hausted's *Rival Friends*. See also Bentley, vol. 5.

Leech, Clifford. "Francis Jacques, Author of *The Queene of Corsica*." *DUJ* 39 (1947): 111-19. It is unlikely that the author of *The Queene of Corsica* was the "F. J." who revised *Hey for Honesty* in 1651.

Tannenbaum, Samuel A. and Dorothy R. *Thomas Randolph (A Concise Bibliography)*. 1947. This checklist of Randolph studies was reprinted in vol. 6 of *Elizabethan Bibliographies*, by Samuel A. and Dorothy R. Tannenbaum (1967).

Bentley, Gerald Eades. "Randolph's *Praeludium* and the Salisbury Court Theatre." In *Joseph Quincy Adams: Memorial Studies*, ed. James G. McManaway et al. (1948), pp. 775-83. A dramatic dialogue in the British Museum manuscript collection is clearly by Randolph and was intended to be performed on the stage of a London private theater, not at Cambridge. The piece proves Randolph's employment as a regular theater poet; he probably "occupied that position for the Salisbury Court theatre in the first year of its existence."

Bowden, William R. *The English Dramatic Lyric, 1603-42: A Study in Stuart Dramatic Technique*. 1951. The songs in Randolph's plays are included in a general survey of the function of music in the Stuart theater.

Røstvig, Maren-Sofie. *The Happy Man: Studies in the Metamorphosis of a Classical Ideal, 1600-1700*. Vol. 1. 1954. Randolph's role in the celebration of the country life and as a transmitter of the Horatian ideal is considered in a comparative context.

Herrick, Marvin T. *Tragicomedy: Its Origin and Development in Italy, France, and England*. 1955. *Amyntas* "may not be the best of English pastoral tragicomedies, but it is surely the most entertaining."

Briggs, K. M. *The Anatomy of Puck: An Examination of Fairy Beliefs among Shakespeare's Contemporaries and Successors.* 1958. *Amyntas* "is a pleasant piece of work, lit by an agreeable and scholarly nonsense that is at times not unlike Lewis Carroll's."

Milburn, Daniel Judson. *The Age of Wit, 1650–1750.* 1966. Randolph's "metaphysical" wit, especially as manifest in a tavern brawl in which he lost a little finger, is analyzed.

Schoenbaum, Samuel. *Internal Evidence and Elizabethan Dramatic Authorship.* 1966. Several doubtful ascriptions, especially *The Drinking Academy*, are considered.

Davis, Joe Lee. *The Sons of Ben: Jonsonian Comedy in Caroline England.* 1967. For Randolph in *The Muses' Looking Glass*, the end of comedy is moral education; the subject matter is two sets of characters exemplifying on the one hand vice and folly and on the other appropriate standards; the artistic method is realistic portrayal of typical vice and folly. Davis also analyzes *Aristippus*, *The Drinking Academy*, and *Hey for Honesty* as Aristophanic comedies, and *The Jealous Lovers* as New Comedy.

Guffey, George Robert. *Elizabethan Bibliographies Supplements.* Vol. 3. 1968. The Tannenbaum checklist (above) is brought up to 1965.

Kelliher, W. Hilton. "Two Notes on Thomas Randolph." *PQ* 51 (1972): 941–45. The first corrects the notes to Thorn-Drury's edition of the poems; the second offers an earlier version of a biographical anecdote first published in *Poor Robin's Jests* (1687).

JOSEPH RUTTER

Townsend, Freda L. "Ben Jonson's 'Censure' of Rutter's *Shepheards Holy-Day*." *MP* 44 (1947): 238–47. Jonson praises this and only three other plays in print; "no critic of Jonson, as lawgiver or as dramatist, can afford to ignore his praise of Rutter's unclassical play."

Richards, K. R. "Joseph Rutter's *The Shepherd's Holiday* and the *Silvanire* of Jean de Mairet." *Anglia* 85 (1967): 404–13. "Rutter's debt to Mairet is further evidence of the busy intellectual commerce between the two capitals in the third decade of the seventeenth century."

Lefevre, André. "Au temps de la reine Henriette-Marie: *Le Cid* a Londres." *RLC* 45 (1971): 74-79. A detailed comparison reveals that Rutter's translation fails to accurately render Corneille's meaning; "une error d'appréciation est donc à la base de son travail."

WILLIAM SAMPSON

Adams, Henry Hitch. *English Domestic or, Homiletic Tragedy 1575-1642.* 1943. *The Vow Breaker* (1625), discussed in the chapter "The Decline of Domestic Tragedies," closely follows a contemporary ballad in its stress on the lesson that perjurers are punished.

Scragg, Leah. "Shakespearian Influence in *Herod and Antipater.*" *N&Q* 15 (1968): 258-62. Similarities in plot and character, and verbal parallels, suggest that Sampson is indebted to Edmund in *King Lear* for the bastard Antipater.

Ayres, Philip J. "Production and Adaptation of William Sampson's *The Vow Breaker* (1636) in the Restoration." *Theatre Notebook* 27 (1973): 145-47. The play was produced often between 1699 and 1733 in truncated forms. Sometime after 1700 a copy of the 1636 quarto was partially marked as a promptbook; the annotations are described.

GEORGE SANDYS

Davis, Richard Beale. *George Sandy's Poet-Adventurer: A Study in Anglo-American Culture in the Seventeenth Century.* 1955. Sandy's life, works, and influence are studied in detail.

Barroll, J. Leeds. "Shakespeare's Other Ovid: A Reproduction of Commentary on *Metamorphoses* I-IV." *ShakS* 3 (1967): 173-256. Selections from Sandys's text are reproduced in facsimile; the introduction speculates on Shakespeare's likely interpretation of passages.

Cutts, John P. "'Till Birnam Forest Come to Dunsinane.'" *SQ* 21 (1970): 497-99. "Within a few years of Shakespeare's *Macbeth* an intelligent seventeenth-century writer is interpreting the moving wood episode as a symbolical restitution of harmony to lawless elements." Sandys uses the metaphor in the commentary on Orpheus in his *Ovid's Metamorphosis* (1632 edition) and mentions Macbeth's story in the same paragraph, perhaps revealing his source.

HENRY SHIRLEY

Cutts, John P. "Henry Shirley's *The Martyrd Soldier*." *RN* 12 (1959): 251-53. A contemporary musical setting for a song in the play is printed from a manuscript in the Bodleian. Bullen's suggestion that Henry Shirley well deserves his anonymity is endorsed as a fair overall assessment.

Huebert, Ronald M. "On Detecting John Ford's Hand: A Fallacy." *Library* 26 (1971): 256-59. The arguments advanced for Ford's hand in the lost play, *The Spanish Duke of Lerma*, which is the source of Robert Howard's *The Great Favourite or The Duke of Lerma* are not conclusive; there are other possible authors. It is, for example, possible that Humphrey Mosley misread "James Shirley" as "Henry Shirley" when he registered the play in 1653.

WENTWORTH SMITH

See John Kirke, above.

JOHN SUCKLING

Harbage, Alfred. *Cavalier Drama: An Historical Supplement to the Study of the Elizabethan and Restoration Stage*. 1936. This remains an influential critical study of Suckling's plays. *Brennoralt* is seen as his best dramatic work.

Wallerstein, Ruth. "Suckling's Imitation of Shakespeare: A Caroline View of His Art." *RES* 19 (1943): 290-95. *The Goblins* reveals something about how Shakespeare was read in mid-century. "Though the play was written with *The Tempest* in mind, the fundamental design and substance of the play are difficult to compare with those of *The Tempest* because of the intellectual and dramatic triviality of *The Goblins*."

Clayton, Thomas S. "Thorn-Drury's Marginalia on Sir John Suckling." *N&Q* 6 (1959): 148-50. The comments in Thorn-Drury's copy of Suckling's works, now in the Bodleian, include remarks on canonicity, date, and allusions.

Beaurline, L. A. "The Canon of Sir John Suckling's Poems." *SP* 57 (1960): 492-518. Echoes in the plays, especially *Aglaura*, are used to test doubtful items. "All of the attributions to Suckling since the *Last Remains* are either erroneous or at least questionable."

Berry, Herbert, ed. *Sir John Suckling's Poems and Letters From Manuscript.* 1960. A significant amount of new biographical material is given in the introduction and commentary.

Clayton, Thomas S. "An Historical Study of the Portraits of Sir John Suckling." *JWCI* 23 (1960): 105-26. Spurious and genuine portraits are considered and some new details are provided about Suckling's life.

——. "Sir John Suckling and the Cranfields." *TLS*, 29 Jan. 1960, p. 68. Lady Dorset (Frances Cranfield), a cousin of Suckling's, perhaps provided copy for the first edition of *Fragmenta Aurea* (1646).

Kaufmann, Ralph J. *Richard Brome: Caroline Playwright.* 1961. Brome's attacks on Suckling, especially over the expense and gaudiness of *Aglaura*, may have been partly motivated by Suckling's gibes at Jonson in *A Session of the Poets*; Brome may also be using Suckling as a representative of all new courtiers.

Beaurline, L. A. "An Editorial Experiment: Suckling's *A Sessions of the Poets.*" *SB* 16 (1963): 43-60. A close textual analysis of the first edition of *Fragmenta Aurea* is included.

Frye, Roland Mushat. "Shakespeare's Composition of *Lucrece*: New Evidence." *SQ* 16 (1965): 289-96. Suckling's "A Supplement to an imperfect Copy of Verses of Mr Wil. Shakespears" may cast light on Shakespeare's writing practices.

Lynch, Kathleen M. *Roger Boyle, First Earl of Orrery.* 1965. "Suckling's influence on the future Lord Orrery's work as a dramatist was to be greater than that of any other author."

Armitage, C. M. "Identification of New York Public Library Manuscript 'Suckling Collection' and of Huntington Manuscript 198." *SB* 19 (1966): 215-16. The NYPL collection and the Huntington item may both have been transcribed by Joseph Haselwood between 1822 and 1823.

Freehafer, John. "Brome, Suckling, and Davenant's Theater Project of 1639." *TSLL* 10 (1968): 367–83. Sir Ferdinando in Brome's *The Court Beggar* "is a take-off on Suckling"; Davenant is also satirized in the play and he retaliated by keeping Brome's plays off the London stages after the Restoration.

——. "The *Italian Night Piece* and Suckling's *Aglaura*." *JEGP* 67 (1968): 249–65. The April 1638 production of *Aglaura* borrowed the scenery from the February 1638 performance of *Luminalia* and Suckling's play was "called *The Italian Night Masque* through confusion with the production from which most of its scenery was borrowed."

Beaurline, L. A., and Thomas Clayton. "Notes on Early Editions of *Fragmenta Aurea*." *SB* 23 (1970): 165–70. Greg is in error; there are three, not two, states of the title page of the first edition and the priority is other than Greg indicates. Francis Kirkman was probably the pirate behind a reprint of the third edition and Greg's account is again supplemented.

Madoc-Jones, Enid. "Mary Bulkeley—The Aglaura of the Poet Suckling." *Anglo-Welch Review* 18 (1970): 196–203. Mary, the daughter of Sir Richard Bulkeley, was courted by Suckling and apparently inspired some of his best writing; the heroine of *Aglaura* is probably based on her.

Suckling, John. *Aglaura, 1638*. 1970. This facsimile edition, in folio size, reproduces the British Museum copy.

Beaurline, L. A., ed. *The Works of Sir John Suckling: The Plays*. 1971. The introduction and commentary establish the canon, dates, sources and analogues, and include definitive analyses of the texts. This and the Clayton edition below are the standard editions of Suckling's works.

Clayton, Thomas, ed. *The Works of Sir John Suckling: The Nondramatic Works*. 1971. The introduction includes the best available account of Suckling's life and the best bibiographical study of the early editions of his collected works.

JOHN TATHAM

Scott, Virgil Joseph. "A Reinterpretation of John Tatham's *The Rump: Or, the Mirrour of the Late Times*." *PQ* 24 (1945): 114–18.

Earlier views about purpose and date are inadequate. The play is a "party satire whose first purpose was to attack the enemies of the London party and whose second purpose was to eulogize George Monk." It was written between 11 February and mid-March 1660.

Wallace, John M. "The Case for Internal Evidence (10): The Date of John Tatham's *The Distracted State*." *BNYPL* 64 (1960): 29-40. The procedures for dating by internal evidence are tested on this play, published in 1650. The title page states it was written in 1641. But the play's design has general relevance in 1650, as does the "temper and compression of the republican elements" and the topicality of one of the characters; thus Bentley's suspicion (in *Jacobean and Caroline Stage*, vol. 5) that the title-page composition date is a "blind" is correct. The play is "wholly satirical."

AURELIAN TOWNSHEND

Dunlap, Rhodes, ed. *The Poems of Thomas Carew with His Masque "Coelum Brittanicum."* 1949. The editor's notes to Carew's poem "In Answer of an Elegiacall Letter upon the Death of the King of Sweden, from Aurelian Townshend . . . " provide biographical information about Townshend and mention his activities as a writer of masks.

Veevers, Erica. "Official Accounts for Two Masques by Aurelian Townshend." *N&Q* 9 (1962): 146-47. Transcribes accounts for *Albion's Triumph* and *Tempe Restored* which previously have not been printed.

———. "A Masque Fragment by Aurelian Townshend." *N&Q* 12 (1965): 343-45. The mask, cited by Bentley (*Jacobean and Caroline Stage*, vol. 5), complemented a performance of Montagu's *The Shepherd's Paradise* (1632/3) by enlivening the play and providing novelty.

Demaray, John G. "Milton's *Comus*: The Sequel to a Masque of Circe." *HLQ* 29 (1966): 245-54. Lawes would have appeared in Townshend's masks *Albion's Triumph* and *Tempe Restored* when they were performed at court in 1632. *Albion's Triumph* has scenes similar to those in *Comus*. But *Tempe Restored* anticipates *Comus* in theme and details; these similarities, as well as Lawes's familiarity with it and collaboration with Milton, suggest that *Comus* is the sequel to *Tempe Restored*.

Palmer, Paulina. "Thomas Carew's Reference to *The Shepherd's Paradise*." *N&Q* 13 (1966): 303-4. Carew "need not be referring to a masque by Townshend, but merely to a set of complimentary verses which he hopes Townshend will write."

LIST OF CONTRIBUTORS

DONALD K. ANDERSON, JR., is Professor of English at the University of Missouri.

RICHARD B. DAVIDSON teaches English at Cincinnati Country Day School, Cincinnati, Ohio.

MICHAEL V. DEPORTE is Associate Professor of English at the University of New Hampshire.

ANN HAAKER is Professor of English at California State University at Fullerton.

TERENCE P. LOGAN is Associate Professor of English at the University of New Hampshire. He wishes to thank Professor Michael C. Andrews for permission to use an earlier version of the Massinger essay.

DENZELL S. SMITH is Professor of English at Idaho State University.

ALBERT WERTHEIM is Associate Professor of English at Indiana University.

INDEX

PERSONS

INDEX

PLAYS

Alphabetization and modernized spelling follow the "Index of English Plays" in Alfred Harbage, Annals of English Drama, 975–1700 *(1940; rev. S. Schoenbaum, 1964). Unusually long titles have been abbreviated.*